# coolcamping

## europe

Sophie Dawson, Keith Didcock, Sam Pow, Paul Sullivan,
Richard Waters and Penny Watson

The publishers assert their right to use
*Cool Camping* as a trademark of Punk Publishing Ltd.

*Cool Camping: Europe*
First edition published in the United Kingdom in 2009 by
Punk Publishing Ltd
3 The Yard
Pegasus Place
London
SE11 5SD

www.punkpublishing.co.uk
www.coolcamping.co.uk

A catalogue record of this book is available from the British Library.

ISBN: 978-0-9552036-8-8

10 9 8 7 6 5 4 3 2 1

# introduction

As the compères of the Eurovision Song Contest like to say: *Wilkommen, Bienvenido, Feestelijk Inhalen, Izreči Dobrodošlico* and, of course, *καλώσ ορίσατε* to *Cool Camping: Europe.*

The latest entry in the *Cool Camping* pop parade is our biggest and boldest book yet, a continent-wide carnival of canvas stretching from the Atlantic to the Aegean and La Manche to Le Med. A mixed-beat combo of Cool Campers with pump-up mattresses and their own espresso makers has criss-crossed Europe in Clios and Polos, on Vespas and Lambrettas, to seek out those special little places that don't appear in the bucket-shop brochures.

So, up on the giant neon scoreboard it's *douze points* from the *Cool Camping* jury to olive groves, Alpine meadows and forest clearings but *nul points* to camping *villaggios* and ugly europarks. We've found the highest campsite in Europe and a little hideaway on an uninhabited island off the Spanish coast. There's a weird hangout in the very heart of Berlin, campsites with ancient Greek ruins and a bevy of yurts and tipis in the likes of Andalucía and the Algarve.

However, the *Cool Camping* revolution hasn't yet shone its head torch into every corner of Europe. And you'll generally find that the tipis, yurts and yoga retreats of Portugal, Spain and France give way to a more traditional style of camping the further east you travel. So, if all that holistic stuff isn't your cup of *ouzo*, then there's plenty of honest-to-goodness camping to be found elsewhere, such is the variety on offer.

And you might find yourself musing about Continental Europe, such a curious concept in the mind of our little-island nation. Folk there live into wrinkle-faced old age because they sleep in the afternoon and don't eat till it's bedtime. They don't binge drink – who could on chilled sherry or fruit beer? – and eat baguettes, pittas and paninis rather than sliced white loaves. They shop at stalls, not malls, and eat things like zucchini. And all with such style.

Europe's also a continent of contrasts, so you can choose the kind of place that suits your taste. The pointy-stoned chill of the northern Protestant lands versus the melon-hued warmth of southern Catholic ones or a diet of *bratwurst* and beer versus a meal of fish and wine. You can whizz about in cars and trains around the spider's web of road and rail links or meander along ancient tracks and pathways on donkeys and carts. It's up to you because, wherever you go, you're never too far away from a *Cool Camping* site and you don't need to be a Strasbourg MEP on expenses to enjoy them.

What you might need to be, though, is a bit of a linguist. You'll find that a little Eengleesh goes a long way in Europe (though please don't just add an 'o' onto the ends of words). And if you find yourself lost for words, there's always Spanglish or Franglais or, at a pinch, Esperanto. Try *Ĉu vi parolas Esperanton?* at a Croatian beach party and see how you go. However, there's no substitute for hailing the natives in the local lingo and you'll find a handy little glossary at the back of the book to help you break the ice and keep conversations going through those awkward pauses when hand gestures just might be seen as rude.

With such a large area to cover, there are inevitably places to which we wish we could have given more room, like Slovenia. And there are also a few places, like Belgium, where sadly we couldn't find anything at all that tickled our fancy. However, we think we've found the best of European camping in all its variety and hope that you'll have as much fun exploring the 80 sites in the book as we had humming kitsch tunes to ourselves across the continent whilst researching it.

The result is a Eurovision of continental camping for you to enjoy.

And that concludes the voting from the *Cool Camping* jury.

# campsite locator

Please turn to page 10 for the key to campsite locations.

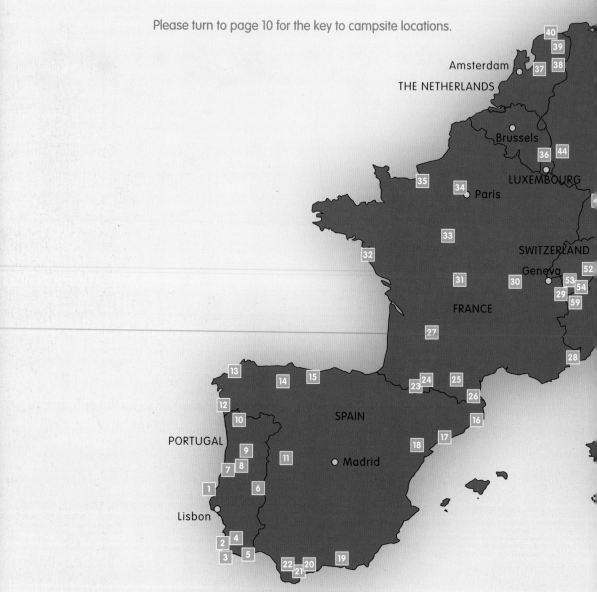

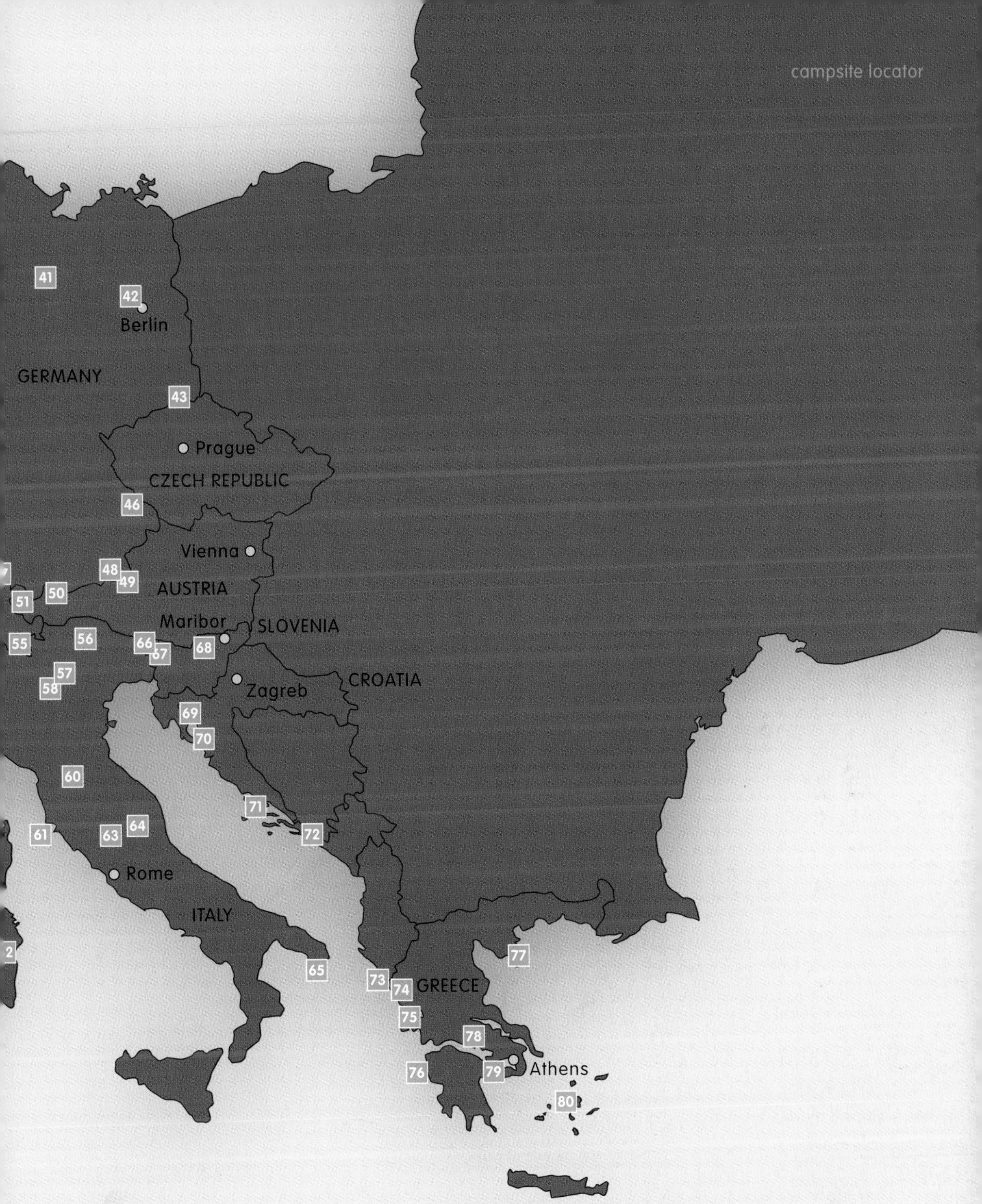
41
42
Berlin
GERMANY
43
Prague
CZECH REPUBLIC
46
Vienna
48
49
AUSTRIA
50
51
Maribor
SLOVENIA
55
56
66
67
68
57
58
Zagreb
CROATIA
69
70
60
71
72
61
63
64
Rome
ITALY
2
65
73
74
GREECE
77
75
78
79
Athens
76
80

1 2

3 4

# cool camping top 5

With the best of Europe outside our tent flaps, it was a Herculean task picking just five campsites to make up the best of the best. So, we bottled it. Here are the seven campsites that make up our top five. The most *bella* of them all.

**1** La Fresneda, Spain                                                                                                p81

Camp under the yawning Matarrañan skies on an environmentally friendly *finca* in Cataluña.

**2** Il Falcone, Italy                                                                                                  p253

Olives and poppies, lakes and villages, off the tourist trail in the heart of Umbria.

**3** CampSpirit, The Netherlands                                                                                        p153

A Dutch island eco-haven, with luxury tipis and yurts and pick-your-own organic veg.
Get in the spirit and chill right out.

**4** Areti, Greece                                                                                                      p298

In the shade of eucalyptus and hibiscus trees, enjoy a life of honey and calamari by the cobalt waters of the Sithonian peninsula.

**5=** Les Romarins, France                                                                                              p119

You'd usually have to break the bank at Monte Carlo to be able to afford views like these. Get them free at Les Romarins, high in the Riviera hills above Monaco.

**5=** Petit Praz & Camping des Glaciers, Switzerland                                                          p210 & p215

Two gob-smacking Swiss Alpine sites with little to choose between them. One is Europe's highest campsite, the other's at the foot of a glacier in a meadow dotted with wild orchids.

# campsites at a glance

# ilha da berlenga

When the Portuguese explorer Vasco da Gama set sail around the Cape of Good Hope in 1497, he made history as the first traveller to plough through the Cape's stormy waters to the eastern coast of Africa. Before this, seamen would navigate by the stars, turning back at the equator when faced with the unfamiliar constellations of the southern hemisphere. Bravely, da Gama had set the benchmark for fellow countrymen to go in search of new land. It therefore seems pertinent that one of the most unusual sites in Portugal requires a little sea adventure all of its own.

Not quite as rough as the waters around the Cape, the passage from Peniche on Portugal's western coast to Ilha da Berlenga is still not ideal for those with wobbly sea legs. On board, the crew, who are well used to this Atlantic crossing, hand out precautionary sick bags, which do get used. The reward for those that endure this choppy half-hour trip is exclusive access to the sublime, crystal-clear waters of Ilha da Berlenga.

Disembarking at the jetty you'll see a tiny cove that's full with two dozen sunbathers. A path leads upwards to a terraced restaurant, then, as it climbs the hill, it sweeps past the stepped camping area (think dinosaur-sized rather than donkey-sized steps etched

into the rocks), before disappearing up and over the vertiginous cliffs. There you pass a lighthouse and then a narrow path leads to the 17th-century Forte de São João Baptista, an impressive-looking fort that sits grandly on an islet joined by a narrow causeway, where you can rent dorm rooms.

People do live on the island, too. A dozen fishermen and their families live in a commune of bungalows, trawling their nets at sea twice daily. You'll be sure to eat like a local and enjoy some of the freshest fish you've probably ever eaten at the Mar e Sol, the island's only bar/restaurant, which opens from breakfast and stays open late, till about until 1am.

In the past, the locals would boat over from the mainland and pitch their tents wherever they fancied. Now that this is a protected nature reserve, the camping falls under the jurisdiction of the Peniche tourist office. In fact, the real bosses of this island are the seabirds – gulls, puffins and cormorants – who breed here in their thousands. It wouldn't be at all surprising to discover that Alfred Hitchcock found inspiration from a spring visit here, when mother birds fiercely guard their hatched eggs, squawking like a 'Hammer House' of feathered vertebrates if you so much as put a foot near their nests.

The campsite enjoys natural shelter from the northerly winds, but make sure your tent is securely pegged down if the wind switches and blows in from the south. Pitches are priced according to size and there are cold sea-water sinks and showers, so you may as well just dive straight into the sea to freshen up. The tourist office advises campers to protect their tents from 'natural bomb raids', which probably sounds a lot more scary than it is. Just ensure you tightly pack any food away in containers and zip up your flaps. Be sure to collect your personal allowance of fresh water at the bar between 8am and 11am (packing a 15-litre water container is as vital as a torch and mallet).

Away from the site, regular boat trips offer some of the best diving in Portugal, so clear is the water here. If diving isn't your bag, hop on a boat to explore the rocky caves and grottoes. And don't go worrying about the journey back to the mainland. Just keep your eyes fixed on the horizon and remember how courageous those Portuguese explorers were over 600 years ago.

THE UPSIDE A remote island with great diving opportunities.
THE DOWNSIDE You're at the mercy of the elements in the squawking company of many many birds.
THE DAMAGE Camping costs €9.25–16.50 per tent per night. Other accommodations available are double rooms at the Pavilhão Mar e Sol (00 351 262 750 331) at €100; and the fort's 15 dorm beds and rooms at €18–81 (00 351 912 631 426, bookings are taken between 6.30pm and 10pm).
THE FACILITIES There are 38 pitches, 2 cold sea-water showers and 3 WCs. A shop (better described as a hole in the wall) sells tinned frankfurters and vegetables, confectionery, ice creams and mini-bottles of water.
FOOD AND DRINK The Mar e Sol restaurant (00 351 262 750 331) serves food all day, including a set €20 lunch menu popular with day-trippers.
FAMILY FUN Swimming in the caves, snorkelling, canoeing and fishing. For all-day snorkelling with lunch €35, call Active Ocean on 00 351 918 820 449.
TREAT YOURSELF Many diving schools sail over from Peniche offering 2 dives a day with lunch (€62; Active Ocean, see FAMILY FUN).

GETTING THERE From Lisbon, take the A8 to Loures/Leiria, exit 14 (À-da-Gorda) onto the IP6 to Peniche. Follow signposts to Ilha da Berlenga to the marina car park.
PUBLIC TRANSPORT Boats leave Peniche harbour at 10.30am returning at 4.30pm (€18 adult, €10 for children aged 5–10, one way). Failing that, hire a private 10-passenger boat, €150.
OPEN June–mid-Sept.
IF IT'S FULL Check for space before you make the choppy crossing. Otherwise, sign up for a surf lesson at the 50-pitch Peniche Surf Camp (Avenida do Mar, 162, 2520–101; 00 351 962 336 295).

**Ilha da Berlenga**, 2520 Peniche, Portugal

t | 00 351 262 789 571 | w | ilhadasberlengas.no.sapo.pt

# quinta dos carriços

You're dreaming of guaranteed sunshine, a beach, peace, privacy, clean facilities and an onsite restaurant for when you don't want to move a muscle – with good transport links. Well, how about this for camping nirvana?

Situated far enough from the overdeveloped tourist ports, but within reach of lively shopping and bar action is this walled, Eden-like campsite. Over the past two decades, the owners have planted seeds and cuttings from their travels, creating botanical mayhem that will make you feel as if you're camping in a garden centre.

Marked plots near the entrance are spacious, terraced along tree-lined avenues. There's a second zone of larger pitches, but wherever you end up you're guaranteed shade – a blessing under the Portuguese sun. Hieroglyphs of naked people signal the entrance to the naturist area. But you needn't expect *Carry on Camping* antics or wobbly bits at every turn; naturists keep out of sight of clothed campers.

If you want to venture further afield, time the 20-minute drive to the lighthouse at Cabo de São Vicente – the most southwesterly tip of Europe (next stop, America) – to catch a majestic sunset that will humble your soul. Closer to home, a short amble will take you to nearby Salema beach – like many on the Algarve, it's full of pink-skinned Northern Europeans wishing that life could be like this every day.

THE UPSIDE  Sunshine, peace and a gorgeous sandy beach.
THE DOWNSIDE  The no-noise policy. So, no music and no rowdy children.
THE DAMAGE  €19.60–21.20 per night for 2 adults, a tent and a car. Hot-water tokens cost €0.70. Studios, apartments and bungalows from €65–100 per night. Dogs cost €2.30.
THE FACILITIES  There are 27 pitches (the best of which are zones 7 and 5) and 14 naturist pitches; plus 13 apartments (sleeping 2–4). Three wash-blocks each have 10 showers, 9 toilets (1 disabled) and 4 urinals. There's a unisex block for naturists. Internet (€4.40 per hour).

FOOD AND DRINK  O Lourenço (00 351 282 698 622) restaurant in Salema serves a fantastic fish supper.
FAMILY FUN  This 'isn't a family campsite' they say, although 'kids who still do what their parents want are welcome'. Let them run off steam at Albufeira's Zoomarine (Estrado Nacional 125, km 65, Guia 8200–864 Albufeira; 00 351 289 560 300; www.zoomarine.com). This huge park has slides, aquariums and exhibitions. Tickets are free for under-4s, €12 (5–10s) and €20 for over-11s.
TREAT YOURSELF  Feel the wind in your hair as you speed along the Med on the look-out for dolphins in their natural habitat on a specially

designed boat with Algarve Dolphins (Marina de Lagos Loja 10; 00 351 282 087 587, www.algarve-dolphins.com).
GETTING THERE  From the IC4 motorway that runs east to west along the Algarve, take the N120 to Lagos and the N125 to Budens.
PUBLIC TRANSPORT  From Faro take the train to Lagos, from where regular buses make the 10 mile (16 km) journey, stopping right outside the campsite.
OPEN  All year.
IF IT'S FULL  For even more peace and quiet check out the *Cool Camping* site at Surfshanti (see p35).

**Quinta dos Carriços**, Praia da Salema, 8650–196 Budens, Algarve, Portugal

| t | 00 351 282 695 201 | w | www.quintadoscarricos.com |

# corgo do pardieiro

Known as the 'bread basket of Portugal', the Alentejo is a poor but golden land that twists and dips its boundaries within the southwest of Portugal. Its countryside looks full-bodied and voluptuous, with lush valleys and dense thickets of trees stretching out far and beyond. Youthful imaginations might compare the lay of the land with Tolkien's Shire, whilst more quixotic minds are sure to find this hilltop hideaway nothing but romantic.

From Corgo do Pardieiro's vantage point, blink and you'll miss the tiny hobbits scuttling about on the horizon. We all know that hobbits don't really exist (right?), but this expanse of wild, overgrown vegetation gives breathing space to many of Mother Nature's real-life creatures. Various owls, snakes, geckos, wild pigs, tree frogs and birds of prey survive amongst the trees. Equally, the airy freedom offers ample room for stressed-out humans to earth themselves spiritually. So, if it's solitude you're after, step inside these woods.

This great expanse of land could actually accommodate hundreds of people, yet only a modest 12 tents are permitted at any one time. Set apart from each other for maximum privacy, they're scattered all over the place – on the top of a hill under an old oak, in the valley amongst the olives or under the cork trees down near the creek. And the majority of shaded plots have great views and picnic tables to boot.

The ideal time to visit is in the spring. Temperatures are pleasantly warm rather than maxed to the oven-blast heights of summer; what's more, the area is an explosion of flowers. The bees keep themselves to themselves, their low buzz humming like a distant motorway as they zoom around nectar-rich blooms. All around the 20-or-so acres, the site sways with plant life in all shapes and sizes.

Imagine how glorious it would be to be woken up in the morning by wafts of freshly baked bread, cooked outdoors in wooden fires, before getting on with the hard task of buttering it for breakfast? Those who like more than their morning bread catered for can order vegetarian evening meals onsite. Committed carnivores, on the other hand, need only head to the village of Amoreiras-Gare, which has restaurants and cafés aplenty where you can sample a *petisco* (snack) and a *copo* (a glass of beer or wine). Nearly every bar and café in Portugal has a huge wide-screen television, so relax – settle down and join in the national pastime of watching soap operas.

Back on site, you'll find solar-powered showers and composting loos in the two outbuilding wash-rooms. Campers will no doubt welcome the completion of the new natural swimming pool that's been under construction. Other than a daily hose-down, there's not much to do at Corgo do Pardieiro to pass the time. After-dark entertainment starts and ends with star-gazing – the galaxies and constellations are the clearest you may ever see. If the quiet evenings have you hankering after something more active in the day, then hire a bike at the campsite and explore the local villages or drive to the sandy, surfer-friendly beaches at Milfontes and Zambujeira, just 25 miles (40 km) away.

So welcoming is the tranquillity of this campsite, though, that it is perfectly understandable why you might put off any adventure until tomorrow. Reading – and dozing – in the shade of the old cork oak will do nicely for today, thank you very much. Today it's just you, the birds and the bees (well, we did tell you it was romantic).

THE UPSIDE Friendly Dutch owners accommodate your every need.
THE DOWNSIDE It's so quiet that light sleepers may well start at every cracking of a twig.
THE DAMAGE In high season, a tent, car and 2 adults is €12.70 per night; 3–10s €1.85 and under-3s go free. Prices go down in low season. There's also a studio that sleeps 2, which starts at €163 for 5 days (low season) and rises to €544 for 2 weeks in high season.
THE FACILITIES In addition to the 12 pitches, there is 1 studio (sleeps 2), 2 washing blocks, and a kitchen with a stove and washing machine. There's also a bread oven, cool blocks, wi-fi, hammocks and a kids' play area. Pets are welcome.

FOOD AND DRINK There's onsite catering for vegetarian and all manner of special diets; meals cost €10–17. Be sure to sample some of the local wines, including Monsaraz and Borba appellations, with your meals.
FAMILY FUN Head out for a spot of wild swimming in the Lago da Barragem de Santa Clara, about 12 miles (20 km) away.
TREAT YOURSELF To a 4-day festival ticket (camping included; €75) for Sudoeste at Zambujeira do Mar in early August (or €40 per day; www.musicanocoracao.pt).
GETTING THERE From Faro airport follow signs for Portimão on the A22, the IC1 towards Lisbon, exit at Santana da Serra towards S.

Martinho das Amoreiras (N503). Turn left to Colos and Odemira (N123-1). Amoreiras-Gare is on the right. Follow the main road and, before the overpass, turn left on the dirt track following the white/blue direction signs (direction Ribeira). After just over a mile (2 km) turn left then right, crossing a small bridge.
PUBLIC TRANSPORT The village railway station is on the Lisbon to Faro route, with 6 trains a day. From Faro it's €17 each way. The owners can pick you up if you ask them nicely.
OPEN All year.
IF IT'S FULL Check out the lovely Quinta Pintados at Monchique (00 351 282 955 320; www.pintados.co.uk).

**Corgo do Pardieiro**, 7630–514 Amoreiras-Gare, Portugal

t | 00 351 283 926 065 | w | www.pardieiro.com

# ilha de tavira

Only a decade ago Tavira was one of the best-kept secrets of the Algarve. Back then the residents of this tiny fishing port would barely notice the few adventurers who travelled east of Faro. Now, it's a different kettle altogether. Boosted by tourism, new properties have expanded the town's borders and the tourist traffic has increased, just as it has all along Portugal's south coast.

Tavira retains much more of its traditional, peaceful charm than most coastal villages, but once you've visited the historical sights on either side of the River Gilão, you might wish to escape to the beach. A 10-minute sea crossing to Tavira Island drops you at a jetty that leads to the only accommodation on the island – the campsite. This fantastic sandy shoreline, stretching for miles and lapped by calm waters, is perfect for anyone who is into tanning or swimming.

Bars and restaurants on the island cater for all tastes, although they tend to close early (there's little nightlife; it's about living al fresco, not at the disco). Portuguese families favour rentable units shielded by tatty canopies, and those who bring their own tents are directed to a nicer tree-lined patch.

The beach sits within the protected Parque Natural da Ria Formosa, so the waters should stay forever azure. If the peace and quiet gets too deafening, hop back to the mainland. Unlike daytrippers, you can return to enjoy a peaceful, deserted sunrise.

THE UPSIDE  It's all about the long, sandy beach.
THE DOWNSIDE  Incongruous wire fences – not an enticing façade for any holiday lodging.
THE DAMAGE  In low season, prices start at €7 per night and per person for a pitch, €80 per week and €140 per month; prices are up to one-third more in high season. Rented tents (sleeps 2–12) cost €21–77 per night. A Tendalit tent (sleeps 2, with kitchen and electricity) from €43 per night.
THE FACILITIES  400 pitches, mini-market, safe (€1 per day), bar (open until 10.30pm), storeroom, BBQ, 4 washing blocks with power points, 20 cold/30 hot showers (€1), disabled WC and 50 sinks. Cashpoint, washing machines (€4), volleyball, Internet (€6 per hour) and a reception.
FOOD AND DRINK  Restaurant Pavilhão da Ilha (Santa Maria Tavira, 8800 Tavira; 00 351 281 324 131) is the best place for the freshest fish.
FAMILY FUN  Plunge down high water slides in Albufeira. Aqualand is open 10am–6pm, May–Sept; adult €18.50 and children €15; www.aqualand.pt). Buses run regularly from Tavira to Aqualand. Your brood will love you forever.
TREAT YOURSELF  Visit the 'capital of the Octopus' – Casa de Polvo restaurant (Avenida Eng. Duarte Pacheco No.3, 8800–537 Santa Luzia; 00 351 96 508 4207) in nearby Santa Luzia serves octopus stewed, fried or sliced like carpaccio.
GETTING THERE  From Faro drive north on the N2, turn right onto the A22 and follow signs to Ilha de Tavira. Ferries run hourly from Rua Jaques Pessoa (8.30am–7.30pm; 8.30am till midnight in July and August), €1.50 return. Water taxis cost €6 per trip.
PUBLIC TRANSPORT  Regular trains run from Faro airport to the north of Tavira town, from where you can catch the ferry.
OPEN  Apr–Sept.
IF IT'S FULL  Just up the coast is a big municipal site Parque Municipal de Campismo de Monte Gordo (Estrada Municipal 511, 8900–118 Monte Gordo; 00 351 281 510 970).

**Parque de Campismo da Ilha de Tavira**, Estrada das 4 Águas, 8800 Tavira, Portugal

| t | 00 351 281 321 709 | w | www.campingtavira.com |

# asseiceira

Marvellous Marvão. Magical, mystical, misty Marvão – all the Ms. What is this Marvão, you may ask? Justifying the excessive alliteration, Marvão is a mountain-top village that will leave you feeling on top of the world, literally. On the far side of a cluster of village houses, the remains of a 13th-century castle lords it over the Alentejo countryside from 900 metres up. Eroded by time and battles the castle's turrets tumble on the edges of a precipitous peak. So, tread carefully along the thick fortified walls; you don't want to topple off with all this excitement…

You can reach these ramparts by car, inching your way along very narrow roads from the other side of the village. Climbing on top of the walls, you, too, will be towering over the terrain, gasping as the earth levels into the lower, flatter plains of Portugal and Spain on either side of you. The setting at Marvão affords 360° views of both of these countries. Walking here with your head literally in the clouds (when it's misty, that is) is a beautifully eerie experience, whatever the time of day.

A small population makes a living from the 20,000 tourists who flock here each year. Better known amongst the Portuguese, this western village isn't on the direct route to anywhere that tourists normally go; it requires a special detour. Day-trippers from Lisbon are able to make the journey, visit the tiny museum, lunch at one of the restaurants and be back in the capital in time for dinner, but it would be a hectic trip. Far more relaxing would be either to stay at least one night at the 5-star *pousada* in the village or, better still, to camp for at least 10 days in the foothills of the mountains.

Located in the spectacular Parque Natural da Serra de São Mamede, Camping Asseiceira ('little hamlet') is a small olive-grove property within walking distance of the bustling village of Santo António das Areias. Simple and compact, it is a truly lovely spot; fresh breezes roll off the mountains and soothe you into a relaxed frame of mind.

The British owner has worked hard to create a mini camping-haven. The front garden is lined with trees on two sides; the roadside edge is framed by a wide-open landscape that stops the site from feeling claustrophobic even with a full house of campers.

Santo António das Areias has shops, hairdressers, an indoor swimming pool and even a disco. Should you ever tire of those, well, there are more attractive medieval villages in the area than the number of days you'll possibly have to fit them all in. Local rivers provide a cheap way to pass the time and swimming at the dam at Barragem da Apartadura has got to top any itinerary, however long or short. And if you turn left out of the gravel drive, you'll be in Spain before you know it – the Spanish border is just 5 miles (8 km) away.

The largest event to roll into town is Feira da Castanha (the Chestnut Festival), which takes over Marvão for one weekend every November. The theme is, you guessed it, chestnuts. Surprisingly for such a little nut, this festival pulls in thousands of people, for all the eating and dancing. However, if you're champing at the bit for some early sun, visit in June when Festas na Relva (the Asseiceira festival) takes place right next to the campsite. The bull run might not be your bag, but watching the village farmers race their donkeys could be amusing.

In a nutshell, it's easy to ardently adore adventurous, awesome Asseiceira.

THE UPSIDE A pretty, tranquil, romantic location that's close to a lot of action, should you need any.
THE DOWNSIDE There isn't enough shade for everyone when it's full, so grab those tree spots.
THE DAMAGE 2 adults, tent and car cost €13. B&B rooms €35–45. Washing machine €5.
THE FACILITIES In total, there are 10 tents, 10 motor homes, a pool and snack bar. Clean showers number 4, as do toilets, plus there are 6 sinks. If you fancy B&B, there are 4 (with 1 en-suite). Internet and wi-fi are €4 in high season.
FOOD AND DRINK Shovel down the tasty Carne de Porco à Alentejana (pork stew with

clams) at the villagers' favourite lunch spot O Pau de Canela (00 351 245 992 650).
FAMILY FUN Karting, rock-climbing and canoeing can all be arranged by an English-speaking company in Portalegre (Desafios Outdoor, 38 Rua Augusto César de Oliveira Tavares; 00 351 245 202 124; www.desafiosoutdoor.pt).
TREAT YOURSELF The posh Pousada de Santa Maria (00 351 245 993 201; www.pousadas.pt) in Marvão offers fine views and fine dining.
GETTING THERE From Lisbon, follow IP1 towards the north, turn off at Junction 7 onto A6/IP7 towards Estremoz. Take the IP2/E802 towards

Portalegre, then Marvão/Spain. After the toll roundabout take the first right and follow the road to Santo António das Areias, passing a petrol station, down the hill.
PUBLIC TRANSPORT Beirã (4 miles/6.5 km away) is the nearest train station with direct connections to Lisbon (www.cp.pt). Daily buses (www.rodalentejo.pt) leave Lisbon at 3pm, returning at 7.45am, taking 4.5 hours.
OPEN All year.
IF IT'S FULL Alegre Camping (00 351 245 964 800; www.alegretravel.eu) is a gorgeous site with 4 pitches near Portalegre. (Minimum stay 3 nights.)

**Camping Asseiceira**, Caixa Postal 2, Asseiceira, 7330–204, Santo António das Areias, Portugal

t | 00 351 245 992 940 | w | www.campingasseiceira.com

# surfshanti

Laurie, the owner at Surfshanti, left Australia's Gold Coast at 16 to go travelling – surfing, more like – around the world. Catching waves all the way up from the southern hemisphere, he ended up in this Portuguese valley. Enrolling volunteers over a period of four years he then repaired, cleared and enhanced the natural lay of the land. Marshes were drained, brambles cleared and sand lugged from the beach to make a valley-view yoga platform and 18 wooden 12-metre-high masts were carved to construct an eye-catching tipi.

Not strictly a campsite, this nature tourism venture, hidden away in the western Algarve, offers a programme of surf and yoga instruction. Before we reveal more, Laurie wants to stress that this is a special, alternative and peaceful haven for paying guests only – it is not a sightseeing destination. So, unless you've booked in, don't even come nosing around his private property, you'll only disturb his, and everyone else's, *chakras* – and that wouldn't be very yogic, now, would it?

Press mentions in glossy mags have caused a rise in the number of tourists turning up unannounced along this stunning coastline, hoping for a glimpse of the much-fêted yurt 'village'. The small compound isn't anything remarkable. What is special is its location: a beautiful valley where little will shatter the tranquillity of your downward dog pose, except the glockenspiel echo of cowbells or the rustle of the wind in the trees. You won't ever regret booking yourself in for a stay.

Having realised his very own Peter Pan childhood dream, Laurie's enchantment is to be shared. Welcomed guests are the lost boys and girls from faraway lands, especially those who've booked into the five-night programme. A giant tipi sleeps four, although you could squeeze 10 inside quite comfortably. Both the Island Tent and the Couples Retreat make fun double bedrooms for couples. You'll feel like explorers camping in the jungle; net walls keep the insects out, but let the fresh air in, enhancing the sense of sustainability and oneness with the outdoors.

Back-to-nature sleeping arrangements are comfortable, but don't go confusing this with luxury camping. Guests are given sizeable beds and share a basic 'bathroom', a brightly painted, open-roof block of two cold-water showers and composting loos. Being an eco-friendly site, only 10 guests are booked in at any one time; the low number makes less of an impact on the environment and results in a more personal stay.

The five-day, full-board programme price includes meals and two yoga classes plus all other extras, such as surfing, board hire and wet suits. Unless the farmer (who swears continually at his cows in the field below) manages to wake you up, make sure you've set an alarm so that you're up and ready to greet the day with everyone else at the 8am sun salutations.

Yoga-phobes can also enjoy Surfshanti. The 'boyfriend going surfing/girlfriend doing yoga' format is particularly popular. In low season, you can treat this place like a campsite without signing up for the classes; the remote location, beautiful setting and proximity to the beach all lend themselves to an ideally situated camping trip.

But most people come here for the waves and the yoga. Surfing conditions in this part of Portugal are renowned and almost guaranteed. Atlantic waves curl as they approach their first taste of land since America, creating optimum conditions for board hounds. Another yoga lesson takes place at dusk, after which everyone gets to eat together outside on a long picnic table.

And as the sun sets, you'll finally twig what this place is all about. The clue is in the name – surf, peace. *Om shanti.*

THE UPSIDE Sunrise, yoga, breakfast, surf, lunch, yoga, sunset, dinner, sleep.
THE DOWNSIDE The early starts won't appeal to late-risers.
THE DAMAGE Full board 5-day/5-night packages with 2 daily yoga lessons, 3 daily meals, staying in the tipi cost €595–735 per week in 2008, but will go up. Extras include €20–45 per person per night, depending on the accommodation you choose. Lessons with a certified surf school are extra, approximately €28 per day. In low season, half-board packages may be available, where you can pay extra for meals

and lessons (see website for details).
THE FACILITIES A 'Taj Mahal' Moroccan lounge, BBQ, 2 hammocks, 2 cold-water showers and 2 composting toilets.
FOOD AND DRINK Breakfast is porridge or cereal, bread and fruit; lunch is a salad/sandwich combo; dinner is a fish and vegetable affair.
FAMILY FUN Hire the retreat's canoes for a downstream paddle to the beach, where you can do some more yoga or have a go at horse-riding (€25 for half a day).
TREAT YOURSELF What better treat is there than fine-tuning your inner being?

GETTING THERE From Faro airport it's 90 minutes by car. Take the A22 towards Lagos and the rest of the directions will be confirmed with your booking.
PUBLIC TRANSPORT Trains run to Lagos, buses go from there to Aljezur, the nearest village, from where Laurie will pick you up. Again, more details on booking.
OPEN May–Oct.
IF IT'S FULL You could always contemplate practising your own yoga with no clothes on! The *Cool Camping* naturist site at Quinta dos Carriços (see p23) is about half an hour's drive away.

**Surfshanti**, Costa Vicentina, West Algarve, Portugal

| | | |
|---|---|---|
| | W | www.surfshanti.com |

# termas da azenha

In ancient Greece, the god of medicine, Asclepius, inspired the construction of many temples that were built in his honour next to 'healing' water springs. About 3,000 kilometres away, and some 3,000 years later, Asclepius is a little-known character amongst the villagers of present-day Soure in western Portugal. Nevertheless, any lack of knowledge of Greek mythology doesn't detract from the locals' appreciation of their own self-proclaimed healing waters. Their luscious landscape is literally bubbling over with springs and the temple, where you can experience their 'curing' powers for yourself, is called Termas da Azenha.

More than just a place to set up camp, this Atlantic-meets-Mediterranean complex (incorporating hotel rooms, a reception, an office, a huge spa treatment room and a bar) is a fascinating find that glimmers at the end of a long road, like a beautiful mirage at the end of a rainbow. The exteriors are all curvy, white-washed walls and spring-yellow columns, whilst the inside is decorated with a wall-to-wall underwater theme.

Mosaics are the big visual attraction of Termas da Azenha. More than 16,000 tiles have been used to create various mermaids, dolphins, urchins and other mystical creatures, creating a stunning walk-through aquarium. Designs are spread out across doorways, on ceilings and into every room on site, and any spot that isn't covered in ceramic tesserae is occupied by a sculpture, picture or poem, instead. So there's plenty to look at. This gallery is being added to constantly – and by guests, too, who can join in the weekly craft sessions.

Also inside, the oh-so-fabulous-looking spa is built around a water spring that the owners believe dates back to Roman times. The (apparently) magical elixir is said to cure eczema. A few soothing hours in the large hall with treatment rooms on each side will do a lot to de-stress your burnt-out soul, at the very least. Whether you opt for a sunken bath or choose to blast your pores wide open in a steam room, you'll probably end most days in one of the marble-tabled massage rooms. As campsite perks go, the spa is a 5-star attraction.

Drag yourself outside – there'll be plenty of time to spend in the spa later – and past the courtyard, past a single line of hotel rooms to the tiny patch of grass, otherwise known as the camping area. It's not exactly the biggest campsite you've ever clapped eyes on. In fact, the space is maxed out with just four families, but it has a fresh feel. Breezes that blow from the Atlantic coast, an hour's drive away, winding their way east to eventually roll over the rice fields right next to the camping spot, engender a pleasingly unpolluted atmosphere. Immersed in water, these expansive plains boost your camping comfort, too, causing the grass to spring to life like a luxury recoiling mattress.

To counter the sedentary nature of the onsite activities, you might want to try to burn off some energy elsewhere. Myriad nature walks can be tried out in the area and the Atlantic coast is great for surfing, whilst Figueira da Foz offers some of the best diving to be had

in the country. After a heavy day's activity, head to Lavos for a sunset drink before checking out one of the beach restaurants there, such as A Pérola do Oceano, a much-loved seafood haunt.

As you breathe in the view of the wetlands from your tent and soak up the calm, relaxed atmosphere, it's hard to imagine doing anything more strenuous than dropping by the spa for yet another massage. You won't always remember that you're in Portugal; you're in the Atlantis of camping sites, worshipping at the temple of good, clean, healthy fun. And what's wrong with that?

THE UPSIDE Where miracles and mosaics meet.
THE DOWNSIDE All these steam baths will require pots of moisturiser; wrinkly skin is so not a good look.
THE DAMAGE 2 people with a tent cost €12.50. Electricity €2.50 per day. There are 5 rentable caravans: €12.50 per day; €85 per week. The owners also rent beds (50) in 4 family houses, 2 studios, 8 hotel rooms and B&B rooms.
THE FACILITIES A shower, a sink and WC. When these become too busy, you may use the 3 spa showers. The spa has steam rooms, sunken baths and 3 massage rooms (warm water, shiatsu and sports massages). There is wi-fi (€4 per hour), a washing machine (€5), an outdoor solar kitchen and the owners will steer their beloved donkey,

Esmé, for €5 a ride. The nearest supermarket is 2½ miles (4 km) away in Vinha da Rainha and a baker visits daily.
FOOD AND DRINK Onsite you can pre-order a 3-course vegetarian evening meal (€12); lunches can be arranged for 5 people minimum. Book a beach meal at Pérola do Oceano (Avenida Mar 23/34, 3080–458 Lavos; 00 351 233 946 127).
FAMILY FUN Surf at Praia do Cabadelo, south of the River Mondego, or stay put to make mosaics.
TREAT YOURSELF To daily dips in the healing waters, of course.
GETTING THERE From Porto take the A-1 towards Porto/Coimbra. Leave the highway at Condeixa. Follow the N1 towards Lisbon and follow the signs to Soure. Go over 2 roundabouts,

cross over the railway line, turn left at the T-junction and right at the next one. After 2½ miles (4 km) you'll see signposts for Vinha da Rainha. Follow the road for just over a mile (2 km) until you get to a T-junction. Facing O Choupal café, turn right and follow this road until you arrive at Termas da Azenha.
PUBLIC TRANSPORT Catch a train from Porto or Lisbon to Soure, where the owners will pick you up for €10.
OPEN All year; but during winter you'll probably feel warmer in one of the hotel rooms.
IF IT'S FULL Make another splash at O Tamanco (00 351 236 952 551; www.campismo-o-tamanco. com) situated near a busy road further south, with its own salt-water pool.

**Termas da Azenha**, Rua João Henrique Foja Oliveira, 3130–434 Vinha da Rainha – Soure, Portugal

| t | 00 351 916 589 145 | w | www.termas-da-azenha.com |

# lugar várzeas

At the turn of the century, Hannah McDonnell and Derek McLean packed their newborn baby and a few belongings into their camper van and, eschewing the urban sprawl of south London, drove towards the hills and valleys of rural Portugal. In the mountainous village of Pracerias, an hour's drive from Coimbra, they bought an abandoned roadside goat shed that they spent two years transforming into a habitable bungalow. After the birth of their second child, they began planning their unique eco-tourism venture.

Taking supreme care to nurture their smallholding, they chopped down the bare minimum in order to zig-zag rows of steps down the hillside. On the valley floor, the couple hand-built a single, magnificent yurt, which they now rent out to guests. Originally the preserve of Mongolian nomads, yurts are the epitome of luxury camping, more commonly known as 'glamping'. Opulent and decadent, this particular beauty is perched on top of a raised platform to level with the natural slope of the land, sheltered by the branches of a sprawling chestnut tree.

Inside the yurt is a riot of colour. Vibrant orange, purple and red covers swathe an old-fashioned, brass-knobbed bed, whilst the turquoise canvas sets off an imposing Egyptian Ankh 'symbol of life' design on the roof. Despite an array of collectible, retro furnishings there's plenty of space to walk around and stand tall. At night, it can get a little chilly, so if you're travelling in low season you might want to pack a woolly hat. However, when the weather is really baking, you can open up the yurt skirts and possibly the roof (it takes a lot of effort and requires Derek's assistance) before lying back on the bed to gaze at the stars.

Vines, olives, figs, lettuces, watercress, broccoli, courgettes, basil and a lot more, grow on the couple's organic allotments. The family's chickens lay your breakfast eggs, which arrive at your door in a hamper stuffed with bread, jam, yogurt, muesli, fruit and a flask of tea or coffee. If you're planning a busy (or lazy) day then you can pre-book dinner, as well. Hannah's home-cooked three-course meals washed down with a bottle of local Dão wine, in your own secluded sanctuary, are hard to refuse.

A solar-powered hot-water shower and a composting loo indicate the couple's strong ecological ideals, but it's the feeling of isolation that is the main attraction here. Private and hidden from the road, the garden

is at your disposal (yours and that of the family's black Labrador, Bula) so you can really relax amongst the fresh scents of pine, eucalyptus, jasmine and orange blossom, without ever having to rejoin civilisation. When you fancy some company, mingle at the large market at Arganil on Thursday mornings where farmers and artisans ply their produce and other creations.

Anyone who's seeking the ultimate escapist retreat or simply looking for a stop-gap on a longer trip through the country would do well to look up Lugar Várzeas. This serene spot makes an ideal destination for honeymooners, whilst longer stays will reward adventurers with wild swimming and hiking trails, donkeys and hiking in beautiful and remote Portuguese countryside.

Hannah and Derek's next project is to build another yurt on the opposite side of the valley, with the same degree of privacy. These former Brixtonians are so laid back that everything they've done appears to look almost effortless. Yet their demeanour belies the massive amount of hard work that they have so far invested in their property. Having built a great self-sustaining lifestyle out of so little, it's fair to say that you'll probably never look at a dilapidated goat shed in the same light ever again.

THE UPSIDE Luxurious, bohemian and secluded relaxation.
THE DOWNSIDE It doesn't come as cheap as regular campsite prices, obviously.
THE DAMAGE Two adults B&B €65 per night including tax. Under-3s go free; 3–12s are €10 each per night. You pay a 50 per cent non-refundable deposit on booking. Cash only onsite.
THE FACILITIES There's a double bed, 2 children's beds on request plus power points, wardrobe, games, books and eco pot-in-pot fridge (2 differently sized terracotta pots sandwiched with coarse sand and saturated with water). Solar-powered shower and composting toilet. Garden table and chairs, badminton nets and hammocks.
FOOD AND DRINK One restaurant well worth the 45-minute trek is Varandas do Ceira (00 351 239 549 833; www.varandasdoceira.com), on the way to Coimbra, which serves tasty Brazilian food.
FAMILY FUN Canoe along the River Douro (00 351 235 778 938; www.transserrano.com).
TREAT YOURSELF Head north of Coimbra and make like a prince or princess at the ornate, 5-star former royal palace, Palace Hotel Bussaco (doubles €135; www.palacehoteldobussaco.com).
GETTING THERE From Porto it's a 2½-hour car journey. Follow the VR1/A28/Porto for A1/IC1 Lisbon, then to Sul (south). Exit at Coimbra North/Viseu IP3. After crossing Rio Mondego, head to IC6/N17 Covilhã (some maps show this as IC7, confusingly). Turn right to N342-4 to Arganil. Through Arganil, turn right at the fountain roundabout and right at the next roundabout for Góis. At the white chapel turn for Pracerias for 3½ miles (6 km) to a stone house on the right.
OPEN Apr–Sept.
IF IT'S FULL Nearby Quinta das Abelhas (00 351 917 147 767; www.portugalsmallholding.org) has a yurt and 10 pitches on its organic farm.

**Lugar Várzeas**, Pracerias, Celavisa, 3300–207 Arganil, Portugal

| t | 00 351 235 208 562 | w | www.yurtholidayportugal.com |

# casa da ribeira

Rugged, wild camping in the company of a self-sufficient community that champions 'green' lifestyles might only appeal to a certain demographic. However, eco-warriors, vegetarians, open-minded, musically minded and plain non-materialistic-minded souls, in particular, are made to feel at home in this valley. Oh, and anyone looking for peace and quiet should definitely turn the page now; camping in Portugal doesn't get much noisier than this.

Two families, musicians and dancers of the touring group, Djamboonda, have reconstructed an old farm building into two modern homes. Tucked away in deepest Portuguese countryside, their land is rugged and wild; like a safari park, but without the animals, you could say. (Although, come to think of it, the family's impressive open-plan living room certainly has enough space to swing a baby elephant.) Next door, you'll find an office space with shelves full of tales from all over the world, and outside, above a stream, a guests' eating area, carved from wood, blends in beautifully with the trees. Then, if you follow the field past the main house, you won't miss the campers' outdoor washing block, the canary-yellow and earth-red colours and murals are striking against the luxuriant bright-green foliage all around.

Casa da Ribeira is well known within Iberian music communities, largely because Djamboonda tour regularly throughout Portugal and Spain but also because there's a high density of performers living in these parts. It's no surprise that the locals call the area 'the valley of the drums'.

To the right-hand edge of the farm, a white construction flashes through the trees. It is, in fact, a huge geodesic dome, illuminated with daylight streaming through its white canvas. The raised wooden platform is the stage for the setting of various festivals, one being the cultural Africa'ki festival, held in late August. It pulls such a good crowd for a sing and a dance that the owners have decided to launch another similar weekend in the summer (see their website for details). A third weekend, where natural therapists congregate to swap notes and learn new skills, is also being planned for 2009.

During the rest of the season, you can expect to share the facilities with up to a dozen other guests. You get the feeling that life flows along as gently as the stream here. If you, like the crew at Casa da Ribeira, are looking for new ways to become more spiritual and less materialistically minded, then a spell here will be sure to cement those beliefs. People who are into adopting

self-sustainable lifestyles are warmly greeted. Are they hugged, too? Well, you never know. The two all-singing, all-dancing couples that live here believe that the world is now on red-alert, public consciousness is evolving accordingly and this campsite is an ideal base from which to mock greedy city bankers (probably).

If you're the type who normally files views like these in a box marked 'new-age waffle', but are attracted by the onsite activities, you could always plan a short stay to see how you get on. Visit during one of the three summer weekend festivals and perhaps you'll become friends with a new dancing partner or a really good reflexologist. You're allowed to cook your own meat in the guests' kitchen; just don't expect it to be offered on the daily changing menu (breakfast onsite is €3 and lunch and dinner cost €7). Should you fancy a night free from chores (and free from carnivore guilt, too) try the recommended mixed grill restaurant in central Tábua. You've got to do all you can to build up those drumming muscles, after all.

THE UPSIDE A musical, community-driven, hippy holiday in a wild, rugged location.
THE DOWNSIDE The discordant sound of tutorials isn't ideal for peace-seekers.
THE DAMAGE €5 per person per night, includes electricity and showers. Festival tickets start at €35 and include camping.
THE FACILITIES There are solar showers, composting toilets, a sheltered dining patio with a basic indoor kitchen, library, bar and picnic tables.
FOOD AND DRINK Self-sufficiency is key here so bring provisions. But for a night off-camp head to Churrasqueira Toino Moleiro (Rua Dr. Fortunato V. das Neves, Edifício Ferro, 3420–324 Tábua; 00 351 235 418 394).
FAMILY FUN Bang the drums or watch a workshop or music festival.
TREAT YOURSELF And your biceps to a rest from all that drumming, and take yourself off for a stroll around Coimbra, an hour's drive away. You only need flex your purse, here; the shopping at this famous university town is great.
GETTING THERE From Coimbra follow the IP3 (direction Viseu) and exit to Tábua. Before arriving at Tábua, head to Ázere, turn left to Vila Seca and after 250m take a left at the modern building, then a right (it's signposted). Follow the dirt track, veering to the left.
PUBLIC TRANSPORT Trains (www.cp.pt) and buses (www.rede-expressos.pt) run from Lisbon to Santa Comba Dão (the journey takes about 3 hours), but you have to get a taxi for the last 5 miles (8 km), for about €12. A direct bus from Lisbon to Tábua runs every Friday evening, returning on Sunday evening.
OPEN May–Sept.
IF IT'S FULL Phone ahead to see if there's space at the *Cool Camping* site of Lugar Várzeas (see p42).

**Casa da Ribeira**, Apartado 92, 3420 Tábua, Portugal

| t | 00 351 235 412 982 | w | www.casadaribeira.no.sapo.pt |

# parque de cerdeira

Portugal is a beautiful country warmed by sunny rays for most of the year. You can cover a lot of ground in a fortnight, driving from the beaches of the Algarve, through the Alentejo countryside, passing Lisbon and up to the north. Tucked away in the northwest corner, close to Spain, is an area that's as ripe for exploration as the south coast.

If you fly into Porto, time your landing to allow for a night in the city. It enjoys a cool art-and-music reputation, plus Porto Wine houses to help you toast your holiday. Next stop is Braga, after which winding roads snake around hills, passing Terras de Bouro, towards Parque Nacional da Peneda–Gerês. On the edge of this mountain wilderness is a striking back-to-nature retreat.

This large woodland site can take up to 600 guests, either in tents or in various rentable accommodations. Unmarked pitches are far away from any roads. Once you've thrown up your tent, head off to the reception to pick up some handy maps and get those sturdy walking boots (and legs) ready for action.

A wealth of walking for all levels means that your days will be busy with hikes of all sizes (or hacks on horseback, if you need to give your feet a rest). There's a small swimming pool onsite for when you feel like having a refreshing dip (you have to pay per half day), but if you'd like a more adventurous work-out then the neighbouring lake Vilarinho da Furna is in a truly stunning setting – and, better still, it's completely free.

THE UPSIDE  A few days spent hiking in the Peneda–Gerês park and you'll be saying, 'Stressed? Who – *moi?*'
THE DOWNSIDE  It's hectic in August; visit during low season for a more relaxed stay.
THE DAMAGE  Two adults, a tent and a car cost from €12.20 per night (low season) up to €17.40 (high season); showers are €0.70.
THE FACILITIES  250 tent pitches. Swimming pool, supermarket, mini-golf, bar, tennis court, TV/games room, Internet and BBQ.
FOOD AND DRINK  A restaurant (opens at 8.30am) supplies scrummy local dishes such as *cozido de Terras de Bouro* (a hotpot of potatoes, pork and cabbage).
FAMILY FUN  Two riding centres close by offer anything from 1-hour lessons to full-day hacks.
TREAT YOURSELF  A 10-minute drive away is O Abocanhado (00 351 253 352 944; www.abocanhado.com). This restaurant's award-winning design is all wooden decking and floor-to-ceiling glass windows. And, in keeping with the nation's sweet tooth, you'll find more puddings than mains on the menu.

GETTING THERE  From Porto it's a 60-mile (95-km) drive. A3/IP1/E1 from Porto to Braga/Valença, exit 8, Braga Sul, then IP9 and A11, and then N101 to Vila Verde then N205-3 to Terras de Bouro. After 6 miles (10 km) you'll see the campsite.
PUBLIC TRANSPORT  Buses (www.transdev.pt) leave Porto every hour for Braga, from where a connecting bus stops near to the campsite.
OPEN  All year.
IF IT'S FULL  Stay in the area just north of Gerês at Parque de Campismo do Vidoeiro (Vidoeiro, 4845-081 Gerês; 00 351 253 391 289).

**Parque de Cerdeira**, Campo de Gerês, 4840–030 Terras de Bouro, Portugal

| t | 00 351 253 351 005 | w | www.parquecerdeira.com |

# el burro blanco

Once upon a time, this campsite's namesake, 'the little white donkey', was the principal means of transportation in Spain. Shifting harvests from the fields and water from the wells, long before roads were laid down in the rural countryside, these four-legged creatures were the lifeblood of agriculture. For a taste of what life was like in Spain before booze shops clogged up the Costas and when donkeys were two-a-peseta, you only need travel to the Sierra de Francia region. In this untouched, remote land is El Burro Blanco campsite.

A three-hour drive from Madrid and Valladolid airports, with Salamanca to the north and the Portuguese border to the west, this area is not densely populated. Locals and tourists are few and far between and even during rush hour you're unlikely to see a lot of traffic, which feels strange given the number of roadside eateries you pass by. Finding Miranda del Castañar, on the eastern edge of El Parque Nacional de Monfragüe, is nicely uncomplicated. Driving down towards the village, arrows point to a dirt track, where further on the right you'll find the campsite easily enough, too.

Keeping nature intact has been the proviso of the three Dutch owners. They've barely touched their nine-acre wood. A trail of trees was cut down to make way for a small track, which leads through the gates down a hill. It joins a natural pathway that guides you into the woods and then up on to a grassy brow of another hill, where the best camping spots – in zone Z – look across the valley to the fortified grandeur of Miranda del Castañar.

Not a lot happens here, the most active creatures seem to be the wildlife: the chorus of local frogs, wasps or crickets can be heard from most of the pitches and little butterflies flutter around the bushes. There are enough majestic trees, wells and foliage to keep all of God's tiny creatures highly entertained. If the threatening armies of big ants put you off pitching up in the woods, just head for a spot at the bottom of the hill or where the village views are, instead.

There's plenty of walking to enjoy outside the campsite. This is countryside that cries out for exploration. A morning walk for a swim in one of the nearby rivers can be followed by a light lunch; it's often too hot to eat much more during the day. You are high up in the mountains here, the sun can be roasting hot, so do pile on the sun cream. The campsite has a bar, which sells drinks only for a couple of hours every evening, as well as bookshelves heaving with classic literature in various languages. Follow an apertif with a stroll through the miniature maze of Miranda del Castañar's streets. Unlike the campsite's eponymous donkey, traditional dinnertimes are still a large part of Spanish culture. Immersing yourself in the ultimate experience of a long, drawn-out feast of tapas, wine and noise in the village is the best end to any day.

As long as you comply with the carefully typed rule sheets that management hands out to new arrivals, then you won't rock anyone's boat. However, noise is a definite no-no: 'if you want noise stay at the airport'. And as for whether this is an ideal spot for couples, here's what they say: 'pre-factored romance is not being offered on principle!'. Make of that what you will. The Dutch trio seem to want very little more out of life except to live quietly in their caravans, conserving and enjoying their land. Their outlook could be infectious; try it and see.

THE UPSIDE Rural Spanish countryside far off the tourist-trail.

THE DOWNSIDE This is not one for entomophobics or 'glampers'.

THE DAMAGE 32 tent pitches €8 per pitch plus €4.80 per person per night; under-6s €3. Four motorhome pitches; electricity €1.50–4.80, depending on the ampage. Washing machine €3.50.

THE FACILITIES Three pristine showers and toilets are housed within a purpose-built, glass-roofed block, where you'll feel cooler inside than out.

FOOD AND DRINK Eat like the locals and tuck in to revueltas (mashed potato, paprika and fried pork skin) at Mirasierra, a 15-minute drive away in the village Moharraz (00 34 234 181 44).

FAMILY FUN Jump in the car for the short drive (30 minutes on the SA225) around the mountains to explore the 4000-year-old cave drawings at Las Batuecas.

TREAT YOURSELF f you're flying from Madrid, a stay in the ornate Hotel Relais Châteaux Orfila – Conde Nast Magazine's 'most charming European hotel 2008' – will make you feel like a prince or princess and at €325 for a deluxe room per night, a pauper, too! (6, Orfila 28010 Madrid, 00 34 917 027 770; www.hotelorfila.com).

GETTING THERE The nearest airports are Madrid and Valladolid. There's less city chaos to endure from the latter; head for Salamanca, follow signs to Portugal/Caceres and take the exit at Aldeatejada Vecinos. Drive through Vecinos and Tamames and take the SA215, which becomes the SA220. Pass several villages then at Miranda del Castañar a painted arrow on the road directs you to the campsite, half a mile (800m) on your left.

PUBLIC TRANSPORT Catch a train to Salamanca, from there there's one bus a day to Miranda del Castañar.

OPEN All year.

IF IT'S FULL You can be noisy at Camping Jaranda, which has a swimming pool and kids' activities (Ctra.C.501 Plasencia-Arenas-Garganta Jaranda, 10450 Jarandilla de la Vera, Caceres, Extremadura, 00 34 927 560 454, www. vayacamping.net).

**Camping El Burro Blanco**, Miranda del Castañar, 37660 Salamanca, Spain

| t | 00 34 923 16 11 00 | w | www.elburroblanco.net |

# islas cíes

Mmmm. Let's see. A group of uninhabited islands off the western coast of Spain, turned into a National Park in 1980 and with limited access by ferry. No roads, so no cars, camper vans or caravans. But there is a campsite. Interested? You should be.

Las Islas Cíes – Isla del Norte, Isla del Faro and Isla del Sur o de San Martín – are just off the western Galician coast, across the bay from the city of Vigo, and are only accessible by a special ferry service. This has the effect of limiting the numbers of visitors each day. To prevent keen campers from pitching up for the whole summer, stays are limited to 15 days at a time and you need to get a *tarjeta de acampado* (camping

ticket) at the camping office at the Estación Marítima de Ría in Vigo before you head over. Once you've arrived, there are handy barrows to help you wheel your gear across from the jetty, and once your tent's up and your kit stowed, you're free to explore your surroundings, like proper Famous Fivers.

Some areas – like the cliffs – are closed off to the public and accessible only by guillemot or gull. But you're more likely, anyway, to emerge from the campsite's trees and head for the curving Playa de Rodas, where the locals often come to sun themselves. They like to think of this as their little slice of the Caribbean and, on a fine day, who's to argue with them?

THE UPSIDE No cars, camper vans or caravans. Just mountains, sea and tents.
THE DOWNSIDE The views are hampered by unsightly tankers moored off Vigo's port area.
THE DAMAGE It's €7.15 per adult and €5.65 per child. Pitches cost €7.45.
THE FACILITIES Decent enough, with hot showers and washing facilities.
FOOD AND DRINK There is a small supermarket and café/restaurant on the site, but for the real experience bring your own food and cook it yourself (though sadly campfires are not allowed).

You also need to take all your rubbish back to the mainland with you when you leave.
FAMILY FUN Bring some binoculars and a Bill Oddie phrasebook and enjoy the abundance of birds.
TREAT YOURSELF There's a lovely *parador* on a rocky promontory at Baiona (00 34 986 35 50 00), due south of the islands. If you can't stay (doubles start at €198), then at least enjoy a meal of local Galician cuisine in its restaurant. There's a special *menú degustación* at €33.
GETTING THERE The ferry company, Mar de

Ons (00 34 986 22 52 72), sails from Estación Marítima de Ría in Vigo, but call in advance for sailing times. In low season there are only boats on Saturdays and Sundays. From June to mid-September the boats are daily. The fare is €17.50 return per person.
OPEN Mid-May–mid-Sept, plus the Easter holidays.
IF IT'S FULL Playa América (00 34 986 36 54 04; www.campingplayaamerica.com) is 6 miles (10 km) south of Vigo at Nigrán. It's fairly sizeable, but is quite cheerful and has a pool.

| | | |
|---|---|---|
| **Camping Islas Cíes**, Ria de Vigo, Pontevedra, Spain | | |
| t | 00 34 986 68 76 30 | w www.campingislascies.com |

# los manzanos

They say you never forget your first time. You were just kids and it was a blissfully warm summer's night. The sun had gone down, the adults were safely ensconced indoors with the curtains drawn and the stars were twinkling up above. And there you were, alone in your very own back garden. Whether it was the era of flares or drainpipes, floppy fringes or Hoxton fins, Slade or Suede, you never forget the first time… you tried camping out in the back garden.

And here on the ritzy lawns of Los Manzanos is your chance to step back in time and experience that back-garden vibe all over again. Because the place is just one huge garden, dotted with trees and shrubs amidst a carpet of shag-pile daisies. In fact, there are so many daisies around the place, you just have to pitch your tent right on top of their bright sunny little faces.

Mind you, Los Manzanos, in Galicia, has one or two things you don't tend to find out back of a suburban semi. Stone statues, for a start. There's one like a cross between an Easter Island maui and a giant stony comb, another like a miniature menhir, the kind of thing you might stumble across when you're yomping on Salisbury Plain. The Galicians love their stones. In fact they love everything that has a touch of the magical and mysterious about it. It surely comes

from the heritage they share with their Celtic-fringe cousins in Brittany, Cornwall and Wales. Galicia is the most western and remote part of Spain; and Fisterra, unlike its almost-namesake in Brittany or Land's End in Cornwall, is indeed at the end of the Earth, at least as far as Europe goes. It's the most westerly point of the continent, where the Romans used to watch the sun set into the sea and wonder where on earth it went.

Another thing you'll notice in Galicia is the number of pilgrims, whose goal is the great gothic cathedral at Santiago de Compostela, just south of A Coruña. Legend has it that the bones of the apostle St James (minus head and hands) are housed at the cathedral. One of the missing hands reputedly turned up in an old iron chest in Reading Abbey in 1786 and is now in a glass case in a church in Marlow, Buckinghamshire. As for his head, well, he lost it in Jerusalem in AD44. So, if you think you might be a budding Dan Brown, this would seem to be a decent starting point for dreaming up a plot of ludicrous implausibility that might just make you millions.

Most of the pilgrims come along the route from the French border, but some come down the Camino Inglés, which starts at Ferrol (birthplace of General Franco) or at the royal sea gate in nearby A Coruña. So don't be

surprised to see crowds of weary walkers in worn-out shoes flop themselves down right on top of the daisies – they've got here the hard way – but at least they'll feel a little less far from home with the familiar back-garden atmosphere at Los Manzanos.

There's a quiet stream meandering down through the site and over the other side of it is a truly sumptuous Spanish restaurant, whose stamp of authenticity is the number of locals who wine and dine there. In typical Spanish fashion lunch continues until late afternoon, or early evening, and the evening shift doesn't start until close to 10 at night. The final post-prandial brandies are sunk at some point during the wee small hours. By this time, of course, you, like the good kid you are, will be tucked up in your sleeping bag and far away in the land of nod.

THE UPSIDE Beautiful garden-camping, with stone statues standing guard.

THE DOWNSIDE It can be a tad noisy. The restaurant crowd departs quite late and there's a pack of dogs periodically barking at each other, plus the occasional plane coming in to land at A Coruña. Apart from that, it's really quiet.

THE DAMAGE €5.90 per adult and €4.60 per child, plus €5.90 for a tent and €6.50 for a caravan, plus another €5.90 for a car. Electricity is €4.10.

THE FACILITIES Well kept and fine when the site's quiet, but a bit of a squeeze in high season. There's a wi-fi network, but you have to be quite close to camp reception to pick it up.

FOOD AND DRINK There's the excellent restaurant (00 34 981 62 72 40) right by the campsite (run by the same people). Inch-thick, melt-in-the-mouth fillet steak with Roquefort is the pick of a wide menu. Food is traditional and dishes 'vary with the flow of the changing seasons'.

FAMILY FUN There are several good beaches nearby, including the Playa de Santa Cruz (the nearest), but the most picturesque is Santa Cristina. Ask for directions at the site – most beaches are within walking distance.

TREAT YOURSELF Try some spiritual uplift by visiting Santiago de Compostela, which is 32 miles (50 km) south of A Coruña. It's the end of the pilgrim route, where the daunting gothic cathedral supposedly houses the bones of the apostle St James.

GETTING THERE Come off the toll motorway at Junction 2F, following the signs for Oleiros. Carry on through the town to the traffic lights. Go straight over and then follow signs for Santa Cruz. Veer right at the mini roundabout, down the hill and turn right onto Avda de Emilia Pardo Bazán. Back up the hill, there's a sign to the campsite on the left.

PUBLIC TRANSPORT Buses run from A Coruña to Santa Cruz, stopping about 10 minutes' walk from the campsite.

OPEN Open for tents Easter–end-Sept. The bungalows are available all year.

IF IT'S FULL Book if you can, though they only take camping reservations a day in advance. There's really nothing else in the vicinity. Best option north is Camping A Lagoa at Valdovino (00 34 981 48 71 22) or much further south is Camping Islas Cíes (see p57).

**Los Manzanos**, 15179 Santa Cruz, Oleiros, A Coruña, Spain

| | t | 00 34 981 61 48 25 | w | www.campinglosmanzanos.com |

# lagos de somiedo

Everywhere with a bit of spare countryside seems to claim that it's one of Europe's last pristine wildernesses. But in the case of the Parque Natural de Somiedo in the Cordillera Cantábrica mountains of northern Spain, it's probably true. Why? Because there be bears up here. And these are not your cuddly Paddington sort either. These guys are the real deal – the kind of sharp-toothed teddies that fancy something a bit meatier than a marmalade sandwich when it's time for dinner. Mind you, they're only little, even on their hind legs, so they're nothing to worry about. The wolves, on the other hand…

These furry friends have stuck around in the mountains of Spain because it's such wild and remote country that there's very little to vex them. The area was made a national park in 1988 and in 2000 was declared a UNESCO Biosphere Reserve, whatever that means. But the result is that it is wilderness preserved and ideal for wildlife. It's just perfect, too, for wandering the *brañas* – high-mountain meadows – with only a Gandalf staff and a half-eaten pack of Hobbit biscuits to keep you company.

Camping Lagos de Somiedo is up such steep and twisty roads that not many humans (and even fewer caravanners) make it up here. If you do the journey by car you'll be clutching for first gear on a couple of the hairpins. The winding roads have a job clinging onto the sides of these deep limestone valleys, carved by glaciers tramping back north at the end of the last ice age, and the resulting rock crumble means you'll have to keep a weather eye out for rock fall. Sometimes it's just a slip of pebbledash, but occasionally you'll find a chunk the size of a baby's head or half-decent watermelon sitting in the middle of the road.

Luckily you leave the rocks far behind when you arrive at the site in the village of Lago. The site's a fairly compact area by the side of a small stream running down from the lake. But with cars confined to an entrance car park, the camping area is blissfully free of clutter and there's plenty of room to spread out and make yourself at home. There's even a discreet little hideaway on its own across the stream, accessed by a rather charming rickety old wooden bridge.

Like everywhere else in construction-crazy Spain, there are cranes erecting new apartment blocks down in the valley in the village of Pola de Somiedo, but Lago is a throwback to an earlier era. The only real signs of modernity up here are the telephone wires strung from house to house, signalling a telecoms revolution that means you can now place trunk calls to Bilbao. Another sign that you're behind the times is that spring comes late in these mountains – the trees can still be budding in May and there can even be flurries of snow – but once summer comes there's everything that you require for that supreme high-mountain feel: birds of prey wheeling through the skies, cow bells clanking on the hills, lazy dogs and horses blocking the road. The locals are enthusiastic bee-keepers, so there are plenty of stripy stingers swigging nectar from the flowers and bumbling around drunkenly looking for a dust-up. And then, of course, there are the bears. And the odd wolf. But at least you can console yourself with the thought that they're likely to be more scared of you than you are of them. Yeah, right.

THE UPSIDE Pristine, remote mountain camping in a village so quiet you could safely take a siesta in the middle of the main street.

THE DOWNSIDE The cows all wear cowbells and don't seem to understand the meaning of bedtime. That grass must be so yummy that they graze all night, wandering through the site dinging and donging as they go. They're also liable to leave you a flat brown present in the middle of the night, so be sure to mind your step if you're out before dawn.

THE DAMAGE A large/small tent is €5.50/€5, plus €4.50 per adult and €3.50 per child (3–10 years).

THE FACILITIES Adequate, but no rosettes are being handed out. There's a rustic wash-block with hot showers and a couple of WCs and a few outside washing-up sinks. That's it.

FOOD AND DRINK There's a dinky little bar on the site, like a mountain refuge hut-cum-wine bar, but if you fancy a bit of posh head back down to Pola and enjoy an evening in the bar at the Hotel Castillo del Alba (00 34 985 763 996; www. hotelcastillodelabla.com). They do good grub there, too, but if you need to get in some fresh supplies, there's always Guillermo's Supermercado in the village.

FAMILY FUN Walk the 4½ miles (7 km) up to the lake. All that fresh air'll do wonders for the kids. Be warned, though; it's about 9 miles (14.5 km) there and back so...

TREAT YOURSELF If you feel like taking things easy, the relaxing option is to see the lake on horseback. El Chugarín (00 34 985 76 36 78) run various rides between 2 and 6 hours in duration. The ride up to the lake is the 4-hour option and costs €25 per person.

GETTING THERE From the A8 coastal road, take the A16 from Riberas and follow the signs for Belmonte on the AS 227 and on to Pola de Somiedo. Once there, turn left down the hill and carry on through the town, following the signs for Valle de Lago. Past the church the road starts to climb the 4½ miles (7 km) up to the village, where the campsite is on your right.

OPEN All year.

IF IT'S FULL There's a fairly basic campsite back down the hill in Pola de Somiedo, though it is likely to fill up before Lagos does. And there's always the Hotel Castillo del Alba (see FOOD AND DRINK).

**Lagos de Somiedo**, Valle de Lago, Somiedo 33840, Asturias, Spain

| t | 00 34 985 76 37 76 | w | www.campinglagosdesomiedo.com |

# la isla picos de europa

Henry Higgins may have taught Eliza Doolittle to aspirate her 'aitches' and not elongate her vowels, but he could have taught her something more meteorologically sound than 'the rain in Spain falls mainly on the plain'. Because it doesn't. If she had a problem pronouncing her Ps, he could have told her that 'the precipitation falls principally on Los Picos'. Which it does.

It would be misleading not to mention the rain here – rather like recommending Scotland and neglecting to mention the midges – because it does have a tendency to fall with alarming frequency. But a good brolly and some stout boots will keep it in its place and in between the rain showers, when the drifting clouds part, you'll find that there's a spectacular mountain wilderness to explore.

The imposing mountains of Los Picos are the much-neglected cousins of the European ranges. In the 18th and 19th centuries, when paparazzi painters were capturing the better-known peaks of the Alps and the Pyrenees, these poor relations just quietly got on with it. They're called the 'Peaks of Europe' because, according to returning Spanish sailors, they're the first landmark you can see from the Atlantic to let you know that you're nearly home.

Despite their visibility, though, these mountains have traditionally been remote and inaccessible. They represent the high-watermark of the Moorish incursion into Spain. This began in AD711 and caused a tide of Spanish refugees to wash up in high valley towns like Potes.

Known as *mozárebes* because of their contact with the Arabs in the south, these folk began *La Reconquista*, the reconquest, following a victory for the Asturian king Pelayo at Covadonga. Columbus had returned from America by the time it was complete, but Asturians are very proud of the fact that their mountain was the first one to be reclaimed, and like so many of the peoples of northern Spain, they remain fiercely independent to this very day.

It's no wonder, when you consider the road up from the coast to the medieval town of Potes. It's as dramatic a gorge drive as you're likely to find anywhere, with huge slabs of rock looming over the road. In some places they literally hang over it. Cheddar Gorge is just a cheesy nibble from the finger buffet compared with this thing – it's the full fondue. Come to think of it, it's so difficult to get here you wonder why Potes needed the 15th-century defensive tower that dominates the town in the first place.

The campsite at La Isla is a short distance (around 1¼ miles/2 km) up the road from the town. It's quite small, just a finger of land beside a gushing river tucked into a valley. Trees dot the pitches around the knuckles, but there's a free camping area at the finger's tip, where you can spread out on the thick grass. Right down by the river there's a small bar with a TV, which seems to be permanently tuned to live bullfighting.

To get a real sense of your surroundings you need to gain some height, so head up the hill to the imposing monastery, from which there are finger-clicking views of the mountains. But for the really dramatic stuff you need to carry on up to Fuente Dé, where there's an even more fantastic view of a great wall of rock rising sheer from a meadow of wild flowers and cowpats.

There's a cable car that runs up to the nearest peak, from which there are high-altitude walks in the pristine Picos. Sure, it may rain. A bit. But it's a small price to pay to stay in the peaks of Europe.

THE UPSIDE Lush green valley-camping, with the sound of the river rushing by.

THE DOWNSIDE The aforementioned abundance of precipitation.

THE DAMAGE For an adult it's €3.75–4.05 and for a child it's €3.15–3.40. Cars are €3.75, a family tent is €3.75 and a small tent is €3.40. At Easter and in July/August there is a surcharge of €10.80 for a pitch.

THE FACILITIES These are to be found in a neat and very clean wood-beamed, red-tiled-roof block by the river. There are plenty of showers and outside washing-up facilities. There's also a pool, with lots of rules (like wearing a bathing cap).

FOOD AND DRINK This is tourist territory so don't expect culinary miracles. The atmospheric Café de Picos (00 34 942 73 81 43 ) on the main street at Plaza Capitán Palacios 20 is an interesting joint with bronze buddhas above the bar and old wooden skis on the walls. It serves a range of tapas, mostly unidentifiable, but then that's half the fun. There's something with anchovies. At least you hope they're anchovies.

FAMILY FUN Not for the faint-hearted is the cable-car ride from Fuente Dé to the peak of Los Picos. Until you see it in action you won't believe how steeply the cable cars climb the 750-metre ascent. It only takes 3½ minutes, but can seem like a lifetime if you're scared of heights.

TREAT YOURSELF Try a night in the Parador at Fuente Dé (00 34 942 73 66 51). It overlooks a meadow of daisies and buttercups at the end of which is the wall of mountain the cable car climbs. Standard double rooms start from €118.

GETTING THERE Leave the main coastal road at Km 272, heading for Potes. Follow the road up through the gorge and through the town of Potes, towards Fuente Dé. Almost 2 miles (3 km) out of town, as the road winds up the valley, the campsite is signposted on the right.

OPEN All year.

IF IT'S FULL Camping La Viorna (00 34 942 73 20 21) is an immaculate and beautiful terraced site with views of the hills. It's on the left as you leave Potes. Or carry on up to Fuente Dé and there's the charming El Redondo (00 34 942 73 66 99), a small meadowy site amidst birch and larch trees up a dirt track just behind the cable-car station.

**Camping La Isla Picos de Europa**, 39586 Turieno, Potes, Cantabria, Spain

| t | 00 34 942 73 08 96 | w | www.liebanaypicosdeeuropa.com |

# cala llevadó

Who says bigger isn't always better? There's loads of space plus loads of campers at Cala Llevadó, but pitching your tent in the intimate cliff-hugging pine forest makes you feel as though the view of the Med is there for you, and you alone.

This sense of seclusion is all down to the setting: a glorious expanse of land on a sloping hillside draped in oaks and pines. On the seafront, giant walls of naked red rock alternate with not two, not three, but four beaches – all worthy of closer inspection. But far from being crowded, these sandy plots, or *calas*, are more like secret pirate coves, hidden between the rocks and almost undetectable until your toes are actually twiddling in their gorgeous sands, wondering if they'll come into contact with any buried pieces-of-eight.

Cala Llevadó itself is hidden away at the end of a tempting, winding path, where kids with buckets and spades clamber amongst the rock pools looking for sea urchins. Further along, Cala d'en Carlos has a graveyard full of old boats that still feel the summer waves, and a little sheltered kiosk, an ideal spot for taking a refreshing beachside beverage. Cala Figuera is smaller, giving all you skinny-dippers a chance to have some privacy. At the other end, Platges de Llorell is a more active hub, which will certainly appeal if you're into scuba-diving, water-skiing, wind-surfing and kite-boarding.

A view onto one of these beaches should be a priority when you're wondering where's the best place to pitch your tent. The idyllic beachfront plots are the ones that you'll find everyone else is heading for, too. So it pays to arrive sharpish. Plots A 67–87, above Cala Llevadó, are amongst the best, beneath shady pine trees overlooking the cove.

Similar sites overlook the other beaches. If you happen to be lucky enough to score one of these, all you'll need next is a couple of deckchairs for a front-row seat, and perhaps a beer or two, as the setting sun bathes that distant blue horizon in dazzling reds, oranges and pinks.

Whilst the campsite seems to go on forever, Cala Llevadó strikes a delicate balance between showing off its natural assets and providing you with everything you'll ever want or need, and a few things you hadn't even thought of. If you do eventually grow weary of sand and salt (perish the thought), take your pick from the campsite's swimming pools, children's playground, outdoor café, bar/restaurant, and tennis, basketball and volleyball courts.

If you feel like venturing further afield, head south to explore the wavy coastline of the Costa Brava. You'll find that it's a heady mix of jam-packed, noisy beach-bum havens, such as Lloret de Mar, and quiet little towns, such as Sant Feliu de Guixols. The curvaceous ocean road between these towns dips in and out of oak-covered hills, revealing views of the Mediterranean around each bend and giving you a scenic detour well worth taking. If you feel like stopping and stretching your legs, you can savour the view from the lookouts, or *miradores*, that dot the roadside. Inland, the city of Gerona, apart from hosting the nearest convenient airport, boasts an old city centre complete with an oversized cathedral and riverside Jewish quarter. Another hot spot, Figueres, is the birthplace of that old devil Salvador Dalí, the eccentric godfather of Surrealism and one of Spain's most famous exports.

An hour away, in Barcelona, Antonio Gaudí's Sagrada Familia is a must-see example of this art-nouveau architect's flamboyant designs. Art historians say that Gaudí was primarily inspired by nature. Who knows? Perhaps he too enjoyed camping out under the trees with the wonderful Mediterranean view all to himself.

THE UPSIDE Proximity to 4 glorious beaches.
THE DOWNSIDE 600 or so plots.
THE DAMAGE €5.50–9.10 per adult and €3.15–4.95 per child (4–12 years) depending on season, plus €5.50–9.10 per car and the same for a tent, depending on season.
THE FACILITIES Endless. Swimming pool, playground, games area, laundry and ironing facilities, hairdresser, bath and shower blocks, Internet café and permanent tents.
FOOD AND DRINK The campsite has a bar and café-cum-restaurant on an outdoor patio, plus a supermarket. For a beach picnic try the chargrilled chickens for sale in front of Can Vilas Restaurant at the campsite entrance.
FAMILY FUN Llorell Beach has children's activities during peak season or visit Tossa De Mar. Its well-preserved old town is set within a walled enclosure dating back to the 12th century.
TREAT YOURSELF If you're in need of a bit of exercise, take a 4-hour (5½-mile/9-km) signposted walk between Tossa De Mar and Lloret de Mar. Sights include the Iberian settlement of Puig de Castellet, the walled site of Tossa de Mar and Santa Clotilde gardens.
GETTING THERE You can spot the campsite easily on the roadside between Tossa De Mar and Lloret de Mar on Ctra. De Tossa a Lloret, Km 3 (or road GI-682).
PUBLIC TRANSPORT Local buses shuttle between Tossa, Lloret, Barcelona and Gerona.
OPEN Early-May–end-Sept.
IF IT'S FULL Head northeast on the GI-682 towards Sant Feliu de Guixols. There is a handful of campsites to choose from along this scenic winding road.

**Cala Llevadó**, Ctra. De Tossa a Lloret, Km 3, Apt. 34 17320 Tossa De Mar, Spain

t 00 34 972 34 03 14 | w www.calallevado.com

# torre de la mora

*Tiene plaza disponible?* It might sound like you've got a mouth full of marbles, but asking for a pitch in the local lingo is a good way of ingratiating yourself with the staff at Torre de la Mora, who get a kick out of hearing Brit campers trying out their Spanglish. But there's another reason for knowing your Spanish ABC – the pitches are alphabetised and it makes good sense to know how to ask for the best ones.

Start with A and B. These slightly elevated locations, just minutes from the sand by foot, look straight down La Mora beach to the tree-topped, red-rock outcrop at the end. The sites are generous and you'll have a spacious pebbled porch to spread out on if you want to put down some temporary roots. Another option for beach frontage is to ask for an E. If you prefer kipping under the trees, try the Ks, where the price you pay for the precious shade is that the pine trees keep dropping their cones whilst you're trying to take a nap. Thankfully, too, the trees are strategically placed on a woody escarpment happily hiding a profusion of bungalows. But at least it leaves the water frontage free for all the tent folk.

Torre de la Mora has the sand and sun thing right down pat. The campsite hugs a section of coast known as the Punta de la Mora, a protected natural environment including cliff faces, forest stretches and some picture-perfect Mediterranean beaches. Down at La Mora the beach – buzz buzz – is a hive of activity, with all the usual suspects jostling for space: surf lifesavers with folded arms like the butcher's best cuts scanning the horizon, sun-baked babes lathering up with factor-8 and kids building sweet little sandcastles by the ankle-deep waves. The beachfront promenade is dotted with cafés and a couple of nicely unpretentious bars. If the latter take your fancy, remember that campsite access from the beach closes at 10pm and if you miss the curfew you'll have to climb over the fence or walk around. Try explaining that in Spanish.

The beach can be somewhat hectic in high summer, when the volleyball net sees some serious action, so you'll be thankful for the protected area running southwest of La Mora towards Tarragona. It's one of the last areas of virgin vegetation along the Med and is a fauna and flora feast – a real treat for all twitchers and nature-fanciers.

One of this stretch's best-kept secrets is Waikiki Beach, an isolated mini-cove surrounded by cliffs and forest. It might sound like it belongs in the Pacific, but it has been voted eighth-best beach in Spain.

It's hard to say whether this is due to, or in spite of, it being a nudist beach, but don't panic, the fashion police don't operate here; you're free to keep your cozzies on if you don't want to scare the wildlife.

If you're a bit of a culture vulture, head for seaside Tarragona. Its pleasant old quarter has a charming central square and streets of boutiques and cafés, where Catalans gather to eat, drink and make merry. It's another good spot for you to brush up on your, by now, superb Spanish. Or if you're old-school head down to the Roman amphitheatre that dominates the beachfront to try out your Latin. If you think that's a tad ambitious, then it's probably best to stick to your Spanish ABCs.

THE UPSIDE Slap bang on a beautiful beach with lifeguards, volleyball, bars – the lot.
THE DOWNSIDE There are a large number of bungalows and mobile homes and you can't reserve a specific site (which means first in, best dressed).
THE DAMAGE Between €13.90 and €28.90 for a single person, car-and-tent package, depending on season. Add €4.30–8.50 for an extra person, car or tent, depending on season.
THE FACILITIES Fully catered with a swimming pool, sports facilities, bar, restaurant, supermarket, well-kept bathroom-and-shower blocks and separate toilet blocks in each camping section.

Organised children's activities and nice play area.
FOOD AND DRINK It's hard to beat the beachside bars along Passeig de la Mora for breakfast or a beverage. For a snazzier meal or drink head into nearby Tarragona to La Taverna (Plaza La Font, 31; 00 34 977 24 95 40) in the Spanish square.
FAMILY FUN Visit the Ancient Roman amphitheatre on the waterfront in the centre of Tarragona. Or take a day trip into Barcelona for a glimpse at La Sagrada Familia, Antonio Gaudí's famed architectural masterpiece.
TREAT YOURSELF Shimmy into Barcelona for a late-night feast at Cal Pep (Plaça de Les Olles,

8; 00 34 93 3107 962), the city's famed tapas bar. You'll recognise it by the queue that snakes out of the door, but it's worth the wait.
GETTING THERE From Barcelona, follow the N-340 or the AP-7 towards Tarragona. Take a turn off to the town of La Mora and follow camp signs.
PUBLIC TRANSPORT Local buses (www.fut.es/~emt) link La Mora to Tarragona 5 miles (8 km) away, where the Renfe (www.renfe.es) trainline connects to Barcelona.
OPEN Mar–Oct.
IF IT'S FULL Los Palmeras (Ctra. N-340, Km 1168, 43007, Tarragona) is a salubrious beachside campsite 1¼ miles (2 km) towards Tarragona.

**Camping Playa Torre de la Mora**, Ctra. N-340, Km 1171, 43008, Tarragona, Catalunya, Spain

t  00 34 977 65 02 77  w  www.torredelamora.com

# la fresneda

Picture this. The sky is a startling blue, save for a lonely cloud sweeping like a white paintbrush stroke across the distant horizon. A bird with a graceful wingspan weaves concentric circles above a small hill crowned in soft, matt-green foliage. The valley is a gently tiered landscape of olive and almond trees lined up like soldiers, flattening out into a yellow, parched landscape, before erupting into a distant wall of red rock. Sounds too good to be true? Wait, there's more.

In the foreground, long afternoon shadows of a row of olive trees fall across the campsite, letting you know it's high time you drew up a pew on the little umbrella-studded patio. From the flat-roofed bar, fashioned from rustic timbers and rugged rock, a friendly face emerges with a glass of cold draught beer.

The Dutch couple who pulled this little piece of paradise together have managed to figure out exactly what camping in Spain should be about. Jet Knijn and Joost Leeuwenberg purchased this 19-acre property in 2002. By recycling tiles and stonework from the original villa the couple built a delightful family home in the style of the region. On the nearby campsite, the washing area, bathroom and tiny bar were also specially constructed to help keep temperatures down and reduce environmental impact. The *finca* not only looks great, but its design got the thumbs-up from the locals, too.

During building, Jet and Joost lived in a caravan with just a solar shower and a composting toilet for company, an experience that turned them into camping-purist converts. La Fresneda has only 28 pitches and to keep the atmosphere really relaxed the couple discourage you from bringing your doggy companions, groups of friends, any hangers-on or other appendages. Lack of permanent *cabañas* is part of this message. Despite the extreme seasonal heat, they don't have a swimming pool, preferring the explorer-style of camping enthusiast rather than those who go for sun 'n' splash-style hols. Well, at least everyone knows where they stand.

And there is plenty of exploring to be done. Ancient paths traverse local medieval villages, wild countryside, rugged canyons and mountainsides. About an hour away, a hot spring and natural-rock swimming pool give you a more-than-welcome escape from the heat. A 4x4 adventure into Los Puertos de Beceite lets you explore this scenic natural reserve, whilst the Via Verde, an abandoned railway track-turned-bike trail, gives you the choice of exploring by bike or on horseback, if that's what takes your fancy. Jet has meticulously catalogued all these adventures in a handy little how-to campsite guide, so no excuses for not getting up to your middle in it.

Meanwhile, back at the campsite, Bar La Roca and the adjoining patio are well placed for early risers to get their espresso fix and pastries for breakfast, and in the evening, draught beer and wine from the local wine co-op slips down a treat. From Thursday through Sunday Joost gets busy in the kitchen making tapas, and on Tuesdays and

Wednesdays a delicious platter of local goat's cheese and charcuterie is served up just as the sun goes down.

In the off-season, when the campsite is closed, Jet and Joost harvest their own olives and take them to the local press. The big ones are saved for scoffing, whilst all the rest are bottled up to make edible souvenirs for the next camping season: a thoughtful pressie to take home to Grandma. Either way, you won't have to leave empty-handed as you'll be given a goodbye gift of locally harvested almonds. A little piece of paradise. In a nutshell.

THE UPSIDE It's perfectly and tastefully adapted to get a full-on Spanish experience.
THE DOWNSIDE At some point you have to go home.
THE DAMAGE €4.50 per adult, €4 per child under 9, €12 per pitch plus 7 per cent VAT. For 7 nights or more: €15 per night for a pitch, 2 adults, electricity (except for Easter, July and August).
THE FACILITIES Immaculate and tasteful bathrooms, a good washing area with washing machines and basins, BBQs, powered sites, a bar and patio.
FOOD AND DRINK Go no further than Bar La

Roca, where the owners dish up tapas 4 nights a week and charcuterie 2 nights a week. There's beer on tap, local wine and a handy espresso machine. Order fresh bread to be delivered to your tent each morning.
FAMILY FUN With keys to La Fresneda village in hand, Joost leads guests on an exploration of its historic buildings, including the medieval gaol, which has ensured La Fresneda's 'monumental protected village' status.
TREAT YOURSELF Another local Dutch couple give refresher and beginner courses in Spanish from €30 (www.eloquentia.es).

GETTING THERE Take AP7 towards Tarragona/ Valencia, then take exit 34 to Tarragona/Reus Este. Turn onto T11 signed Reus/Alcañiz then onto N420 towards Alcañiz. Exit onto N232 at Restaurant Las Ventas for 300 metres towards Vinaròs/ Castellón before taking A231 towards Valjunquera/ Valderrobres. The campsite's signposted.
OPEN Mid-Mar–early-Nov.
IF IT'S FULL Not many places can compare, but Camping Lake Caspe (Crta. N-211, Km. 286,7; 50700 Caspe; 00 34 976 63 41 74; www.campinglakecaspe.com) is worth a try, about an hour away by car.

**La Fresneda**, Partida Vall Del Pi, 44596 La Fresneda, Teruel, Spain

| t | 00 34 978 85 40 85 | w | www.campinglafresneda.com |

# balcón de pitres

Hold on to your lunch. The twisting road to Balcón de Pitres is stomach-churningly winding, but rest assured, this temporary discomfort should give you a few hints about the eye-popping views that lie in wait for you up here in La Alpujarra mountains on the southern slopes of the Sierra Nevada.

With 175 grassy plots, many of them blanketed in wild flowers and shaded by a thick canopy of trees, there's a good chance of being able to pitch your tent on a mountain-view site. And what a view. It stretches at least 180° and looks over the Orgiva valley towards the Contraviesa mountain range. The site's squint-worthy southern orientation makes sure that you enjoy afternoon sun to the max. The town of Balcón de Pitres, 10 minutes' walk away,

has the small flat-roofed white villas that you see all over the area. Their character is equally matched by the surrounding environment, which has been declared a nature reserve, a national park and Biosphere Reserve by UNESCO. This is due to the wonderful profusion of plant species found only in this neck of the woods.

If you're feeling footloose and fancy-free explore the terrain via the 2-mile (3-km) Pitres-to-Ferreirola walk. It traverses the lovely Bermejo river and passes through the little villages of Mecina, Mecinilla and Fondales. If you're a fan of mountain-biking and horse-riding, you'll find both. Otherwise take advantage of the tranquil campsite, where a swimming pool and beer garden are a legitimate distraction from the view.

THE UPSIDE  The view and the tranquillity.
THE DOWNSIDE  The facilities look a little tired, unfortunately.
THE DAMAGE  It costs €5 per adult, €3.50 per child, €4.50 per car, plus 7 per cent VAT.
THE FACILITIES  Swimming pool, bar/restaurant, bathroom blocks with hot showers, laundry service and a grocery.
FOOD AND DRINK  The campsite has a restaurant and an enticing beer garden. If you go into Pitres for breakfast, try out the oversized

tostado con tomate, aceite y jamón at Restaurante La Carretera.
FAMILY FUN  Nearby Orgiva hosts a Thursday-morning market in the town square.
TREAT YOURSELF  To dinner in Orgiva at Restaurante Casa Robles (Avda. González Robles, 10, 18400; 00 39 609 36 44 12), where the hospitable owners cook up a wonderful feast of local favourites such as ajo blanco salmorejo (a white garlic gazpacho) and bacalao (delicately cooked salted cod).

GETTING THERE  From Granada, take the E-902/A-44 towards Motril. Exit onto the A348 to Lanjarón and Orgiva. Just before reaching Orgiva, turn left onto A-4132 to Balcón de Pitres.
OPEN  May–Oct.
IF IT'S FULL  Backtrack to Camping Puerta de la Alpujarra (00 34 958 78 44 50; www.campingpuertadelaalpujarra.com) near the Balcón de Pitres turn-off on the A348 between Lanjarón and Orgiva. Its views are pleasant, albeit not as lofty.

**Balcón de Pitres**, Crta. Orgiva-Ugijar Km 51, Pitres, La Alpujarra, Granada, Spain

| t | 00 34 958 76 61 11 | w | www.balcondepitres.com |

# tipi ronda

Tipi Ronda sounds like a bunch of wigwams in a Welsh valley – you can almost hear the male voice choir tuning up – but thankfully, at least as far as the weather is concerned, it's actually located in Andalucía. Neither location is the tipi's natural habitat, but who cares about that?

Dutch owner Marion Wieske and family developed their serene hillside *finca* knowing it would make a fantastic spot for anyone looking for an authentic taste of rural Spain. And so it does. Though why they thought tipis would help is anyone's guess.

There are two tipis for hire, each on its own secluded little perch in the olive grove. Your first treat on arrival is a bottle of local *vino tinto* and the best place to pop the cork is on the private outdoor patio, just a short step from your tipi door. From here you can savour the view, which is quintessentially Andalucian. The rolling hills, striped with olive trees, create a patchwork of pale greens that stand out like the missing bum pockets on a pair of old jeans.

Inside your tipi are all the things you expect to find in a simple conical tent – decked floors, soft beds, fluffy duvets, clean linen and space for hanging your clothes. The natural skylight formed where the wooden poles merge gives you a window to view the stars at night. Perhaps it's a gentle reminder that, despite all the creature comforts, this is still camping, so don't forget to put your shoes on when you stagger out to the loo in the middle of the night.

Or, if you fancy a dip, it's a short stroll down a pebbled pavement dotted with dried black olive droppings to the swimming pool – a blissful aquamarine oasis. Poolside sunloungers provide the perfect place to make serious inroads into *Don Quixote*, though you'd have a pretty deep tan if you lay there until you'd finished it.

Once you've had the chance to kick back and are ready to go and tilt at a few windmills, you'll find that there's plenty to explore in the area. The *finca* is just a few minutes' drive from the remains of the Roman town of Acinipo, which sits amidst wild flowers on one of the highest hillocks in the area. A brisk ramble to the top will reward you with a great view of the ancient amphitheatre, which – just like Bruce Forsyth – is in surprisingly good nick for its age.

You'll find another dose of history at Cueva de la Pileta, where you can see some of Andalucía's most ancient caves, complete with Stone-Age carvings, by candlelight.

All you hikers, walkers and horse-riders are spoilt for choice, having the Serranía de Ronda mountain range, and Grazalema and Sierra de las Nieves *parques naturales* on your very doorstop. This last's claim to fame is Torrecilla, the highest point in Andalucía at nearly 2,000 metres, which makes for a rewarding climb. That is, if you're not already feeling on top of the world.

Before you leave the area, you really must spend at least a day in Ronda, a historic town best recognised by the dramatic arches of the Puente Nuevo bridge spanning El Tajo gorge in the town centre. The town was the sometime home of Ernest Hemingway, who set part of his Spanish Civil War novel *For Whom the Bell Tolls* here. Of course, the war is now thankfully long gone, and the place is a treat, with its graceful avenues of orange trees, cobbled streets and a plethora of excellent tapas restaurants for when exploring leaves you somewhat peckish and in need of a nibble.

THE UPSIDE This is an isolated rural setting, which has all the creature comforts you could possibly want.
THE DOWNSIDE Only 2 tipis are available for hire.
THE DAMAGE The rate May–June is €55 per person, and July–Oct €65 per person (same rate for kids). The minimum is 2 nights' stay.
THE FACILITIES There is a swimming pool and outhouse with a clean and modern toilet, shower, kitchen and pergola and there is also a good play area and a trampoline for the kids to bounce around to their hearts' content.

FOOD AND DRINK On the road to Ronda there's a roadside bar and café, which is worth a visit. In the opposite direction the little town of Ventaleche has a 'silent' bar run by Maria. Look out for the patio with tables and chairs.
FAMILY FUN Explore the nearby town of Ronda, famous for its bullring, which has guided tours and a dramatic gorge-spanning bridge.
TREAT YOURSELF To a wonderful ride in a balloon over Ronda (€160 per person for 1-hour flight; www.balloonflightsspain.com). If you feel it's then time for some fine dining, reserve a table at Michelin-starred Restaurante Tragabuches

(bullring, Calle José Aparicio 1, Ronda; 00 34 952 19 02 91; www.tragabuches.com).
GETTING THERE Follow the A-374 towards Ronda. Between Km 25–26, turn left onto the MA7402. After 7 miles (11 km) you'll see a ramshackle house on the left. Turn right here onto a unmade road. Tipi Ronda is the first *finca* on the right after the road turns left.
OPEN May–Oct.
IF IT'S FULL There are 2 other 'tent-free' *Cool Camping* sites within an hour's drive: either upscale Hoopoe Yurt Hotel (see p91) or rural La Huerta Yurts (see p97).

**Tipi Ronda**, Apartado de Correos 471, 29400, Ronda, Málaga, Spain

| | t | 00 34 951 16 60 30 | w | www.tipironda.com |

# hoopoe yurt hotel

Don't scoff. This isn't just camping for toffs. Hoopoe Yurt Hotel might not involve leaking tents or air mattresses that deflate in the wee small hours, but it's still camping. It's just very stylish, boutique camping, for those of you who want to take the softie-route, just for a change.

The 'hotel' is actually made up of a miniature yurt village of 13 Mongolian-style yurts, generously spaced on seven acres of rugged Andalucian mountain. Five of the yurts form the family home of the owners Henrietta and Ed.

Like the Tardis, yurts are bigger on the inside than you'd think – and each one has a unique theme. For example, there's the Mongolian, decked out in earthy red and orange rugs. There's a large double bed and an eclectic mix of traditional Mongol furniture, including bedside tables and a dresser. All that's missing is a Mongolian Sonic Screwdriver. In fact, you can hardly call this camping at all. Then there's the Jaipur yurt, made from latticed chestnut wood, where you can dream yourself back in time for a bit of old-style Raj decadence.

All Hoopoe's yurts have overhead and bedside lights as well as sockets for charging mobiles and laptops, and in keeping with the hotel's green approach, it's all solar-powered. But wouldn't you rather leave your laptop in the office and tell your boss you'd forgotten your phone? You're on holiday, after all.

Outside, you have a private shaded area with garden furniture and your very own swinging hammock for relaxation that goes more than skin-deep. Stylish wooden outhouses provide private composting toilets and bathrooms for each yurt. About the closest thing to roughing it you'll find at Hoopoe is stepping out amidst the oak trees for a midnight trip to the loo with only the star-studded sky and a couple of curious owls for company.

Most visitors to Hoopoe tend to stay for a week or longer, and it's easy to see why. When you're not lounging on the deck near the kidney-shaped swimming pool or enjoying a massage under the oaken canopy, you can relax on luxurious cushions in the cosy pergola and order up a selection of tasty snacks from the in-yurt menu. This certainly beats rubbing two sticks together, and who needs campfires anyway?

The campsite itself is arranged on a gently sloping hillside covered in Spain's quintessentially gnarled cork trees, the

kind with heavy foliage and thick red bark that regenerates when it's harvested. In spring the landscape is carpeted in pink, purple and yellow flowers and grasses. If you can summon the will to move at all, the combination provides the perfect territory for short walks and explorations.

You can see the mountains of Grazalema from the campsite and this terrain, along with the nearby Sierra Ronda, makes a playground for you to go horse-riding, mountain-biking, bird-watching and hiking. Even caves with Paleolithic paintings are there for the investigation. You can hire local guides for all these pursuits and if you ask

nicely Hoopoe will even put together a scrummy picnic for you to take with you. No need to starve here.

In the sleepy town of Cortes de la Frontera, within walking distance, you can stay limber with your own private yoga lessons, mug up on Spanish or taste-test the local tapas. Just remember, though, that everyone is very strict about siesta time – come two o'clock in the afternoon everything grinds to an abrupt halt, and you should, too. And given how laid-back everything is at Hoopoe, you'll sometimes struggle to stir again afterwards. This is the kind of camping that all of us could deal with.

THE UPSIDE Luxury camping in a rural setting. No children.
THE DOWNSIDE With only 5 yurts, bookings are essential. No children.
THE DAMAGE £95 per couple, per night, including breakfast.
THE FACILITIES Private bathroom and toilet, swimming pool, al fresco dining, room service.
FOOD AND DRINK Hoopoe serves 3-course dinners 4 nights per week, breakfast daily, plus there is an all-day snack and drinks menu. The food is all grown in the kitchen garden or locally.
FAMILY FUN No children are allowed, so 'family' fun isn't really on the menu, making this place 'campo relaxo' whatever you do.
TREAT YOURSELF Hoopoe arranges massages on a bed beneath the oak trees. They'll also pack you a hamper for picnics in the countryside.
GETTING THERE Hoopoe hands out directions once a booking has been made. The website gives directions from Málaga, Jerez and Gibraltar.
PUBLIC TRANSPORT Trains to Cortes de la Frontera run between Granada and Alcaceres, and from Ronda. Pick-ups from Cortes de la Frontera by arrangement.
OPEN Mid-Apr–mid-Oct.
IF IT'S FULL There are 2 other 'tent-free' *Cool Camping* sites – Tipi Ronda (see p86) and La Huerta Yurts (see p97), but don't expect the same level of luxury.

| Hoopoe Yurt Hotel, Apartado de Correos 23, Cortes de la Frontera, 29380 Málaga, Spain | | |
|---|---|---|
| | t 00 34 951 16 80 40 | w www.yurthotel.com |

# la huerta yurts

Ever wondered about that well-known connection between Uzbekistan and Morocco? Well, this is it. Here is a campsite that lets you sample Moroccan flavours, both culinary and visual, and traditional Uzbekistan yurt-style accommodation – all in southern Spain. A bit of a stretch? Well, you'll be surprised to hear it works a treat.

La Huerta means 'fruit garden' or 'orchard' in Spanish and it has to be said that whoever conjured up the name wasn't wrong. Located in a 'secret' valley between the Hacho and Crestillina mountains and the pueblo of Gaucín, the La Huerta property, or *finca*, is striped in rows of gnarled old orange and peach trees that look as though they've been there for ever. The orchard is so bountiful that the soft thud of fat fruit falling into the wild grass is a constant background sound-effect. Constant, too, is the delicious smell of something strangely reminiscent of marmalade as the oranges gradually ripen. Enough to make you homesick? Well, not really.

Running across the corner of La Huerta is the Rio Genal, a pristine creek hidden like a prized gift amongst the poplars and wild cane. It's so clean and clear that you can forget about the campsite's so-so shower facilities and bathe here *en plein air* instead,

surrounded by the sights and sounds of the magical oak forest that blankets the surrounding hills. The little pebbled beaches provide pleasant spots to spread out your towel and sunbathe with a good novel or go otter-spotting in the knee-deep shallows.

In the midst of this paradise stand two traditional Uzbekistan yurts, neatly fenced off, no doubt to protect you from the wild pigs in search of those yummy oranges. Inside, the yurts are rustic, with quaint wooden floors criss-crossed with dappled sunlight and stocked with sufficient warm blankets to keep your whole family, or bunch of mates, snug for an entire winter. The Moroccan décor is a charming nod towards Andalucía's Moorish history and the owners' own forays into nearby Morocco.

Owners Penny and Kit Hogg are an English couple who have lived in Spain for more than 10 years and adopted the same laid-back approach as the locals. They've set up the campsite so that you feel more like visiting friends than travelling strangers: you are free to use the family kitchen and run the gauntlet of its comings and goings; the bathroom facilities are annexed off the main house; and meals are shared. On the porch of their two-storey villa, Penny serves up a traditional Moroccan *tajine* feast and the communal table brings guests together, inspiring many lingering late-night conversations. Another high point is Kit's wood-fuelled natural sauna, designed and built by his own fair hands. The idea is to work up a sweat in the little cubbyhole-like structure before cooling off in the creek.

The Hoggs say that most visitors make the trek down the 2½-mile (4-km) dirt road and rarely feel the urge to make the return journey until home-time comes along. That's not to say that there isn't a lot to do in the area. So if you feel like exploring, not far south the Mediterranean beaches of the Costa del Sol and the Rock of Gibraltar beckon, just a day-trip away.

Closer to the campsite, about 20 minutes away, the exquisite little *pueblo blanco* (white village) of Gaucín features a ruined Moorish castle, an atmospheric lookout giving you a good view of the La Huerta valley. When the castle is lit up at night you can see it from the porch whilst Penny serves up your dinner. Whoever it was who planted this orchard all those years ago sure knew a good spot when he saw one.

THE UPSIDE Tranquillity, isolation and excellent hospitality.
THE DOWNSIDE There are only 2 yurts (which are looking a little tired, it has to be said), but they do sleep 8–10. Dinner is a little pricey if you have kids in tow.
THE DAMAGE €35 bed and breakfast per person (kids as well), plus €20 for optional dinner.
THE FACILITIES Owners' kitchen and annexed bathroom facilities, wood-fuelled sauna and a freshwater creek perfect for bathing.

FOOD AND DRINK Penny cooks a mean Moroccan *tajine* for dinner. Help yourself to breakfast in the kitchen. In nearby Gaucín, Pura Vida organic shop and café (Calle Convento, 166; 00 34 952 15 13 69) has a great selection of local food for self-catering and dining-in plus coffee, wine and plenty of other supplies. And they're lovely people to boot.
FAMILY FUN Penny and Kit conduct mini tours down the shallows of the Rio Genal looking for wildlife. The creek will occupy kids for hours.

TREAT YOURSELF Time your stay for Gaucín's August 'Feria' and the exciting 'Running of the Bulls' festivities.
GETTING THERE La Huerta is 30 minutes from the AP-7 motorway junction on A377, including a 2½-mile (4-km) dirt track. You will be given specific instructions after making a booking.
OPEN May–Oct.
IF IT'S FULL There are 2 other 'tent-free' *Cool Camping* sites within an hour's drive, Hoopoe Yurt Hotel (see p90) and Tipi Ronda (see p86).

**La Huerta**, Gaucín, Andalucía, Spain

| t | 00 34 952 11 74 86 | w | www.andaluciayurts.com |

# tipis indiens

All small boys whoop like Red Indians at some stage in their infancy. Some boys don't leave it with a simple rain dance in the playground, and instead pursue their intrigue further. When, as a teenager, you're spending all your time knocking out native North American Indian arrowheads, it soon becomes clear that this hobby has turned into an obsession. Years later, when you open up your very own tipi village and see the delight of every visitor who comes, you know that it was time well invested.

Francis Caussieu grew up here in the Barèges Valley and spent a little time travelling abroad before inheriting two countryside barns on the outskirts of the little village of Gèdre. He decided to carry out renovation and hire them out as *gîtes* throughout the year.

He also built himself a house further down the mountain at Esterre, where he spent time sitting and watching the seasons unfold before him like a slow-motion nature programme. Reflecting on a childhood spent tearing around mountains by day and watching spaghetti Westerns at night, Francis concluded that if he was never actually going to be Clint Eastwood or Burt Lancaster, he could still, at the very least, have his own film set.

In January 2004, the search for a local craftsman to make tipis began. In the Alpes-de-Hautes-Provence region, Francis found someone with a passion to match his own. Together they chose designs that were easy to assemble; then, they set about the harder task of finding a logger who'd select the strong woods needed to create the sturdy dwellings. By June 2006, just a month before his first visitors were due, Francis was the proud owner of six tipis.

Each construction has two double beds and a small sofa bed with a thick, wooden chest, snug duvets, a table and a few Indian artefacts thrown in for good measure. The tipis are extremely cosy because the beds take up most of the space. There's a homely barn where you could stash a few belongings, although you would be sharing these facilities with the other tipi guests. You can shower, cook, watch TV in front of a small furnace fire or eat at the dining table – enjoying the best of both worlds: camping like an Indian and dining like a king.

Most campers prefer to be within sight of the mountains in the evenings and as night falls they'll stack up firewood for a campfire singsong with their friends and neighbours. Apart from its immediate location, with stunning views of the Cirque de Troumouse, you're surrounded by a landscape alive with goats and marmots. The village, Gèdre, has a pool, an ice-skating rink and a bob luge, which all remain open during the summer holidays. The village is also blessed with some excellent eateries, the best of all being La Brèche de Roland, where you should make a reservation early on in your stay, as the beef filet with melted ewe's cheese sauce may well lure you back for seconds.

Outside Gèdre you drive past some truly gorgeous scenery. There's the ski station town of Luz-Saint-Sauveur in the north, where riverside cafés are jollied up by colourful street bunting. Then, further south, at Gavarnie, is the highest waterfall in France, a worldly wonder situated just before the French–Spanish border. If you visit at the right time, avoiding heavy traffic, you can park up and then walk into one of the best natural amphitheatres in Europe.

It'll be hard not to do your best Red Indian war-whoop cry here, but we wouldn't advise you to go disturbing the deafening silence.

THE UPSIDE You're high up the mountains, living like a Red Indian.
THE DOWNSIDE Goats with their droppings and coughs can be a disconcerting wake-up call.
THE DAMAGE Prices for tipis in July and August for 1 night cost €85, €195 for 3 nights and €490 per week. In May, June and September, the weekly rate drops to €330 (apart from the last week in June, which is €390).
THE FACILITIES One *gîte* is available to all tipi guests with TV, sofas, a kitchen with *fondue* and *raclette* sets, washing machine, iron and 2 shower rooms. Guests must bring their own sheets and pillowcases, or you can hire linen for €5 per bed. Cleaning is an optional €10 per tipi.
FOOD AND DRINK La Boutique des Cirques in town (place de la Fontaine) has all kinds of local produce and crafts for sale. La Brèche de Roland (00 33 5 62 92 48 54) is the centrally located village steak specialist.
FAMILY FUN The goats were bought especially to please tourists and the kids can't get enough of them. A 5-minute drive down the mountain to Gèdre is an outdoor pool, an indoor ice-skating rink (open July and August) and a bob luge (open July–Sept).
TREAT YOURSELF To a sunrise walk into the amphitheatre of Gavarnie. There's no doubt it will render you utterly speechless. Or you could book a balcony-view room at Hôtel Vignemale (00 33 5 62 92 40 00; www.hotel-vignemale.com) and open the curtains for a similar effect.
GETTING THERE A very pretty drive, the D821 to Argelès-Gazost, leads to the D921 through Gèdre. At the village end, turn right, then take the first left towards Saussa. Passing Camping Les Tilleuls on your left, continue until you see a few car park spaces on the right, and just after that is a small 'Tipis' sign on your left. It's a steep drive down, and it was a rocky one last year, but Francis said he'd be laying a smoother surface in time for the new season.
PUBLIC TRANSPORT The SNCF train station at Lourdes is 26 miles (42 km) away with a bus service to Luz-Saint-Sauveur. From there you could order a Taxi Caussieu (Francis' brother; 00 33 5 62 92 97 56).
OPEN May–Oct.
IF IT'S FULL A short distance back downhill is the smaller *Cool Camping* site of Les Tilleuls (see p104).

**Tipis Indiens**, 8 rue des Carolins, 65120 Luz-Saint-Sauveur, France

| t | 00 33 6 15 41 33 29 | w | www.tipis-indiens.com |

# les tilleuls

Generations of the Millet family are so consumed with catching up on their gossip, they barely glance at new arrivals inching down the driveway towards their patio table. When they do notice you, they'll fix you with the friendliest of smiles. Could they really be so used to the voluminous valley vista stretching out beneath them, that their eyes are not permanently fixed on the horizon? Surely no amount of time would weary one's appreciation of such a spectacular sight.

The view below is a chocolate-box mountainscape revealing the extraordinary terrain of Campbielh, Coumély and Le Cirque de Gavarnie, dotted with old stone houses like a random scattering of Lego bricks. The Millets understand that such a fortunate location should be shared to be fully enjoyed, and so for many years have been allowing campers to experience the views from their garden (1,100 metres above sea level). What's more, campers don't have to fight to be first with a front-row seat, as the garden has been divided into four tiered levels, which all look down over the hamlets. And high-season travellers might want to pitch under one of the few trees, as there's nowhere else to hide from the sun on this campsite.

Perching high up on this privileged ridge, you'll feel like a bird of prey surveying the scene below – and Les Tilleuls is the perfect place to build your nest.

---

THE UPSIDE  Cracking valley views.
THE DOWNSIDE  Cars are allowed onsite next to the tents, which seems a shame as the site would look even prettier without them.
THE DAMAGE  There are 25 pitches costing from €12 for 2 adults with a car.
THE FACILITIES  Next to the vegetable garden is a very modern and clean block containing 4 showers, a sink, a basin for washing clothes and 5 toilets. Pets are allowed.
FOOD AND DRINK  The artisan shop on the road heading into Gèdre from the north sells Fleur d'Amour, a sherry-type apéritif *pour rester amoureux*, a bargain at €12 (La Tannière,

Pragnères, 65120 Gèdre; 00 33 5 62 92 49 11).
FAMILY FUN  A 5-minute drive down the mountain to Gèdre is an outdoor pool, an indoor ice-skating rink (both open July and August) and a bob luge (open July–Sept).
TREAT YOURSELF  To a helicopter ride with Pyrénées Copt'Air (Jean-Philippe Duprat, 64230 Poey-de-Lescar; 00 33 5 59 68 65 19). A 15–20-minute aerial view of the mountains and lakes costs from €120 for 2 people. The drive back north towards Argelès-Gazost to Hautacam will take less than an hour, but in good weather it's a scenic route you'll not tire of.
GETTING THERE  Follow the D821 to Argelès-

Gazost then the D921 through Gèdre. At the village end, turn right, then take the first left (to Saussa). Follow the road and keep a look out for the almost hidden left turn down to Camping Les Tilleuls.
PUBLIC TRANSPORT  The SNCF train station at Lourdes is 26 miles (43 km) away with a bus service to Luz-Saint-Sauveur.
OPEN  Early-May–20 Sept.
IF IT'S FULL  The *Cool Camping* site of Tipis Indiens (see p100) further up the mountain has tipis for hire. If all else fails, the family on the other side of the road from Les Tilleuls allows campers on their tiny garden ledge. The facilities are pretty poor, but it's cheap, from €4 a night for 2 people.

**Camping Les Tilleuls**, Saussa, 65120 Gèdre, France

| | t | 00 33 5 62 92 48 92 | e | millet.rosalie@wanadoo.fr |

# belrepayre trailer park

Perry looks like a clown. He has the voluminous nose and wide expression, plus those distinctive side tufts of hair that you usually associate with clown wigs (the ones with the bald patches on top). So you won't be terribly surprised to learn that he's a semi-retired circus performer, who in fact worked for the industry's renowned impresario Gerry Cottle. He's the son of a legendary actor, he'll pull insightful quips out of his hat during general chit-chat and he owns a life-size collection of London Transport memorabilia. But best of all, he's a creative genius who, together with his wife, has pulled off what for most would be like a pie-in-the-sky dream – Europe's first Airstream trailer park.

How does a son follow in the footsteps of the late Michael Balfour, a regular feature on British TV drama and comedy in the 1960s and later a star of many big-budget Hollywood movies? In Perry's case, you don't; you jump in with both oversized clown feet and form a father-and-son touring clown troupe – who were known as the Hazzards. Michael, Perry and his brother toured their theatrical gang show all over the UK in between acting assignments, travelling as a family in a 90-year-old caravan; then later on, when Perry had his own brood, they upgraded to a double-decker bus. If anything ever influenced Perry's life path, it was growing up amongst illustrious acting circles ranging from Saturday matinée actors, the Children's Film Foundation, to the slapstick performers, the *Carry On* crew.

Living in the 1970s also made a mark, one that Perry never wanted to wash off. With his dad's advice – to always stay either one step ahead or a few steps behind fashion – ringing in his ears, Perry and his wife Coline put down roots and set about transforming an idyllic spot in the Ariège foothills of the Pyrénées into a themed trailer park. A novelty concept with incredible mileage, you could call it fashionable, but pioneering would be more accurate.

Over the past two decades the couple have gradually amassed a collection of 15 Airstreams, restoring each one in turn, then kitting them out in retro fabrics and fitting paraphernalia unearthed at flea markets. The model names of trailers are determined by their size and, apart from an Airstream diner, which they stumbled across under the Eiffel Tower and turned into the Apollo bar, all their vehicles hail from America. They found a 1972 Sovereign in a nudist camp in Florida, a 1970s Tradewind model in New Mexico and a rare 1950s Silver Streak Clipper in Arizona.

Perry likens being inside an Airstream to being in the womb; designed like a capsule, they make people feel safe and cosy.

The interiors are truly wah-wah: all swirly patterns, knitted cushions and retro crockery. As well as a tiny bathroom, fitted kitchen and wardrobes, each one has an atmospheric black-and-white TV, an eight-track music system, a video player (ours came with a tape of *The Avengers*) and a mini-garden with a captivating fringed umbrella and sunloungers.

BelRepayre's strong seventies theme is heightened with retro bunting and artistic touches all over the site, particularly in the Apollo bar-disco room. People really trip back in time here. Some guests bring 1970s clothes with them: floral or Hawaiian shirts, full skirts and flares are *de rigueur*. Perry dresses up when he turns into DJ Bobby Lotion to spin seminal New York or Italian disco along with chart-topping hits of the decade. He reckons people lose 35 years here. Which, if true, really would leave some of us feeling deliciously ga-ga.

THE UPSIDE  Step back to the 1970s at this unique retro caravan park. Cool, man.
THE DOWNSIDE  Turning up in your battered Rover and parking it next to a trailer might, rather embarrassingly, spoil the look.
THE DAMAGE  Airstream trailers, vintage caravans and campers (retro tents preferred please). A pitch and 2 people €18–27 per night. BelRepayre's Airstream hire costs from €75 a night to €650 a week (sleep up to 4). Extra charges for sheets (regular or silk!), towels, dressing gowns and cleaning.
THE FACILITIES  There's lots: sauna, yoga room, ping-pong, badminton, bike tracks, outdoor cinema screen, DJ bar-disco, evening food (high season only), a small shop selling organic

produce, hot tub and communal showers. And Perry's son might perform a few magic tricks.
FOOD AND DRINK  Mirepoix has an exemplary farmers' market every Monday on place du Maréchal Leclerc. For something a bit more upmarket, head for the fabulous restaurant Le Comptoir Gourmand (Cours du Maréchal de Mirepoix; 00 33 5 61 68 19 19), where you can feast on everything from mussels to monkfish in a converted barn before stocking up on regional produce in their deli.
FAMILY FUN  This is really a playground for the grown-ups, but as Perry says, he welcomes *tout le monde* 'as long as they're nice'. Rambles through the bordering Bélène Forest should burn off some energy. Else notch up a gear and burn some rubber

at the go-kart track near Carcassonne (00 33 4 68 25 67 07; www.winkart.fr).
TREAT YOURSELF  To a hot tub in view of the snow-capped mountains, followed by a massage, then share a bottle of champagne under the stars (€30 for tub for two, massage €20–90).
GETTING THERE  It's near Mirepoix. Once booking's confirmed you'll receive directions. This secretive approach prevents curious tourists from disturbing everyone's privacy. Perry may be able to pick you up from the airport. If you arrive in your own classic car you'll get a 10 per cent discount.
OPEN  May–Sept.
IF IT'S FULL  On the D625 from Mirepoix to Bénaix you'll find Camping Le Mathibot (00 33 5 61 01 86 36), a simple 6-pitch field behind a farm.

**BelRepayre Airstream & Retro Camping**, Near Mirepoix, France

| | t | 00 33 5 61 68 11 99 | w | www.airstreameurope.com |

# mas de la fargassa

An organic fruit farm that lives off its land – selling plums, apples, strawberries, gooseberries, raspberries, pears and 120 kilos of organic bread each week – needs some assistance, and the Dutch–English proprietors get it by offering work placements to people of all ages. In exchange for free accommodation and food, the land is cultivated, the donkeys walked, brushed and fed, the bread kneaded every Friday (ready to sell at the wonderful Céret market on the Saturday) and the fires are lit at night.

Watching workers from all over the world busying themselves and relaxing so well together lends a really cool, traveller vibe to this location. Actually, the location is cool enough without them, and turns over as a family-friendly business in the height of summer. But anyone who's trekked to far-fetched lands will be impressed with the journey to get here. Some people rate the view of the Gorges du Mondony as their holiday highlight, others will always regret having looked down. On a more positive note, the smaller the vehicle, the less your vertigo-induced fear (mobile homes are a definite no-go).

It took Jeroen and Madhu two years of travelling down never-ending roads to find their dream home. One day, 11 years ago, they caught a glimpse of chimney smoke rising through a clearing in the trees. The owner of that particular home wasn't selling, but next door they spotted an isolated, dilapidated forge that had been uninhabited since the 1930s. They snapped it up along with the surrounding 600 acres, then set to work transforming rubbles of stone into fully functional, modern accommodation. Nowadays, they hire out a *gîte*, a chalet and a pigsty, which in total sleep 18 people.

Madhu and Jeroen launched the camping bow in their arrow some seven years ago with their Dutch-designed De Waard Albatros tents. Six equipped tents named after the trees they're next to ('Holly', 'Plum' and so on) sit by the stream or on a raised level overlooking the garden; plus, there's space for people to put up their own canvas. They built a covered eating area, where 50 people have been known to crowd around dining tables for the vegetarian evening meals. You can also swim in the river – making dams is apparently the holidaying proclivity of older Dutchmen – else just sit back and cook marshmallows over the fire. It feels quite exciting to be so near to Spain in dense woodland. Whenever you fancy a change of national scenery, just hike over the border; there are two-hour and five-hour organised walks available. If you came in your own 4x4 you'll be able to make it over rocky terrain by car, maybe passing a few wild boars on the way. Madhu arranges regular group outings, where you can hike to a Spanish restaurant for dinner, after which cars will thoughtfully bring you back. These trips are usually snapped up as it's good to stretch your legs without the added anxiety of getting lost in the woods. Lately, Madhu has been overseeing the construction of a second pigsty (perhaps better described as a two-person, one-room studio). Whilst Jeroen's been working on a tree-house development overlooking the Spanish border. The couple have come a long way from Amsterdam, where they previously ran a successful tea shop. It's a long way from anywhere, in fact. Their amazing, combined feat borne of patience, hard labour and assiduous planting enables them to sustain a living in this remote, unusual borderline setting. Hats off to them for living the (self-sufficient) dream.

THE UPSIDE  Organic living and river swimming.

THE DOWNSIDE  The narrow mountain road has a precipitous drop and it's not for the faint-hearted. Nor is it for those who like nipping out to the shops.

THE DAMAGE  Six equipped tents are €450 per week. The chalet (sleeps 5–6) is €550 per week. Two apartments (sleep 2 or 9) are €350/€1025 per week. Campers with their own tent are charged €9 per person per night, €25 for a family (there's no camping, though, in July and August).

THE FACILITIES  The shop sells campsite basics (bread, milk, coffee). There are hot showers, a kids' play area and a shared BBQ.

No pets are allowed, but they have their own cat, dog, chickens, donkeys and ponies.

FOOD AND DRINK  Home-baked bread, jams, chutney and organic vegetables and fruits are at your fingertips.

FAMILY FUN  Madhu offers regular guided donkey and pony rides.

TREAT YOURSELF  To a traditional Catalan festival, where everyone parades in costume and kicks up their heels with a song and dance. Various local events take place over the summer.

GETTING THERE  Hire a car or take a bus to Amélie-les-Bains. Heading out of Amélie-les-Bains, take the first sharp left onto the D53 (signposted Montalba & Mas Pagris), and after

500 m bear right. Continue for 3 miles (5 km) and at the junction, turn right following signs for Mas Pagris; 1 mile (1.5 km) after Mas Pagris turn right onto the short dirt track that leads to the farm.

PUBLIC TRANSPORT  You can get a bus from Perpignan to Amélie-les-Bains. It's a 2-hour walk from there, or they may be able to pick you up.

OPEN  Mid-Mar–end-Oct; other accommodation open all year. May is a great time to see Céret's cherry blossom in full bloom. Always phone beforehand as the site fills up fast.

IF IT'S FULL  There's not a lot in the area, but back in Collioure is the seaside resort of Les Criques des Porteils (00 33 4 68 80 35 53; www.lescriques.com).

**Mas de la Fargassa**, Montalba, 66110 Amélie-les-Bains, France

| t | 00 33 4 68 39 01 15 | w | www.fargassa.com |

# les ormes

Can't make it to Africa this year? Then make Les Ormes your next-best option. Six years ago, two Dutch couples spied a gap in the travel market, threw in their office jobs and began importing desert tents from South Africa for their newly acquired plot of land in the Lot-et-Garonne. Inspired by a luxury tent hotel they spotted in Tanzania, their quest was to create an authentic, but comfortable, camping experience aimed at affluent 30-somethings who had once enjoyed spending holidays under canvas in their own childhoods. With plenty of creature comforts thrown in, Les Ormes allows them to replicate the experience, in style, with their own families.

Twenty-five desert tents are spaciously plotted within a forest of *ormes* (elm trees) – in a setting not too dissimilar to the jungles of the Congo…provided you use a little imagination. There are various configurations to choose from: the Gibsons have large terraced awnings, four of them also have tree-tents for the kids; the Takla-Makan is a tent for two, with a sleeping and a living area; whilst the Mojaves have stunning valley views. All tents have hip interior touches, comfortable spring beds and fresh linen. They look very chic indeed, but for an even more impressive water-cooler story to share back home, stay in the 360°

rotating Tournesol (this means sunflower) chalet. This is cleverly built on a ring with wheels, so that you can turn it gradually during the day. You might want it to face the sun in the morning, but then you can move it back into the shade when you're feeling a little overcooked later on. If you think that's a bit of a classy touch, then the owners' next project – floating chalets on a man-made pond – is sure to blow us all away. Let's hope the campers don't get sea-sick!

For the more traditional tenters amongst us there are 90 spacious tent pitches up for grabs, spread out along hilly and flat fields. It's a good idea to camp as near to the wonderful bottle-green lake – which offers boating and carp fishing next to the candy-coloured swimming pool – but as far away from the huge, central facility block as you can. A bastion of many a French campsite, rows of changing rooms and cubicles act as a bustling crossroads to the campsite's various destinations, so it gets a bit noisy there early in the morning.

Offsite, Dordogne's buzzy town of Bergerac, half an hour away, boasts 12 appellations of red, white and rosé and dozens of winemakers who'll be keen to welcome your custom. Once the key port for distributing wine to the UK, a role since passed on to

Bordeaux, you can now find good value for your money here. Take your time to hunt down your favourite taste by touring the Bergerac Wine Route (La Route des Vins de Bergerac), a map of picturesque vineyards set against backdrops of castles, paper mills and walled villages. OK, so it would take you a while to complete the whole tour, but then who's in a rush?

The nearby village of Saint-Étienne de Villeréal isn't as remarkable as the many beauties lying further north in the Dordogne region. On the bright side, this makes the area feel less like a tourist trap (with less traffic!) and more an unspoilt slice of real France. There are many villages and markets waiting to be explored for tasty food to cook back at your desert tent – maybe you'll find some South African cocoa beans to whip up a thick French–African hot chocolate recipe.

Your time in this laid-back base is very much your own. And whilst it may not quite have the exotic safari style of a true African camp, it feels a continent away from the larger commercial campsites that can be spotted clogging up watering holes across France.

THE UPSIDE Extremely comfortable safari-style camping.
THE DOWNSIDE The site is huge (over 60 acres) and takes an hour to walk around.
THE DAMAGE The 90 tent pitches are €10 per night, and €7 per person (over age 8). Off-season, over-50s are €14 and families €21 all-in. Weekly hire of basic tents and the quirky Tournesol is between €335 and €550. The safari-style tents start at about €420 and go up to €925 for the top-of-the-range Takla-Makan.
THE FACILITIES Everything you could possibly need: a barn restaurant, reception area, tennis court, table tennis, *boules*, fishing, volleyball, lake, small animal farm, a swimming pool Zanzi-Bar and near by, a splendid 18-hole golf course.
FOOD AND DRINK Take the D660 to Château Les Merles (00 33 5 53 63 13 42; www.lesmerles.com) in Mouleydier for 8-course banquets in the restaurant or less in the bistro. In an area famous for sweet dessert white wine, produced from a mixture of Sauvignon and Semillon grapes, *the* place to taste it is Château de Monbazillac (Route de Mont-de-Marsan, 24240 Monbazillac; 00 33 5 53 63 65 00; www.chateau-monbazillac.com).
FAMILY FUN Run off some energy together in the wide open spaces at Parc en Ciel (00 33 5 53 71 84 58; www.parc-en-ciel.com).
TREAT YOURSELF To some top nosh. Chef Vincent Arnould earned his Michelin star at Le Vieux Logis, Trémolat (00 33 5 53 22 80 06; www.vieux-logis.com).
GETTING THERE From Bergerac it's a 40-minute drive to the campsite. Take the N21 from Villeneuve or Bergerac and turn off at the D2 towards Saint-Étienne de Villeréal. The campsite is well signposted from there.
OPEN Late-Apr–mid-Sept.
IF IT'S FULL Campsite Le Moulin de David is just up the road at Monpazier. It has a pool complex with a lake, waterfalls and slides (00 33 4 99 57 21 21; www.moulin-de-david.com).

**Camping Les Ormes**, 47210 Saint Étienne de Villéreal, France

| t | 00 33 5 53 36 60 26 | w | www.campinglesormes.com |

# les romarins

Imagine waking up in the morning, unzipping your tent and watching sunrays skid across the azure ripples of the Med. Then imagine sipping your coffee whilst spying the private yachts of millionaires snaking in and out of Cap Ferrat harbour. Welcome to Les Romarins campsite, a sure winner of the *Cool Camping* award for Best Sea View in France – if such an award existed. *Cool Camping* Awards? Now, there's an idea that's sure to catch on.

High up in the hills between Nice and Monaco, Les Romarins is in the most remarkable of settings, where each of the 41 pitches boasts panoramic Mediterranean views. But it's the vibe as well as the view that gets into your soul – with no swimming pool, kids' activities or any loud entertainment, this really is a place to come and chill.

You'll need a car, though, not only to get to the site and nearby attractions, but also to whizz around the three *corniche* roads that cling to the curves of the coastal cliffs. The *Basse Corniche* snakes through the seafront Riviera towns, the *Grande Corniche* takes a faster, straighter line across the cliff tops, but it's the *Moyenne Corniche* that's said to be one of the most romantic drives in the world. Choose some suitable cruising music

and put your foot down; this is the stuff of car ads and movie chases, with slaloms, hairpins and more of those big, blue views around every bend.

The *Moyenne Corniche* will take you to the village of Èze, a pretty, medieval place perched high on a rock 475 metres above the sea. Its fortified castle was sadly destroyed in the 18th century (obviously not quite fortified enough), but the ruins now house the Jardin Exotique – a garden filled with exotic plants and cacti, with another stunning Riviera backdrop. There are many other interesting coastal towns to explore nearby. Villefranche-sur-Mer has one of the most beautiful bays along this stretch and has retained many of its ancient charms. You could easily spend a day sunbathing on the sand and pebble beach, becoming acquainted with the architecture of its 16th-century citadel or just sipping coffee by the harbour as the fishing boats bob and knock in the handsome dock.

Of course, you can't come here without visiting those Riviera jewels, Monaco and Nice, both just a short drive from the site. Where tiny Monaco is flash, swanky and swish, Nice is more traditional and relaxed with a characterful old town of narrow alleys to explore and plenty of places to sample local seafood specialities – without the superstar price tag. Nice also has a long, pebbly beach with comfortable sunloungers available for hire and waiters on hand to bring refreshments, but a bit of effort and a good map is all that's required to find the smaller, quieter beaches amongst the cliffs and coves between Monaco and Nice. When you've had your fill of glitz and glamour, Les Romarins is a stunning location to come home to at the end of the day. The hill on which the site rests is dotted with

rosemary and olive trees, providing plenty of shade from the hot sun. The owners, who live onsite, ensure that the select clientele respect the tranquil nature of the place, and whilst the facilities are somewhat low-key, there is a snack bar with a panoramic terrace, a chill-out room and renovated wash-rooms. There's even an ironing board available to press that starched white shirt when you're getting ready for a visit to the casino in Monaco – or perhaps for that all-important awards ceremony.

THE UPSIDE  Chilled-out campsite views just don't get better than this.

THE DOWNSIDE  The small pitches and quiet vibe aren't really suitable for families.

THE DAMAGE  Pitches cost €17.20–20 per night for 2 people and a tent (depending on season). An extra adult costs between €5.45 and €7.10; children (under 5) are €3–3.70.

THE FACILITIES  There's a panoramic terrace and modern toilet block, and there's also a washing machine and public telephone.

FOOD AND DRINK  With only snacks and breakfast available onsite, the closest place for a meal is Èze, which fortunately has plenty of cafés and restaurants. Château Eza (rue de la Pise; 00 33 4 93 41 12 24; www.chateaueza.com) is a romantic

hotel with a wonderful Michelin-starred restaurant; for a less-expensive option try Le Troubador, which serves great meat and lamb dishes in an atmospheric medieval house and once entertained Robert Mitchum.

FAMILY FUN  Apart from the nearby beaches, Les Artistes du Soleil in Nice (16–18 boulevard de la République; 00 33 4 93 52 55 89) is an artistic and ceramic centre that has kids' workshops operating on Wednesdays and during the school holidays. The Mini Center (4 rue Rancher; 00 33 6 18 21 06 20) in Vieux Nice organises activities for children.

TREAT YOURSELF  To the heady mixture of romance and roulette at one of Monaco's famous Monte Carlo Casinos (www.casino-monte-carlo.

com). If you don't have the money (or the jacket and tie) to hand, perhaps a scuba dive might be a memorable souvenir of the Côte d'Azur (00 33 4 93 89 42 44; www.nicediving.com).

GETTING THERE  From Nice take the Corniche André de Joly (D6007) and follow the Moyenne Corniche; turn off onto avenue des Caroubiers and at the end turn right along Grande Corniche, following signs for La Turbie; the site is over a mile (2 km) from here on your right.

PUBLIC TRANSPORT  Buses run regularly from Nice and Monaco to Èze.

OPEN  Mid–late-May and mid-June–mid-Sept.

IF IT'S FULL  No other site comes close to the views, so change your dates and make a reservation.

**Camping Les Romarins**, 250 ave des Diables Bleus, Grande Corniche, 06360 Èze, France

| t | 00 33 4 93 01 81 64 | w | www.campingromarins.com |

# le grand champ

In the foothills of the legendary Mont Blanc mountain range, directly beneath the towering peak of Aiguille du Midi, you'll find Camping Le Grand Champ – and what a great find it is. Run by Françoise Dudas and her family, the site is in a tip-top location, 1,000 metres up in the sky, with mountain views wherever you look.

The jagged and oft-snow-topped blocks of rock that dominate the horizon in every direction make this place feel a bit like Shangri-La: a secret valley, cut off from the world and stranded in happy seclusion. And whilst the spike-strewn view is the most obvious of the site's charms, there are plenty of other reasons to recommend Le Grand Champ as one of the most appealing of all Alpine camps.

The beautiful terraced garden boasts pretty pitches, all grassy and green, and separated by a neat-but-natural jumble of trees, bushes and hedges. Even though there's actually room for up to 100 tents or caravans, you'd never guess that this was such a large site since the layout of the gardens gives it a very intimate feel. Whilst groups are welcome at the site, they are directed to set up camp in a separate area, and this ensures that the other tenters can enjoy their peace and privacy at all times.

Françoise and the gang do everything in their power to make sure the site functions perfectly. The facilities are in decent shape, with three sanitary blocks (sinks and showers, hot and cold water), access for disabled visitors, washing machines and electricity; there's even a basic but cosy little communal room should the weather turn nasty. And if you're running low on supplies, just pop along to the reception, where you'll find a few essentials on sale. Fresh bread is delivered every day during the summer months, just in time for breakfast.

The nearest supermarket is in the town of Les Houches, almost 2 miles (3 km) along the road. Comprised of a number of hamlets, Les Houches has a certain Alpine charm, as well as great ski slopes, a lake and castle ruins. Climbing fans will enjoy the town's indoor wall, whilst walkers can begin the Tour du Mont Blanc there.

Nearby, Chamonix is a far cry from the peace and tranquillity of the site – but, it's a bit of a mixed blessing. With its myriad cafés, restaurants, tourist facilities and activity centres, it makes a fantastic hub for anyone wanting to make an exploration of the region. But (and you could hear a 'but' coming), with up to 40,000 people a day in the surrounding valley during peak season,

it has a resort atmosphere that erodes its more natural charms.

Although this area is best known for its ski slopes, it offers something for every kind of thrill-seeker. In fact, it would be easier to list what it doesn't have: you can hike, cycle, climb, raft, kart, golf, abseil, glide, swim, snowboard – and that's just for starters. *Entrées* could include canyoning, hot-air-ballooning, paint-balling and off-road mountain-biking. And why not round the menu off with a sedate ride in a helicopter, a horse trek or a game of *boules*? If you should

tire of all the activities and feel in need of a well-earned rest, then Chamonix offers the opportunity to be indulgent as well as active. There can't be many campsites in the midst of a natural wonderland that also offer cinemas, beauty salons, casinos and shopping so close by.

At the end of your hectic day, just zip up the tent flaps on that vertiginous view, snuggle into your sleeping bag and join Le Grand Champ's version of the mile-high club – snoozing happily at altitude in this freshest-of-fresh mountain air.

THE UPSIDE  Drop-dead gorgeous site on the doorstep of Mont Blanc.
THE DOWNSIDE  Self-sufficiency is the name of the game here. And depending on where you pitch you might hear some motorway noise.
THE DAMAGE  It's €4.50 for a pitch, €4.30 per adult and €2.20 per child (under 7).
THE FACILITIES  In keeping with the site these are fairly basic – just a small shop and decent sanitary provisions.
FOOD AND DRINK  Apart from the classic Savoyard specialities (*fondue, raclette, tartiflette* and *farcement*) you can find most kinds of food in this area. However, a decent local option is the hotel-restaurant Les Gorges de la Diosaz in Servoz (00 33 4 50 47 20 97; www.hoteldesgorges.com), which serves good classic French dishes and has

a great terrace to sit on. But if you want something that's a little more swish, Les Granges d'en Haut (00 33 4 50 54 65 36; www.grangesdenhaut.com) is a contemporary spot above Les Houches with novel twists on French classics and some very good brunch options.
FAMILY FUN  There's so much for families to do here, it would be hard to fit everything in. Options include Les Gaillands in Chamonix, a natural climbing crag great for children and beginners (follow the 'Taconnaz, Bossons' signs from Chamonix and the wall is on your left, opposite the lake); and a tree-based activity centre (00 33 6 62 67 28 51; www.arbreaventure-montblanc.com).
TREAT YOURSELF  To a romantic dinner at Hameau Albert 1er (38 Route du Bouchet, 74402

Chamonix-Mont-Blanc; 00 33 4 50 53 05 09; www.hameaualbert.fr).
GETTING THERE  Les Bossons is located directly off the E25/A40 just over 3 miles (5.5 km) from Chamonix. The site is signposted from the village.
PUBLIC TRANSPORT  Chamonix is accessible by train and bus from most major French towns. From Chamonix, you can catch a bus to the nearby shops, just over half a mile (1 km) away. There's also a railway station at Les Bossons just over a mile (2 km) away.
OPEN  May–mid-Oct.
IF IT'S FULL  Glacier d'Argentière, 161 chemin des Chosalets, 74400 Argentière (00 33 4 50 54 17 36; www.campingchamonix.com) is one of Chamonix's more scenic and *naturelle* campsites.

**Camping Le Grand Champ**, 167 chemin du Glacier de Taconnaz, Les Bossons, 74400 Chamonix-Mont-Blanc, France

| | t | 00 33 4 50 53 04 83 | e | campinggrandchamp@hotmail.com |

# les roulottes de la serve

*Roulottes* – covered gypsy caravans originally designed for nomads – are now officially *en vogue* with campers throughout France. Whilst some sites are content with bunging a few standard-issue caravans in a field and charging a nightly rate, others offer an altogether more distinctive experience.

Les Roulottes de la Serve is one such place: three *roulottes*, tucked away in an Arcadian setting, on a super-rustic farm that's out of the way of everything. Rewind 20 years and owners Pascal (Pat) and Pascaline had some horses that needed a field. They bought a derelict 19th-century farmhouse and devoted their lives to restoring it. And the horses were over the moon – they got much larger fields than they'd hoped for.

Pat and Pascaline were offered their first *roulotte* by a local merry-go-round owner (you couldn't make it up). They put it in the field, alongside the horses, and decided they liked it so much they wanted a couple more. Fast-forward 15 or so years and – following an eight-month jaunt through Africa and India – the pair now have three *roulottes* and some seriously good interior décor ideas. *Et voilà!* Les Roulottes de la Serve was born.

The site is beautifully off the beaten track. An engaging climb through the undulating hills of Les Ardillats in the middle of the Beaujolais countryside leads to a narrow country lane and a dense garden of trees, plants and meadows. A wooden cart brimming with apples sits beneath a tree. A huge Saint Bernard dog basks in the golden sunlight. Horses worry gently at lush green grass. It's a painterly tableau.

Tucked behind the garden are the three brightly coloured *roulottes* and the farmhouse, now more or less fully restored. You can choose your *roulotte* according to taste and price: *Des Amoureux* wears a nostalgic 50s interior; *Des Manèges* is more reminiscent of the 20s; *Des Etoiles*, the biggest, is decorated with sequinned cushions and natty trinkets from the Orient.

Whichever you choose, you'll have a comfortable night's slumber and the satisfaction of sleeping in a tasteful little space that comes with its own en-suite bathroom – all in a field! Breakfast, normally taken in the farmhouse's fabulously rustic dining area, can also be delivered to your caravan for a reasonable extra charge.

The surrounding Beaujolais region is awash with vineyards and farms, which of course means an abundance of great cheeses, meats and wines – an excellent reason to get out and sample the wares. Thankfully you can walk or cycle all the over-consumption off easily enough as there are plenty of options to strike out and explore the countryside.

The site lies on the 500-year-old St-Jacques de Compostelle pilgrim route, and there are plenty of interesting places to stop in at during your jaunts. Organic wine-lovers will enjoy Domaine du Crêt de Ruyère (www.cretderuyere.com). It's a small but perfectly formed vineyard set in the hills above Villié-Morgon and is run by Cathy (who is English) and Jean-Luc Gauthier.

There are also a few local towns worth exploring. Nearby Avenas has a nice little church (and a great restaurant, see below). Fishing trips can be arranged at attractive Beaujeu (6 miles/10 km), the capital of the Beaujolais (ask at reception). And just 19 miles (30 km) away is Cluny, with its world-famous Benedictine monastery. And do try to sneak a peek at Pascal's workshop. A carpenter and furniture-restorer by trade, he decided to try his hand at making customised *roulottes* and he now sells them all across France.

Far from simply depositing a few caravans in a field, the folk at Les Roulottes de la Serve celebrate the finer aspects of this unique lifestyle and provide an authentically rustic experience.

THE UPSIDE Unique caravan-in-a-field experience.

THE DOWNSIDE It's a little hard to find – you need to keep your eyes peeled for the signs – and there's no direct public transport to the site.

THE DAMAGE The *roulottes* are individually priced for 2 people per night, including breakfast, from €50 (smallest) to €60 (largest).

THE FACILITIES Toilets, showers and a kitchen for guests' use is in the farmhouse, where breakfast is also served.

FOOD AND DRINK The main local restaurant is the Auberge du Fût d'Avenas (69430 Avenas; 00 33 4 74 69 90 76). It's set in an old farmhouse and run by a hip young French couple (Émile and Julien), who speak great English and cook up daily set menus based on fresh ingredients. Plus, there are markets in Cluny (Saturdays), Villefranche (Mondays) and Belleville (Tuesdays).

FAMILY FUN For the kids there are lots of safe tree-climbing options and *voie verte* (literally 'green path') cycling in the area. And the Association de Rollers Clunisois (00 33 3 85 50 29 96) offers lessons for both beginner and experienced roller-skaters.

TREAT YOURSELF To a hot-air balloon ride across the Beaujolais. Montgolfière Air Escargot is based in Cluny (00 33 3 85 87 12 30).

GETTING THERE From Lyon take the A6/E15 to Mâcon. Turn off onto the D18 at Belleville. Follow the D18 towards Avenas/Ouroux. The site is signposted from Avenas.

PUBLIC TRANSPORT Trains and buses serve Belleville. Pick-ups can be organised in advance.

OPEN Apr–Oct.

IF IT'S FULL There aren't many other campsites in the region, but there's a wonderful wood-and-stone B&B (Ferme du Planet; 00 33 4 74 04 64 89) just along the road in Ouroux. It's all hand-built (Pascal helped with the wood) and is run by the local vet and his family. Prices for the ridiculously comfortable rooms range from €50 to €60.

**Les Roulottes de la Serve**, 69860 Ouroux, France

| | t | 00 33 4 74 04 76 40 | w | www.lesroulottes.com |

# tipis at folbeix

Can you keep a secret? They say there are two kinds of really great campsites: those that you want to tell everyone about and those you want to tell no one about and keep for yourself. Nigel and Sheila Harding's tipis at Folbeix, in the enchanted forests of La Creuse, definitely belong to the latter category. So, can you keep a secret? OK, then let's begin.

The real attraction of this site is that it's a haven of environmentally conscious living. Nestled in a coppiced wood are six snowy-white tipis, each on a raised platform of pine decking made from Forestry Stewardship Council wood and illuminated at night by candle lanterns and solar-powered lights. And if you're still in the dark about the essence of this place, grab one of the wind-up torches available, because sustainability and self-sufficiency are crucial watchwords here. It's a philosophy that's particularly apt in La Creuse.

This deep, dark region of France is where they used to speak Occitan, the old Romance language from the time of Dante. It's the language in which travelling troubadours would sing of their lost loves and favourite taverns. Although it is rarely spoken nowadays, there are vestiges of it in the thick local accent, full of rough, strangled vowels, characteristic of the cross between the languages of 'oc' and 'oil' (that's the languages of the Languedoc and of northern France). And if this all sounds like something from *The Lord of the Rings,* don't worry. Although it's a rich soup of sounds, it's still recognisably French and you'll soon pick it up. But the fact that the accent is so thick is a sign that this area of France has been pretty much left to its own devices for hundreds of years.

Whilst roads were being built all around it, La Creuse was bypassed by the French and by tourists alike. So, the old Gallo–Roman remains were left untouched, the dialect hardened and the forests grew. And what a playground it has produced. There's horse-riding, fishing, cycling and walking in abundance. If you've come by car (and can offset the carbon) then take a drive between Le Bourg d'Hem and Beausoleil in the region known as Le Pays de Trois Lacs (the country of three lakes). The road plunges down through wooded gorges to one of the trio of lakes whose peaceful waters reflect the surrounding forests.

It's ironic that the recent construction of better road links means the area is now opening up as a tourist destination. All the more reason to keep the secret to yourself and get out here whilst it's still off most people's holiday radar. As others inhale the smell of cheap jet fuel and onboard alcopops, you could be breathing in the sweet, musty smells of the forest and some lovely fresh air.

Each of the tipis is set in a different part of the wood and apparently some of the people who come here disappear into the trees at the beginning of the week and aren't seen again until it's time to leave. They sit, they watch and listen to the wildlife snuffling about in the undergrowth and they go and play in the mudbath in the middle of the wood, where deer also come to frolic. However, it's worth wandering back to the Hardings' house every now and again. For a start, you can help yourself to fresh herbs from the garden to pep up whatever's cooking over your campfire. And, what's more, you won't want to miss out on Sheila's industrious output of jams, chutneys and beverages of varying descriptions (and of varying levels of alcoholic potency). They're the perfect accompaniment to the lifestyle you'll find in your pearly white tipi in the luscious, silent forests at Folbeix.

THE UPSIDE A wonderful, natural site with discreet areas for each of the tipis and an eco-friendly philosophy to match.

THE DOWNSIDE With only 6 tipis, it's essential to book.

THE DAMAGE €350 per week or €170 for a 3-day break for up to 2 adults and 2 children. The tariff includes a continental breakfast with home-made jams and fresh bread collected from the village each morning.

THE FACILITIES The new block (built in 2008) features toilets, showers, baby-changing and cooking facilities, and also a dining area.

FOOD AND DRINK The theme is very much one of self-sufficiency and eating locally grown produce. There is a market every Friday just up the road in Châtelus-Malvaleix, which also has a boulangerie and pâtisserie. But if you pine for a night out, try La Bonne Auberge (see TREAT YOURSELF below).

FAMILY FUN Play hippos in the mudbath. Just remember to use plenty of the eco-friendly detergent available onsite to wash afterwards.

TREAT YOURSELF To a local dinner at La Bonne Auberge (1 rue de Lilas, 23600 Nouzerines; 00 33 5 55 82 01 18; www.la-bonne-auberge.net). It has a delicious dessert option of local cheese known as Creuseois, made from unpasteurised milk. Délicieux.

GETTING THERE In keeping with the philosophy of minimal environmental impact, the site is not signposted and is easy to miss. Heading east from Guéret on the N145, turn off at the sign for Ajain and head for Ladapeyre. In the village take the D990 towards Châtelus-Malvaleix. Folbeix is a mile (1.5 km) or so up the road and is little more than a collection of houses on either side of it. The site is on your right just as you enter Folbeix. Pull in at the ivy-covered house.

PUBLIC TRANSPORT There is a railway station at Guéret, from where the Hardings can arrange to pick you up for the 15-minute journey to the site.

OPEN May–Sept.

IF IT'S FULL There's a fine site owned by English couple Neil and Linda Flinton at Fleurat, midway between Guéret and La Souterraine, called Camping Les Boueix (23320 Fleurat; 00 33 5 55 41 86 81; www.campinglesboueix.com).

**Tipi Holidays in France**, Folbeix, France

| t | 00 33 5 55 80 90 26 | w | www.vacanesdetipienfrance.com |

# la vendette

Part of the Huttopia chain's Indigo brand of sites, Camping La Vendette is as good as it gets for beachside camping. Given that it is located only a little south of Brittany, just below the mouth of the Loire, Noirmoutier is just like a slice of the Mediterranean. It's no surprise that Renoir came here in the 1890s to paint the shimmering greens and purples of the pine shade.

From the whitewashed villas with terracotta roof tiles and blue wooden shutters to the cool blue waters and abundant woods, this place seems to be a couple of hundred miles north of where it should be. When the weather's right, you can lie back and watch the children paddle in the still waters, whilst out in the sheltered bay little boats bob at anchor. And you'll certainly ask yourself 'who needs the Med?' It all just seems a bit too good to be true.

Admittedly the site is a bit of a hike out of town by the main roads, but there's a handy short cut through a nature reserve along a road that's closed to traffic. The town itself has sleepy streets of sun-bleached houses, a medieval castle and a Romanesque church, which was formerly part of a Benedictine abbey. Sure, the place has its share of tourists and postcard shops, but it retains a certain cutesy charm.

Back in Renoir's day, Île de Noirmoutier was accessible only by boat or by a cobbled causeway called the Passage du Gois, which was submerged at high tide. Nowadays there's a bridge connecting the southern tip of the island to the mainland, though it makes for a longer round-trip than cutting across from Beauvoir-sur-Mer. However, if you get your timing and the tide right, it's still a whole lot more fun to drive across the causeway. Luckily the island's remoteness and the difficulty of access mean that the tourists don't arrive in droves.

In town there's a fine terrace café. You can spend hours relaxing under its yellow awning watching the world go by whilst you sip a *petite noisette* and chew ruminatively on a delicious *pain au chocolat*. Fortified and refreshed, you can then stroll out to the open-air saltpans, which form the backbone of the local economy.

Just like Far-Eastern paddy fields but without the green shoots of rice, the marshes have been dug into square channels in which sea water is trapped and allowed to gradually evaporate under the scorching sun. You can buy the resulting *fleurs de sel* in town, along with the local fishermen's latest catch. After that you can head back to the site to cook up a really tangy treat.

Choose a beachside pitch or retreat deeper into the shady pines – there are no manicured lawns with hissing sprinklers on this site. Certainly not. Just kick a few pine cones out of the way and pitch your tent between the trees (*Pinus pinaster* if you're at all arboreally inclined – they were planted in the 19th century, apparently to help anchor the sand, which, it has to be admitted, is a little shifty – especially for tent pegs).

The whole area, known as the Bois de la Chaize, is a magical tangle of trees alive with birdlife. After your seafood supper, if you turn left out of the site and follow the road through the wood of pine, ilex and mimosa, you'll emerge from the trees between a flat water meadow and a sheltered bay, and you might just be treated to a fantastic view of the silhouette of castle, church and town against the setting sun. Perfect.

THE UPSIDE Fantastic pine-shaded site right on a quiet beach. You just can't get a better-located seaside site than this.
THE DOWNSIDE Waterside pitches get booked solid in summer, so book early.
THE DAMAGE A pitch is €12.90 for 2 adults, tent and car (€19.10 in high season), plus €3.20 per additional adult (€4.40) and €1.50 (€2.50) for children (2–7 years). Electricity is €4.
THE FACILITIES Not quite up to the standard of the Huttopia site at Versailles (see p143), but pretty good. Plenty of hot showers, toilets and other washing facilities. The washing machines and driers take tokens *(jetons)*, from reception.

FOOD AND DRINK There's a *boulanger* who comes to the site every morning with fresh bread and other goodies. Catch him outside reception at 8.30am. For a great dining experience, go to Le Grand Four on the corner above the castle (00 33 2 51 39 61 97; www.legrandfour.com). It's a beautiful ivy-clad building, with a couple of tables outside, fabulously lorded over by the huge castle walls. Set menus start at €20.
FAMILY FUN Time your arrival or departure with the low tide and take the famous Passage du Gois to or from the île. Be warned, though, that you don't want to dawdle or the rising tide will get you…just like in *Chitty Chitty Bang Bang*.

TREAT YOURSELF To some salt. That's right – there is a thriving salt industry on the island and there's a marvellous little shop opposite the castle on rue de Grand Four called Château de Sel.
GETTING THERE The sites (there are several along Les Sableaux) are well signposted from the main road through the town. La Vendette is the last on the left, with a large blue banner.
OPEN Early-Apr–early-Oct.
IF IT'S FULL Right next door (but without the same access to the beach) is the municipal site of Le Clair Matin (00 33 2 51 39 05 56). It's a perfectly nice site with a few shady pitches and some around a cleared lawn next to the road.

**Camping La Vendette**, 23 Allée des Sableaux, Bois de la Chaize, 85330 Noirmoutier-en-L'île, France

| t | 00 33 2 51 39 06 24 | w | www.camping-indigo.com |

# les roulottes

The Loire valley, one of France's principal tourist destinations, is disappointingly littered with gargantuan caravan parks displaying stickers of affiliation from just about every caravan club in the EU. So, you'll thank your lucky stars when you find Monsieur Arnaud Séné, just outside the little town of Huisseau-sur-Cosson, near Blois.

Les Roulottes is a collection of old-fashioned gypsy caravans in a quiet backwater of the countryside that's deliberately difficult to find. Arnaud, the quietly spoken but very welcoming proprietor of the site, doesn't advertise or put up signs. That just encourages the idly curious and passers-by, he says. No, like some kind of Harry Potter test, first you have to find the place and only then do you deserve to come here. Why? Because Arnaud takes his three caravans extremely seriously and they are all the genuine article.

There's a 1970s two-person caravan in peaceful shades of mauve and olive and a stately, bright red-and-green 1930s triple with elegant raised double bed set into rich woodwork. The two come as a *gîte* package with a third *roulotte*, a 1950s model – also bright-red and green – that serves as compact kitchen/diner and bathroom. And, as if that weren't heritage enough for

you, Arnaud has just finished restoring a magnificent wooden-wheeled 1890 caravan – a hugely romantic self-contained unit for two with en-suite bathroom. Couples with kids can rent it alongside a teensy-tiny 1980s caravan designed with wee ones in mind.

Nuzzling up to the banks of a river so slow that it looks like a long pond, the site nestles into a small sunken clearing below the road and the bridge, surrounded by trees. It's as private as you could wish for and as quiet as a Marcel Marceau sketch.

The caravans are arranged facing a strip of grass with the charcoal ring of an open cooking fire. At night you can sit here whilst cooking up a feast and imagining the strains of a gypsy violin as the sun goes down and the silence deepens around you. And if it's your turn to cook (again), keep everyone amused by telling them the story of Denis Papin. He was born in nearby Chitenay in the 17th century and actually invented the pressure cooker.

In the morning, after the first night of unbroken sleep you've probably enjoyed in ages, you may just want to lounge by the river watching a fishing rod occasionally twitch. Or chill in the hammock that's strung between the trees, stick a piece of grass in

your mouth and pull your hat down over your eyes (and who's to say you haven't earned it?). But, don't linger long as there's plenty to be getting on with. This is, after all, the Loire valley and you're only a short drive away from Blois, which is one of the finest towns the length of the river.

Before entering Blois, stop on the southern bank and take in the view of the famous *château*. For architectural buffs, there's plenty to whet the palate, with everything from Gothic to Renaissance to classical revival on show. Once in the town, try not to get too lost in the huddled streets of the old quarter and find your way to the Tour Beauvoir, which dates all the way back to the 11th century. This is where it all started and the ideal place to learn that the ensuing 900 years of history in Blois are more full of mystery, intrigue, murder and treason than a wet holiday weekend spent playing Cluedo with the in-laws. A colourful past, indeed, but not a patch on the present – in the form of the brightly painted four-wheeled cabins back at base.

THE UPSIDE A simple, unaffected and genuine taste of the gypsy lifestyle.

THE DOWNSIDE You need to bring your own bed linen; and with only a handful of *roulottes*, it's essential to book ahead.

THE DAMAGE €450 per week in July and August, reducing to €310 the rest of the year. For a 5-night stay, rates are €380/€250; and weekend (Sat–Mon) rates are €200/€150. Prices are for the trio of *roulottes*, sleeping 5 in total.

THE FACILITIES Limited to a small toilet and shower in one of the *roulottes*, though they are clean and functional. There are bikes and canoes to use whilst you're at the site.

FOOD AND DRINK Bring your own to cook on the open fire. There is a hob and microwave in one of the *roulottes*, but you'd be a fool not to use the real thing. Otherwise head into Blois, where the locals' favourite restaurant is Au Bouchon Lyonnais (25 rue des Violettes, Blois; 00 33 2 54 74 12 87), serving a mix of local cuisine and, as the name implies, dishes from the most gourmet of French cities, Lyon, in a charming dining room of old wood beams and stone walls.

FAMILY FUN Take the kids to circus school: L'École de Cirque Micheletty (00 33 2 38 55 13 98; www.ecoledecirquemicheletty.com) at nearby St-Jean de Braye has juggling, acrobatics and lessons in the art of clownship.

TREAT YOURSELF To a day out at Chambord, visiting the magnificent *château* (the most-visited one in the region) and its extensive woods (www.chambord.org). It's only a short drive away, but worth a full day. If you can, stay there until sundown, when a series of coloured floodlights illuminates the *château*.

GETTING THERE From Blois, follow the D33 towards Huisseau-sur-Cosson. As you approach the town, you will see Château des Grotteaux. Take the left turn and carry on past the entrance, following the road round behind the *château*. Where the tarmac runs out, take the unmade road to your left, through a small tunnel, and you will find the gated entrance to Les Roulottes immediately on your left.

OPEN Late-Mar–Christmas.

IF IT'S FULL There's a pleasant campsite in Huisseau-sur-Cosson itself (just past the cemetery) – Camping de Chatillon (6 rue de Chatillon, 41350 Huisseau-sur-Cosson; 00 33 2 54 20 35 26).

**Les Roulottes**, Les Marais, 41350 Huisseau-sur-Cosson, France

| t | 00 33 6 67 74 94 93 | w | www.lesroulottes.net |

# huttopia versailles

Sir Thomas More's 1516 treatise on the ideal society, *Utopia*, may seem an unlikely basis for a corporate camping set-up. But that is exactly what the owners of this site of tents, *roulottes* (old-fashioned gypsy caravans) and huts claim – a little hut Utopia. Hence Huttopia. Get it? Never mind – it sounds much better in French anyway.

The company takes a philosophical approach to a kind of camping that harks back to a simpler time, when people lived in harmony with their natural surroundings. Of course, few people nowadays will be familiar with the work of Sir Thomas More, but think of Al Gore in a doublet and hose and you'll probably get the general idea.

The idea is to provide an authentic natural environment, as little altered by human hands as possible – so no clearing of trees, levelling the ground or landscaping the gardens. The result is just a naturally contoured patch of forest on the periphery of Paris, perched up on a hill at the edge of the wood by Viroflay.

The beautifully designed huts at Huttopia are actually quite spacious *cabanes*, sleeping up to six people. The *roulottes* are much snugger affairs, accommodating up to four in a double and a couple of bunks. But if you just can't sleep without the sound of rippling canvas above your head, you can opt for one of the *canadiennes*, the five-person fixed tents available for hire.

Or, naturally, you can always bring your own. The company claims that it puts a priority on canvas campers and restricts the *cabanes* and *roulottes* to no more than 30 per cent of the available pitches.

However admirable the approach, though, we all know that no ideal society is perfect. Even in More's *Utopia* each household was allowed to keep a couple of slaves (not available here) and in the end, of course, Henry VIII chopped poor Sir Thomas's head off. There are a few compromises with the utopian concept here, too.

For a start, there's an environmentally unfriendly swimming pool next to the bar/restaurant, though in the heat of a Parisian summer it's a luxury that only the most puritanical environmentalist would shun. And then there's the slightly 'corporate' air that pervades the whole place. You'll be conscious that the staff – young, enthusiastic and friendly though they certainly are – are actually employees of a large company, rather than owners running their own site.

Putting such minor quibbles aside, though, it all works surprisingly well and there's no doubt that this is a fantastic site. It certainly makes for a different take on a weekend trip to Paris. It's only 20 minutes by train from the centre of the city and a mere 20 minutes' walk from the palace at Versailles, which is well worth a visit.

Any indignation you may have felt about all the water used for the swimming pool might be transformed into burning self-righteousness at the sight of all the fountains, sprinklers and sculpted lakes in the palace gardens there. Such beauty just isn't natural, you might say. Yes – but just look around you. These are probably the most stunning gardens in the world. And somewhere between the unspoilt nature at Huttopia and the manipulated perfection at Versailles is, after all, where most of us are quite content to live.

THE UPSIDE  A real attempt to promote a philosophy of minimal interference with nature. THE DOWNSIDE  Its proximity to Paris means that it attracts an unwelcome share of beer-and-BBQ Brits looking for a cheaper option than a budget hotel in the capital. As a result, the camping area can be quite noisy late into the night. THE DAMAGE  High season (July and August) it's €32 for a tent, two adults and car, plus €8.50 per additional adult and €4.30 per child (2–7 years). Low season, prices dip to €22.70 for a tent, 2 adults and car, plus €6.20 per adult and €3 for a child. Electricity ranges from €4.60 to €6.80 depending on season and ampage. *Cabanes*, *roulottes* and *canadiennes* are available only for a minimum of 2 nights and range from €59 to €169 per night. THE FACILITIES  Three substantial blocks of clean, well-maintained facilities. There are open-air urinals (men only!) and plenty of toilets, plus dish- and deep clothes-washing sinks. There's also a free Internet terminal in reception. FOOD AND DRINK  There's a bar and restaurant next to the pool serving reasonable but unexciting pizzas, steaks, salads and beers. But this is Paris (well, almost), so there are gastronomic delights a-plenty just a short train ride away. FAMILY FUN  Though the gardens at Versailles are free to enter, it is worth paying €13.50 (€10 after 3pm) to tour the palace itself and even paying the extra euros to see the Grandes Eaux Musicales, when the fountains are turned on and choreographed to music. This only happens at weekends, however, and it's best to see it at night. TREAT YOURSELF  To a copy of Sir Thomas More's *Utopia*, available from all good bookshops. GETTING THERE  Avoid Paris's *périphérique* (ring road) if you can. Head away from the palace of Versailles along the broad avenue de Paris. After it bends left, there are two sandstone gatehouses on either side of the road. Turn right here onto avenue de Porchefontaine. Go under the railway line and carry on along rue Costa until you hit rue Rémont. Turn left and then right onto rue Berthelot. Huttopia is at the top of the road on the left. PUBLIC TRANSPORT  The RER C regional train station of Porchefontaine is a few minutes' walk from the site. Frequent trains to and from Paris take approximately 20 minutes. There is also a B-line bus stop on rue Yves Le Coz at the bottom of rue Berthelot, which goes to and from the Palace at Versailles and a bus No 171 from avenue de Paris about 5 minutes' extra walk. OPEN  Late-Mar–Nov. IF IT'S FULL  There is another Huttopia site at Rambouillet (Route du Château d'Eau, 78120 Rambouillet; 00 33 1 30 41 07 34).

**Huttopia Versailles**, 31 rue Berthelot, 78000 Versailles, France

| | t | 00 33 1 39 51 23 61 | w | www.huttopia.com |

# le brévedent

This is surely one of the classiest campsites in France. Set in the grounds of a Louis XVIth hunting lodge, with pitches around a mirrored lake, amidst apple trees and on the fringe of a wood, the *château* of Le Brévedent has been in the same family for 400 years and has been used for camping for four generations. Raphaël Guerrey, who has recently taken over the running of the place from his mother, runs the site with his wife and small (fifth-generation) son.

Camping came about at Le Brévedent in part because of the ruination caused by World War II. The lodge had been occupied by the Germans and was badly damaged when a passing Allied bomber inadvertently dropped its payload on its way to crashing in the woods. In order to help pay for the repairs, the Marquis de Chabannes La Palice – Raphaël's great-grandfather – decided to plant apple trees to harvest the fruit, began extracting lime from the woods to sell to local farmers and invited campers to come and stay in the grounds as well.

Further encouragement came in the form of an organisation set up in 1957 by Georges Pilliet to help the owners of French *châteaux* preserve their family heritage. Le Brévedent became a member of the Castel group of campsites in 1965 and now looks upon the fellow owners as a second family. If only something similar had happened back home we could all be camping on the lawns at Chatsworth and Cliveden right now.

Of course, there was a little added *cachet* at Le Brévedent, as the idea of staying with a French Marquis proved an unsurprising hit. It did lead some campers into delusions of grandeur, however. One early visitor was discomfited to discover that dinner jackets were not obligatory evening attire. He had assumed that dinner with the Marquis required a certain degree of formality.

Rest assured there's no dress code here now, and you'll find a welcoming, laid-back attitude from everyone you meet. The Guerrey family are endlessly entertaining companions for an evening in the bar in the lodge, which Raphaël opens every night from 9pm.

Whether it's the history of the lodge, the family – which traces its roots back 1,000 years – French politics or the deficiencies of British farming, they're happy to chat to their guests, many of whom are now such regular visitors as to consider Le Brévedent a second home. Raphaël's also a talented musician and is partial to jamming with anyone who happens along with a guitar.

In fact, he's even gone so far as to organise musical evenings in front of the floodlit house for anyone who wishes to participate. These sessions don't last too long into the night, though, and you're more likely to be disturbed by the plop of the occasional apple dropping from the trees onto the grass than by anything else. And, when morning comes, you'll probably be roused by the sound of the baker's van arriving with the first batch of fresh bread. If the sound doesn't get you, the smell will. Try staying in your sleeping

bag when the aroma of warm *pains au chocolat*, still soft and gooey from the oven, is wafting across the grass. You'll be up like a shot and climbing into your *culottes* before you can say *'sacre bleu!'*.

Still, it'll be the only time in your stay at Le Brévedent when you break into more than an amble. That's just the kind of place it is. Because when you've been around for as long as this place has, what's the hurry?

THE UPSIDE  A fascinating family, a beautiful house, a lake and a garden full of apple trees.
THE DOWNSIDE  It's hard to think of one.
THE DAMAGE  €9 for a tent or caravan (€7 in May, June and September) plus €6.70 per adult (€5.20 low season); €4.50 per child (7–12 years) (€3.35); and €3.50 per younger child (€2.20). Electricity is €3.20 or €2.45 per night, depending on the season.
THE FACILITIES  These are immaculate. One of the newly decorated blocks could easily grace the pages of an interior design magazine. Good hot showers, pearly white lavatories and plenty of excellent washing facilities.
FOOD AND DRINK  The usual *boulangerie*, *pâtisserie*, and so on can be found in the charming village of Blangy-le-Château. The small bar in

the lodge sells cider made by a local farmer called Edward Maclean (yes, he's originally from Scotland). Whilst you're here, try the brew called Apéro, a mixture of cider, blackcurrant and calvados; it might sound like snakebite, but it's far classier. There is also a restaurant onsite, but if you want something special, see TREAT YOURSELF below.
FAMILY FUN  There are 2 children's play areas on the site with swings, climbing frames and a roundabout. In the gardens there's an ancient tree that's great for climbing; if that's not enough, the Kids' Club organises daily activities.
TREAT YOURSELF  To a slap-up meal. A former one-star Michelin chef called Bernard Vaxelaire, having tired of the glitz and glamour of his Paris restaurant, runs a fantastic place called Les

Gourmandises (rue de l'Abbaye; 00 33 2 32 42 10 96) in the nearby town of Cormeilles.
GETTING THERE  Take the A13 *autoroute* from Paris (or join it from the A29 over the Pont de Normandie from Le Havre), heading for Pont l'Évêque. Take the D579 for just over a mile (2 km) and turn left for Manneville-la-Pipard. Follow the road to Blangy-le-Château and turn right in the village and Le Brévedent is just over a mile (2 km) down the road. The site is on the left, just after the road leading to the church.
OPEN  Late-Apr–Sept.
IF IT'S FULL  There's another Castel Camping site at Château Le Colombier (14590 Moyaux; 00 33 2 31 63 63 08), about 6 miles (10 km) to the southwest. It's slightly larger, but the same idea, set between a *château* and an ornate dovecote.

**Castel Camping Le Brévedent**, 14130 Le Brévedent, France

t  00 33 2 31 64 72 88    w  www.campinglebrevedent.com

# val d'or

Think of Luxembourg and you think of, well, not very much really. At first blush it's one of those anonymous little places with little to boast about – no famous sports stars or A-list celebs in rehab and not even a laughably poor record in the Eurovision Song Contest to spice up their image. They've won it five times. Perhaps the most interesting fact about the country is that its area is 999 square miles. But out into the countryside of the Ardennes, tucked away in the trees in the valley of the Clerve river, you'll find some of the finest acreage of that 999 square miles – the little goldmine of Val d'Or in Enscherange. The friendly Dutch owners took over the site in 1991 and have turned it into an enchanting little oasis of greenery, with the river running through it, which is perfect for kids to play in. There's room to pitch by the river or, over a wooden footbridge, there are more spacious pitches hidden away behind high hedges, if you fancy a little peace and quiet.

Not that the place is a riot at the best of times. The village has a population of 140 and there's only one tiny bar, Bistro Beim Renée, so small you feel you're invading someone's sitting room. But it's the perfect place for a sing-along, with brownie points on offer to anyone who can remember the lyrics to Luxembourg's last Eurovision winner, Corinne Hermès's memorable 1983 chart-topper *'Si la vie est cadeau'*.

THE UPSIDE Trickly riverside camping in the green heart of a Grand Duchy.
THE DOWNSIDE A railway line runs right by the campsite. To be fair, it's not that busy – they're mainly local trains and they don't run at night – but it's a bit of a downer.
THE DAMAGE €5 per adult and €2 per child, plus €10 for a pitch.
THE FACILITIES Not bad – though you need a digital gizmo from reception (for which there's a €25 refundable deposit) in order to get any hot water. Charge it up with cash and watch the balance on it decrease at a rate of €0.03 every 10 seconds. That's if you don't get soap in your eyes from trying to shampoo too quickly.

FOOD AND DRINK There's nothing in the village apart from the tiny Bistro Beim Renée. The nearest supermarket is an Aldi at Marnach, so it's best to stock up there and self-cater.
FAMILY FUN There's everything you need right onsite. There's the river, for a start, and loads of play areas with various swings, and so on. But the real star is a wooden and metal water feature: prime the pump and water flows into various channels and turns water wheels. It will keep the kids quiet for hours.
TREAT YOURSELF No don't. For once take a leaf from Winnie the Pooh: 'Sometimes', he says, 'I sits and thinks. And sometimes I just sits'.
GETTING THERE It's about an hour's drive from the city of Luxembourg. Head up the A7 through Ettelbruck and on to Hosingen. Follow the signs for Enscherange and as you reach the village the entrance to the site is on the right over the railway line. Parking is at the other end of the village.
PUBLIC TRANSPORT There are hourly trains to/from Luxembourg city (45 mins) on the main line to Liege/Luik in Belgium. The station is under a mile (1.5 km) from the camping. The owners can pick you up if you contact them and arrange something in advance.
OPEN Apr–early-Nov.
IF IT'S FULL There's a plush site right by the River Clerve at the historic town of Clervaux (33 Klatzwee, Clervaux; www.camping-clervaux.lu).

**Camping Val d'Or**, L-9747 Enscherange, Luxembourg

| t | 00 352 92 06 91 | w | www.valdor.lu |

# campspirit

You know you're onto a good thing when the only means of getting to a campsite is by boat. Not only does this mean no cars, but also no cares. Leave both on the mainland before taking a gentle 15-minute chug across the waters of Lake Veluwe to the peaceful reed-enclosed retreat of the wonderfully named CampSpirit. Situated on De Kluut island, the campsite is a delightful mish-mash of canvas dwellings from all over the world. Take your pick from seven Native American tipis (one serving as the communal lounge), a Swedish tipi, three Sahara tents, a Mongolian yurt and a very special Kyrgyz yurt. And the Eastern wedding tent, all the way from Pakistan, provides the perfect space for the relaxing workshops held throughout the year.

Opened in summer 2007, CampSpirit has been a labour of love for its dedicated creators Janneke and Doron. They painstakingly shipped the dwellings over one by one and constructed them right from scratch, before embarking on making every piece of furniture themselves. Having travelled around Africa to get a few ideas, they wanted to set up something different from the average Dutch campsite, and they've certainly succeeded. This is a carefree, comfortable sanctuary, where you don't need to worry about setting up tents or lugging cooking equipment around. In fact, you don't need to bring much with you at all, except for a few items of clothing, essential personal stuff and some nourishing fresh food. Plus, perhaps, a copy of Thoreau's *Walden*. Everything else is already here – for you to use. So sit back and relax.

The dwellings are spread across half the island; the other half remains untouched, part of a nature reserve protecting the lake's many birds. The tipis accommodate two to six people, whilst both yurts take four with ease. All tents are equipped with proper beds, boasting thick, comfy mattresses and covered with beautiful ethnic blankets – so you'll sleep like the proverbial log. There's also a stove, every piece of crockery and equipment you can think of, plus a few others you can't, and a small larder stocked with groceries. Blossoming vegetable and herb gardens are close at hand to raid at any time, so if you feel a little peckish in the middle of the night, you can always creep out and pull up a radish.

Three Sahara tents provide the perfect digs for people travelling alone, and there's a separate cooking tent and picnic table with a view to encourage a communal spirit amongst singletons. But don't worry if you find this approach too hearty. You may feel more than happy just being a hermit – and why not? The campsite's ethos is such that if you want time out from the rest of the human race, no problem; but if you feel inclined to mingle, then the communal tipi is just the place for a good old natter around the campfire.

CampSpirit's special atmosphere makes it less of a campsite and more a laid-back sanctuary. In fact, it's so laid back it's practically horizontal. With its island setting, protected by a wall of swaying reeds, the camp has an immediate calming effect on the soul. Only 50 people are

allowed on the island at once, and you'd want to take most of them home with you afterwards. With a woodland grove dotted with swaying hammocks beneath shady boughs, a picturesque little harbour and endless places to wind down on a sunny day, you can't help but feel completely chilled. CampSpirit probably represents camping at its very coolest.

It's no surprise, then, to see some seriously sad faces on those poor souls boarding the boat for their journey back to the mainland – to pick up their cars, but hopefully not too many of their cares.

THE UPSIDE Luxury 'camping' on an island retreat, complete with real fires in the tipis.
THE DOWNSIDE Like a lot of lovely treats, it's not cheap, and the ferry only crosses between island and mainland 4 times a day.
THE DAMAGE Best to check out their website as prices vary from one person in a Sahara tent for a weekend in low season at €55, to 4 people in the Kyrgyz yurt for a week in high season for €599. There are extra costs for bed linen – €6 per person – and tourist tax at €0.75 per person per night.
THE FACILITIES Four well-maintained toilet and shower cubicles, dishwashing facilities, some clothes lines and a tiny shop that stocks dry and canned goods. Each tipi has a cooking stove, equipment and crockery; and there's a communal cooking tent for the Sahara tents.
FOOD AND DRINK Basiliek Restaurant in Harderwijk (Vischmarkt 57a, Harderwijk,

00 31 341 41 52 90; www.restaurantbasiliek.nl) is featured in the Netherlands' top 100 'Beautiful 2008' restaurant review. Sumptuously presented culinary delights are served at this Michelin-starred restaurant, which in the past was a chapel.
FAMILY FUN Sailing lessons are available at Molecaten's Flevostrand recreation park across the lake (00 31 320 28 84 80; info@flevostrand.nl) or there's Walibi World adventure ride park in Biddinghuizen for adrenalin-junkie roller-coaster riders (00 31 321 32 99 99; www.walibiworld.nl).
TREAT YOURSELF They have a large workshop tent onsite, where anyone can join in the activities, from painting and yoga to mosaic-making and reiki therapy, and from re-balancing techniques to making African power shields. The workshops are a regular feature, though they do not run every day.
GETTING THERE Take the A1 from Amsterdam towards Almere/Amersfoort for 6 miles (10 km),

then take the exit onto A6 towards Almere/Lelystad for 20 miles (33 km), leave at exit 10, onto the Larserweg/N302. After 6 miles (10 km) take a left onto Gooise Weg N305. After just over a mile (2 km) turn right onto the Karekietweg. Take another right at Harderbosweg/N306 for a third of a mile (0.5 km). Carry on past the Flevostrand campsite and take a left on Strandweg until you reach the harbour. Park and take the ferry over to the island (see CampSpirit website for ferry times).
PUBLIC TRANSPORT Catch the train to Harderwijk, then the 147 bus to Flevostrand, followed by the boat over to the island (ferry times available on camp website).
OPEN May–Sept.
IF IT'S FULL If you haven't booked ahead at CampSpirit then Molecaten recreation park has a campsite near to the beach (00 31 320 28 84 80; www.molecaten.nl/nl/flevostrand).

**CampSpirit**, De Kluut island, Strandweg 1, 8256 RZ Biddinghuizen, The Netherlands

t 00 31 630 36 47 23 | w www.campspirit.nl

# camping de roos

A *zwembroek* (if you're a guy) or *badpak* (if you're a girl – though what's with the 'bad'?) is an absolute must for a stay at Camping de Roos. Also known as bathers, swimmers, bathing suits, trunks or cozzies, unless you fancy a skinny-dip, these items are wardrobe essentials for a refreshing dunk in the River Vecht, which meanders through this sprawling campsite. So be sure you pack at least one or two.

Located within an area of outstanding natural beauty between the towns of Ommen and Beerze, the campsite occupies an expanse of sloping clearings surrounded by dense woodland, boasting friendly neighbours such as roe deer, nightingales and woodpeckers.

Despite the site's capacity of 276 pitches, many of them taken by caravans, the careful layout means you rarely get that unpleasant overcrowded sensation. The pitches are extremely roomy, and the undulating land scattered with trees, bushes and winding paths creates the illusion of a much smaller site, with more than enough room to go round. But if you'd rather a complete slice of countryside peace and quiet, two designated *trekkersvelden* are on hand to provide just the sanctuary you might be needing. Tucked away amidst the ground's chunkier trees,

they are exclusively reserved for anyone who's come by bike or on foot. The site's sensible 'no-car' policy, with vehicles only allowed onsite for unloading and loading, helps maintain that natural feel.

In fact, preserving the natural beauty of the site is a priority at Camping de Roos, as it's a rare honour to be granted permission to run a campsite in a protected area. Timed showers and recycling bins, plus gentle requests not to pick the lovely flowers ensure the site remains as kind to its environment as possible. There's also an onsite shop chock-full of healthy foods, planet-friendly cleaning unguents and the most local of local produce, of which ice cream made at a nearby farm is worth several return trips.

The merry tinkle of children's laughter is a constant backdrop here, with the owners taking the term 'child-friendly' to a whole new level. It's almost guaranteed you won't hear the familiar 'I'm borrrred' when there's a volleyball court, a football pitch, a kite-flying field, *boules* ground and dinghies dotted along the river bank; as well as a kiosk where kiddywinks (along with sweet-toothed mums and dads) can get their fill of tasty treats. Even on rainy days there's plenty of indoor fun to be had. But the firm favourite has got to be the swimming opportunity, well…jumping into water and splashing around. The river's tributary forms the ideal spot for a children's pool – even boasting its own mini-beach – and when the weather's fine they jump, dive and 'bomb' from its little pier.

The surrounding area is criss-crossed with cycle routes in the 'river-dune' landscape, formed at some point during the last ice age. You can hire bikes from the site, and a short pedal will find you plunged deep into wonderfully quiet woodland. Or if you'd like to dispense with wheels completely,

the Vecht Valley walking path passes right through the campsite, covering a fair old trek of 44½ miles (72 km) in total, taking in some top-of-the-range countryside.

This site's enviable location means that, even with numerous amenities and kids' activities on offer, it still exudes a tranquillity that can be hard to find at other European sites. And if it takes you a while to tune in to the country vibes, try floating along the cool river, with blue skies and fluffy clouds above and grassy banks on either side, to enjoy a bit of Mother Nature at her finest.

THE UPSIDE Stunning woodland location around the River Vecht. It's relaxing, environmentally friendly and heaven for kids.
THE DOWNSIDE With 276 pitches it can get pretty busy. As it's very family-orientated it's not the ideal place for couples wanting a romantic retreat or some adult-only time.
THE DAMAGE The basic rate per pitch per night is €16.50 for 2 adults, a tent/caravan/camper and parking space, and €13.50 in the low season, with extras per night for another person (over 3 years of age) €3.50, auxiliary tents €1/€2, tourist tax of €0.80 per person per night, electricity €2.60, sewerage €1. There are also packages available.
THE FACILITIES An onsite shop, which stocks organic and local produce as well as hot pizzas and vegetable pies. A small tea room and kiosk on a terrace near the river tributary. There's also an onsite launderette complete with iron and

board. Handy cooling elements and freezer packs are available. There's also a payphone and free Internet. The loo blocks are heated, with each shower doling out 5 minutes of hot water. Dogs are not allowed on the site.
FOOD AND DRINK For mouth-watering pancakes try the De Gloepe farm restaurant in Diffelen (Rheezerweg 84a; 00 31 523 25 12 31; www.degloepe.nl).
FAMILY FUN Take the kids on the Wolf Trail adventure walk through the woods. Games are played throughout the 1½ mile (2.5 km) route, and each child gets a rucksack full of descriptions, assignments and a magic sweet that will apparently turn them into a wolf (sounds like fun). Info and rucksacks (€5.95) available at Ommen's Tourist Info Centre, Kruisstraat 6, Ommen; 00 31 0900 112 23 75; www.vvvommen.nl.
TREAT YOURSELF Take a canoe trip along the

River Vecht to experience the valley's beautiful scenery. A bus will take you to the starting point and from there you travel at your own pace back to Ommen (00 31 529 45 19 24/45 14 33).
GETTING THERE Head from Amsterdam on the A1 towards Almere/Amersfoort. Take exit 14 for A28 towards Zwolle. Just past Zwolle, get off at exit 21 for the N340 to Ommen. In Ommen, turn right onto the bridge and turn left onto Zeesserweg, which becomes Beerzerweg. The campsite is approximately 6 miles (10 km) along the road on the left.
PUBLIC TRANSPORT The closest you'll get is Ommen if you come by train, and it's a long old walk to the site from there.
OPEN Mid-Apr–early-Oct.
IF IT'S FULL Along the same road, towards Ommen, you'll find Camping De Vogelsangh (00 31 546 67 30 80; www.devogelsangh.nl).

**Camping de Roos**, Beerzerweg 10, Beerze–Ommen, 7736 PJ, The Netherlands

| t | 00 31 523 25 12 34 | w | www.camping-de-roos.nl |

# thyencamp

Paul and Marjo Tienkamp's son makes no bones about calling his parents 'hippies' these days. A city lawyer himself, he's watched them hang up their suits in favour of beads, beards, shorts and sandals, to join a clutch of environmental groups and run an art gallery and campsite in the grassy flatlands of Drenthe.

The campsite offers 30 pitches spread over a Kermit-green lawn interspersed with fruit trees, shady oaks and berry-laden hedges. It's the only carbon-neutral camping site in the Netherlands and the owners run it at a loss to make quite sure that it stays sustainable – such is their passion for all things environmental. However, luckily they refrain from hopping on soapboxes, waving green flags at campers or lecturing anybody about their carbon footprint. Theirs is a far more subtle demonstration of how to take care of the planet by taking small, simple steps that don't cost the earth – a quiet conviction that enhances the calm, unspoiled nature of this camping retreat.

As well as generating electricity with windmills and solar panels, they've implemented the more wallet-friendly step of using low-watt LED bulbs, one of which was purchased a whopping 25 years ago and is still glowing strong. They have also planted three walnut trees in both the sheep paddock and the garden. A true symbol of sustainability, walnut trees live for 250 years plus, sucking in oodles of $CO_2$, producing tasty nuts and providing shiny, durable furniture wood along the way.

Running the campsite and gallery may now be a far cry from his former life as a city insurance manager, but this is definitely the hippified life for Paul, and many happy campers return year after year to enjoy his campsite's serenity, its philosophy and simple views of green and ochre fields. A dyke playing home to ducks separates the camping lawn from next-door's field, with its lazy grazing Friesians.

When the sun comes out campers sunbathe on the clover-carpeted grass and enjoy afternoon snoozes beneath shading boughs. If all you can hear are the sounds of the breeze rustling through the leaves or the spluttery coughs of a nearby tractor, you can feel your city stresses evaporating as quickly as the morning dew.

A small children's play area keeps kids happy when they're not off on family days cycling, fruit-picking and sightseeing around the pleasant countryside. And there's a computer for anyone in need of a cyber fix.

If you are an art-lover, art of all kinds is on show everywhere at Thyencamp, both indoors and out. Funky sculptures keep you company on the picnic tables whilst you munch your lunch and bird statues in the garden add an eccentric but graceful presence. Inside, gorgeous paintings adorn corridor walls and special exhibitions brighten up both attic space and recreation hall. What better place to retreat from the evening chill and enjoy a glass of organic beer? And in the mornings the air is thick with the delicious aroma of fresh-baked bread from the local bakery. All you do is place an order in the evening and Paul collects the precious doughy cargo in his old, liquid-gas-fuelled car the next day.

In the midst of a slow-paced country life in Drenthe, where cyclists outnumber motorists, Camping Thyencamp epitomises the laid-back, ecologically striving and charming Dutch outlook that makes the Netherlands a truly refreshing holiday destination. It would be hippy-critical not to give it a hearty seal of approval.

THE UPSIDE Scenic, peaceful, guilt-free camping with the added bonus of lovely owners.
THE DOWNSIDE Leaving.
THE DAMAGE Caravans/folding trailers are charged €4.50, camper buses/vans are charged €5.50. Tents are €4 and hikers' tents €3. Charges per person are €3.50 (children under 3 go free, as do pets, but please contact Paul and Marjo about bringing your furry friends along first). Dogs must be kept on leads onsite. Tourist tax per person is €0.80 and environmental tax per person is €0.25. Anyone arriving by bicycle gets a 10 per cent discount. Electricity costs €2.50. There's also the option of staying in the onsite sustainable caravan for €20 (minimum 3 days).
THE FACILITIES Lovely, pristine, bathrooms (well-stocked with loo rolls and Ecover soap) comprising 2 toilets and 2 showers each for men and women, inside the main house. Washing (€3) and drying (€2) machines are available. Fair trade

eco drinks and ice creams are sold at reception. There's also a small children's playing area.
FOOD AND DRINK Hooghalen's bakery, Fledderus, is a gold mine of tasty treats and is a must for all campers. Fresh bread, rolls, pastries, cakes and scrummy ice cream flavours flow in abundance in this cosy place, with its sunny outdoor terrace.
FAMILY FUN Hire bikes or get into your walking boots to enjoy Drenthe's flat, beautiful scenery. Near to the campsite you can explore Hijkerveld, the old Celtic fields in the region. The walks vary from 3 to 9 miles (5 to 15 km) long.
TREAT YOURSELF Indulge in some fruit, freshly picked from local trees and vines. Sturing's farm, along the road to Hooghalen, is a real goody-bag of home-made jams, wines, cheeses and fruit, glorious fruit! They also stock farmyard eggs, which make the perfect breakfast accompaniment to the fresh bread.

GETTING THERE From Amsterdam, take the A1 towards Almere/Amersfoort. Change to the A28 to Zwolle at exit 14. Keep on the A28 towards Assen, passing Hoogeveen until you see signs for Smilde and Hooghalen. Turn off the highway and drive through Hooghalen along Laaghalerveen for about 1½ miles (2.5 km) and you'll see a sign for Thyencamp to the right. The site is about a third of a mile (0.5 km) up the road.
PUBLIC TRANSPORT Buses just don't get this far into the countryside. The best bet is to take a train to Assen. Paul or Marjo will kindly collect you from the train station if you organise it in advance.
OPEN Mid-Apr–Oct.
IF IT'S FULL On the Laaghalerveen road between Hooghalen and Camping Thyencamp, there is a 'mini camping' called De Vogelpoel (00 31 593 59 29 45; www.devogelpoel.nl), which consists of camping pitches in the owners' garden.

**Camping en Galerie Thyencamp**, Laaghalerveen 23, 9414VH Hooghalen, The Netherlands

| t | 00 31 593 59 23 30 | w | www.thyencamp.nl |

# lauwerszee

Cycling in the UK is often synonymous with taking your life into your own hands. Big, boisterous buses, few cycling lanes and cross motorists can make it a hanging-on-by-the-seat-of-your-pants ordeal. Happily, such scenarios are unheard of in The Netherlands, where cyclists have priority over everyone else. Whether you're four or 84, the preferred method of transport here is sedate pedalling.

One of the country's top locations for enjoying a bit of biking is around Lake Lauwersmeer and its surrounding National Park. Twitchers will delight to hear that this area's home to over 140 species, to be spotted flapping and wheeling overhead or paddling in the lake.

An easy pedal away is tiny Vierhuizen, watched over by its large wooden windmill. At the other end you'll find Camping Lauwerszee, tucked behind its owners' cosy restaurant, where local diners (just the men, thankfully) boast the kind of bushy moustaches that'd have the likes of Ned Flanders burning with 'tache-envy.

The campsite resembles a landscaped garden, with brightly coloured hedgerows and huddles of trees providing tent-privacy, whilst sprinkles of flowers, host to butterflies, adorn the spacious lawns. Its laid-back ambience makes it the perfect place to relax after a good day's exploration in the saddle.

THE UPSIDE Peaceful, spacious camping with a lake within cycling distance.
THE DOWNSIDE It's sticks-ville here so don't go expecting much in the way of entertainment.
THE DAMAGE One night for 2 people with a tent or caravan and car is approximately €13, with an extra €3.25 per adult, and €2 per child under 12, or dog. Electricity costs €2.90.
THE FACILITIES There's a new toilet and shower block. There's a play area for kids and bikes are available to hire.
FOOD AND DRINK The Herberg Restaurant on the site is well known in the area for its tasty treats.

The menu is entirely in Dutch, so be adventurous and go for something untranslatable.
FAMILY FUN Go to nearby Anjum to visit the tiny mustard museum and candle-making factory (where you can make your own candles).
TREAT YOURSELF Try a ghostly Full Moon Excursion around the mudlands of the lake. The walk begins at 11pm and finishes at 2am.
GETTING THERE From Amsterdam, take the A1 towards Almere/Amersfoort. After a short while, turn onto the A6 past Lelystad towards Groningen (at Heerenveen it changes into the A7). Leave at exit 33 (marked Zuidhorn/Boerakker) and turn left,

following the N388 through Boerakker, Grijpskerk and Zoutkamp. Two miles (3 km) past Zoutkap, turn left onto the Hoofdstraat and the campsite is about ½ mile (1 km) down the road on the right.
PUBLIC TRANSPORT Take the train to Groningen and then hop onto the Arriva 65 bus towards Zoutkamp for the 1½-hour journey. The bus stops outside the church at Vierhuizen.
OPEN Apr–Oct.
IF IT'S FULL This is unheard of, according to the owners, but just to be on the safe side, Camping de Rousant is near the lake (00 31 595 44 71 50; www.rousant.nl/camping) at Zoutkamp.

**Camping Lauwerszee**, Hoofdstraat 49, 9975 VR Vierhuizen, The Netherlands

| t | 00 31 595 40 16 57 | w | www.camping-lauwerszee.nl |

# uhlenköper

'The hiiills are aliiive with…the sight of heather?' Yes, from August through till September, Germany's Lüneburger Heide region hits its purple patch. Its heathlands are transformed into oceans of mauve so expansive that Prince could write songs about them. There are heather festivals and annual crownings of heather queens, and tourists overwhelm local towns and villages.

Amidst this violet fury lies Uhlenköper, a tranquil eco-site ensconced in the itsy-bitsy village of Westerweyhe, near Uelzen. Run by Gertrud and Thomas Körding, this three-acre site has been carved up into areas for *dauercampers* (permanent residents), caravans and larger tents, tenters and cyclists. In between flow the site's public areas: a solar-powered reception (with shower block, restaurant and bio-shop), modest playground and – *pièce de résistance* – a spanking new swimming pool with sections for swimmers and paddlers.

Offsite fun can be had cycling, kayaking on the Ilmenau or checking out Natur Park Sudheide, where you can glimpse the black-haired rams with white bodies that resemble woolly pints of Guinness. If nothing else they make a change from all that purple.

THE UPSIDE Relaxed, eco-friendly site with a pool; good access to the Lüneburger Heide region.
THE DOWNSIDE The camping area is smallish and the pool is open to the public at certain times.
THE DAMAGE For 2 people and tent plus car the cost is €19, and plus 2 kids it's €23. Without a car the cost is €17 and with 2 kids it's €21.
THE FACILITIES Uhlenköper Camp has won awards for its eco-commitments and the facilities reflect this – no chemicals in the pool, bio food in the shop, free herb gardens and solar power where possible. The shower block is clean and modern; the restaurant offers a decent selection of meals.
FOOD AND DRINK Apart from the onsite restaurant (terraced in summer), you can grab a tasty schnitzel at the village restaurant Dorfkrug (a 2-minute stroll – take your dancing shoes and join in the weekly square dance on Sunday evenings), otherwise the nearest spots are in Uelzen. For local produce, the Bauckhof farm (00 49 581 90160; www.bauckhof.de) sells everything from free-range eggs to sausages and cheese.
FAMILY FUN The pool, which has a shallow section for younger children, provides ample playing opportunities. The site owners are qualified canoe guides and can take you for a family trip along the river – or you can hire your own canoes and bikes on site and do your own thing.
TREAT YOURSELF Upgrade your eco-accommodation. Hotel Kenners Landlust (00 49 5855 9793; www.kenners-landlust.de). This bio hotel in Dübbekold offers organic food, shiatsu massage and a pool and sauna for total relaxation.
GETTING THERE From Hamburg take the B4 and continue along the A255, following signs for A1/Bremen/Lübeck, then continue along the A1. Take exit 39-Maschener Kreuz and merge onto the A250 towards Lüneburg/Maschen. Continue on the B4 (signposted Uelzen and Lüneburg), taking the exit onto the B4. Take a right at K40/Westerweyher Strasse, follow the K40, turn left at Am Waterbusch, then a slight right at Festplatzweg.
PUBLIC TRANSPORT Take the Deutsche Bahn to Uelzen Bahnhof/train station. Then, hop on the 1973 bus towards Weinbergstrasse/Ebstorf, getting off at Westerweyhe train station. Follow the footpath, taking a left then straight on into Altes Dorfstrasse, keeping the school to your right.
OPEN All year.
IF IT'S FULL Campingplatz Rote Schleuse (00 49 31 791500; www.camproteschleuse.de) is in Lüneburg, at the River Ilmenau and has a natural pool, a laid-back atmosphere and excellent access to Lüneburg.

**Uhlenköper**, Festplatzweg 11, 29525 Uelzen, Germany

| t | 00 49 581 73044 | w | www.uhlenkoeper-camp.de |

# tentstation

Question: What do cabaret, camping, abandoned swimming pools, techno and former divided cities have in common? Normally not a great deal, but in the case of Berlin's Tentstation, rather a lot. Whilst you may balk at the idea of setting up a tent in the middle of a city – it does seem to undermine the notion of 'getting away from it all' somewhat – you might rejoice at the chance to grab some cheap, funky accommodation in one of the buzziest capital cities in Europe.

Tentstation genuinely offers the best of both worlds: a green-ish oasis in the middle of a concrete jungle that strives to be comfortable and original. Of course, having a massive abandoned swimming pool as the centrepiece of your site already goes some way towards ensuring uniqueness, but Tentstation's staff go further – showing movies in its capacious pit, setting up badminton nets, putting on concerts, turning the smaller pool into a sand-pit for kids and a volleyball area for older kids and adults...

The disused nature of the site's facilities (it was transformed from an old outdoor swimming park), many of which are heavily scrawled with graffiti (to chime in with the old sections of the Berlin Wall still on show in the city, perhaps?), gives Tentstation a

bit of a scruffy look. But you'll soon rumble that its overabundance of aerosol art and crumbling concrete belies the fact that the site is actually very well maintained.

Run by a dedicated team of 20- to 40-year-olds, an air of 'anything goes' – typical of Berlin – is the order of the day. The two-acre site offers space for up to 125 tents, and pitches are arranged within the green meadows around the swimming pool; they're not marked out – so you can just throw your tent up wherever there's room.

There's a bar open during summer, which comes in handy for concerts and DJ sets, and the rectangular shower block is the one used by the swimmers back in the day – it does have a municipal feel, but on the upside it's large enough to cope with the influx of guests. The bar also serves up breakfasts and snacks, and you can also borrow a grill from reception if you fancy a BBQ.

Perhaps the best thing about Tentstation, though – apart from the fact it's for campers only – is its proximity to the thrills and spills of the big city. A 10-minute stroll will get you to Berlin's Hauptbahnhof, the centre of the city's notoriously efficient and reasonably priced rail network. From there the *Stadt* is your oyster: world-famous sights such as Brandenburger Tor and the Reichstag are a mere 15-minute pootle; you can shop to your heart's content in Ku'Damm (there's secure storage for valuable shopping hauls back at Tentstation); check out the boutiques and cafés in trendy Mitte; stroll around picturesque Prenzlauer Berg; or hang out in the more 'alternative' areas of Freidrichshain and Kreuzberg.

At night Berlin really comes alive, with a slew of cocktail bars, clubs catering for every known genre of music, great live venues and one of the best techno scenes in the world. Berghain, one of the city's most notorious venues, doesn't even get going until 7am, meaning it's a toss-up between tea and techno for breakfast. Urban camping just doesn't get any better than this.

THE UPSIDE Urban camping in the heart of one of Europe's hippest cities.
THE DOWNSIDE The site looks a bit scruffy and the facilities are unusual, to say the least.
THE DAMAGE A tent and 2 adults costs €32, and children aged 5–10/11–17 pay €5/8 each.
THE FACILITIES There's some stuff to do on site, such as play badminton or volleyball in the pool, hang out at the bar during concerts or play table tennis. In summer there are open-air cinema shows, live bands and DJs.
FOOD AND DRINK The bar sells breakfasts and snacks during summer. There's a Plus supermarket 5 minutes' walking distance away, an Italian budget restaurant, Mediterrano, 7 minutes away. To combine decent food with a splendid array of art, take a 10-minute stroll to the excellent Hamburger Bahnhof art museum and indulge in some healthy,

fresh food courtesy of celebrity chef Sarah Wiener (00 49 30 7071 3650; www.sarahwiener.de).
FAMILY FUN One of the pools (the smaller one) at Tentstation is full of sand for kids and kidults to play in. There's also volleyball and badminton in the main pool, and there are table-tennis tables scattered around. The city itself offers lots of opportunities: from bike tours (00 49 30 2404 7991; www.fattirebiketoursberlin.com) and boat tours (00 49 30 5363 6088; www.sternundkreis. de) to children's museums (00 49 30 8009 31150; www.labyrinth-kindermuseum.de). There are also flea markets in Mauerpark (Sundays), Boxhagener Platz (Sundays) and Strasse des 17. Juni (Saturdays and Sundays).
TREAT YOURSELF Why not get a bird's eye view of the city? Hi-Flyer (00 49 30 5321 5321; www.air-service-berlin.de) has several different

types of flying machine, from helicopter and balloon to a floatplane and even a bomber.
GETTING THERE Follow signs for the inner city and/or the Hauptbahnhof (Berlin's central train station). Turn left from Invalidenstrasse to Seydlitzstrasse after 100 metres. Another 100 metres along you'll find Tentstation parking on the right side of the street. The entrance to the camping site is behind the car park on the left side, opposite the entrance to the indoor bath.
PUBLIC TRANSPORT From Berlin's Tegel catch bus TXL (dest. Mollstrasse/Prenzlauer Allee) to Hauptbahnhof (about 20 minutes). Then, as above.
OPEN Late-Apr–early-Oct.
IF IT'S FULL Campingplatz Krossinsee (00 49 30 6758 687; www.dccberlin.de/campingplatzkrossinsee.htm) is a pleasant spot near a lake, though it's a bit further from the city.

**Tentstation**, Seydlitzstr. 6, 10557 Berlin, Germany

| t | 00 49 30 3940 4650 | w | www.tentstation.de |

# thorwaldblick

It's true that it's much easier to pronounce the official name of Germany's Saxony Switzerland region – Sächsische Schweiz – after downing several strong schnapps. But don't do this the moment you arrive – there's simply way too much to explore before you start opening any bottles.

The region was given its name because of its similarity to Switzerland's rugged landscape. Containing both the Ore and Lusation ranges – as well as the Elbe river – the Sächsische Schweiz is one of the most mountainous areas in Germany. If you like climbing around on rocks, you'll find its fissured, craggy landscape ideal; with over 1,000 climbing peaks it's become something of a mountaineering Mecca. It will also suit you if you are into hiking, biking, kayaking or just about any other outdoorsy pursuit you can think of.

Set at the far edge of this natural wonderland, within the Saxony Switzerland National Park, is Camping Thorwaldblick. Cosy and intimate would be apt words for this diminutive campsite, which has been up and running since 1996. Run by the down-to-earth Peh family, there's only room for 20 or so tent-carrying souls (caravans and mobile homes are located on the other side of reception), but the campers get to inhabit a lovely garden-like area fringed with fruit trees and surrounded by fields.

The site has only basic amenities (reception, toilets, washing facilities), but tiny Hinterhermsdorf – once the proud winner of a 'Germany's Most Beautiful Village' award – is just down the road. Despite its size, Hinterhermsdorf is a popular holiday haunt, boasting lots of handsome half-timbered houses and plenty of fresh mountain air. Plus, it has all the usuals: butcher, baker, restaurants and a mini-market.

The Saxony Switzerland National Park covers two areas of 35-odd square miles (90 sq km), most of it covered in beech and conifer forests and criss-crossed with trails, peaks and voluptuous vistas. Apart from hiking and biking your way through this top-notch rural scenery, you can make a beeline for such specific stop-offs as the striking 13th-century fortress Festung Königstein (a 30-minute drive), the equally dramatic Stolpen castle (a 45-minute drive) or the famous Bastei bridge (another 45-minute drive), with its distinctive rock formations and grandiose views.

For urban thrills, head to nearby Dresden (a one-hour drive), which wasn't nicknamed the 'Florence of the Elbe' for nothing.

It offers an array of rebuilt Baroque architecture (it was controversially fire-bombed by the Allied Forces at the end of World War II), world-renowned museums and a truly engaging buzz. It makes for a fantastic day trip and, since it's one of the greenest cities in Europe, it's a decent option for families, too.

If that's not exotic enough for you, strike out in the other direction across the Czech border. Right next door lies the Šumava National Park (a natural continuation of the Saxony Swiss one), with plenty of charming Czech villages. A two-hour drive will bring you to dark, mysterious Prague.

But you don't need to go quite so far to enjoy yourself: there are hikes and bike rides aplenty nearby. And whilst the onsite facilities are limited, there's an adventure pool in Neustadt (about 12 miles/20 km away) and a relaxation swimming pool and adventure park in Sebnitz (6 miles/10 km away). You can canoe on the Elbe or hike up to the Weifbergturm (a 40-minute walk) for a panoramic view of the Ore and, on a clear day, even the Czech Krkonose mountains.

When you're done exploring, head back to your intimate garden retreat, cook up some food on the stove and relax. Now, what was that about cracking open some bottles?

THE UPSIDE Intimate campsite with great access to both the Sächsische Schweiz National Park and the Czech Republic.
THE DOWNSIDE There's only space for 20 or so tents, and not much in the way of onsite facilities.
THE DAMAGE Two people, a tent and a car cost €11.80; 4 people, a tent and a car cost €18.
THE FACILITIES The facilities are humble but adequate – a small playground; a room with sinks; fridge; cooking facilities; and washing machine.
FOOD AND DRINK You can order bread and brötchen from the nearby bakery, as well as steaks and bratwürste (sausages) for a BBQ, plus ice cream, beer, wine and soft drinks. The closest shop is Dorfladen (open until 8pm) in Hinterhermsdorf. Also in Hinterhermsdorf are restaurants such as Erbgericht and Wanderstübel, which offer traditional food. Gasthof zur Hoffnung is a bit nicer. Sebnitz has a Bauernmarkt on Mondays

and Wednesdays (9am–6pm).
FAMILY FUN The site has a small playground with a sandpit, swings and a table-tennis table. In Hinterhermsdorf you can hire a horse-cart and take a tour around the local countryside or try a ceramics painting course (ask at reception for details). In Sebnitz, the Forellenschenke (www.gasthof-forellenschenke.de) has an obstacle course, adventure park and minigolf.
TREAT YOURSELF For serious relaxation, try the Toskana Therme spa (www.toskanaworld. net) at Bad Schandau, where you can unwind in a wonderful setting. There is also a gliding school in Pirna (www.aeroclub-pirna.de) if you want to earn some romantic air miles.
GETTING THERE From Berlin take the A100 towards Dresden, continuing on the A113 (following signs for Frankfurt (Oder)/E36/Treptow/Dresden). Follow the A13, taking exit 10-Dreieck

Spreewald, following the A13 before merging onto the A4. Take the motorway slip road Burkau onto Bischofswerdaer Str, through Neustadt, Sebnitz and Hinterhermsdorf, following signs to the site. From Dresden, take the B170 and join the A17 towards Pirna., taking the B172 all the way to Basteiplatz/S165, where you turn left and carry on until you arrive at the site.
PUBLIC TRANSPORT You can catch a train to Sebnitz or Bad Schandau. From there the site runs a shuttle service direct to the campsite, and there are also public buses that stop outside – normally once a day, depending on the season.
OPEN All year.
IF IT'S FULL Ostrauer Mühle (www.ostrauer-muehle.de) is the only other campsite within the national park. It's larger and more commercial than Thorwaldblick but is well run but has equally great access to the surrounding area.

**Camping Thorwaldblick**, Schandauer Strasse 37, 01855 Hinterhermsdorf, Germany

| t | 00 49 35 9745 0648 | w | www.thorwaldblick.de |

# vulkaneifel

The Vulkan region may sound like the kind of interplanetary place Dr Spock might hang out in – or even hail from – but it's not. It's Germany's only volcanic region, a low mountain range in a southwestern section of the Rhineland-Pfalz (known as the Eifel), which lures tourists with its water-filled craters (the so-called 'eyes' of the Eifel) and tantalising landscapes.

Natur-Camping Vulkaneifel lies in the centre of the region, just over half a mile (1 km) outside the village of Manderscheid in Bernkastel-Wittlich. Owner Wolfgang Moritz has been in charge for 30 years, starting it initially as a children's summer camp and gradually expanding into a campsite for all.

Moritz, a keen advocate of Rudolf Steiner's Waldorf Schools, submits to Steiner's ideas of anthroposophy, though those not sold on Steiner need not worry. Apart from an emphasis on bio products in the children's canteen, the use of natural materials around the site and a 'free' environment for children to be themselves, you wouldn't notice.

The centre of the campsite is still given over to the Jugendferiendorf, or children's village, a collection of multi-coloured huts set around a landscaped area. The camping pitches are situated along a series of quiet, green terraces shaded by fruit trees, slightly away from the site's centre. The pitches are categorised as A, B and C, according to their size. The north side has the biggest and quietest pitches, and is the most popular with campers, though the southern pitches are perfectly pleasant, too.

The facilities are clean and modern with separate shower blocks for men and women, outdoor sinks and a small kitchen. In keeping with the child-friendly ethos, there's also plenty of green space to relax or run around in, plus a badminton court and playground, BBQ area and a boutique tipi in a field brimming with red poppies.

This easy-going pleasantness is all in contrast to how the Eifel region was 400 years ago, when it was ravaged by plagues, witch-hunts and feuds – you know, all that cheery Middle Ages stuff. They say almost 300 people were executed as witches between 1528 and 1641, though these days you're much more likely to be dining on a juicy steak than being burned at one.

Nearby Manderscheid is a comely spa town with 1,300 or so inhabitants. Though it's generally coy on the sightseeing front, it does offer some convenient facilities for campers – a couple of supermarkets, some restaurants, and an enthusiastic tourist office – as well as a truly stunning castle, some sections of which are said to date right back to the 10th century.

The real draw, though, is the volcanic region, which since 2004 has been part of the UNESCO Global Geoparks. Most of the area is easily accessible from the campsite and is interlaced with a web of walking and cycling trails, some of them literally starting at the site's front door. The Geo-Route Manderscheid, for instance, is an 86-mile (140-km) walk, which takes in a lot of the region's highlights. Cyclists will marvel at the Maare-Mosel-Radweg path, which runs from Manderscheid along an old railway line and takes you either to the lovely town of Daun or to the beautiful Mosel river, a great place to check out some local wines. Towns like Koblenz make a wonderful stopover, as does the ancient city of Trier. As luck would have it, there's even a road that joins the two together – the Mosel Wine Road – how totally logical. Even Spock couldn't fail to enjoy himself here.

THE UPSIDE Great family-friendly site with a natural vibe and great access to the fascinating Vulkaneifel region.
THE DOWNSIDE There are a lot of kids hanging out here, but many of the pitches are far enough apart so that those without can enjoy some P&Q.
THE DAMAGE Each pitch is €4–9, depending on size, plus €7 per person; children under 8 are free and ages 8–13 are €1 each.
THE FACILITIES Facilities are good and include a large shower block, washing machine and dryer, a small kitchen for campers, kiosk in reception, badminton net, BBQ area and playground.
FOOD AND DRINK The canteen serves tasty, bio-friendly meals, but only at specific times (breakfast 8–9am; lunch at noon; dinner at 6pm). You can also cook in the dedicated BBQ area.

For farmyard delicacies head to the Vulkanhof in Gillenfeld (00 49 65 739148; www.vulkanhof. de), which has a nice selection of mustards, jams, goat's cheese and the like.
FAMILY FUN The site is geared towards children and families so finding entertaining stuff to do here is not a problem. The Manderscheid Tourist Board (www.manderscheid.de) run regular geological excursions around the area, and the site works with a range of independent companies to arrange everything from raft-building and orienteering courses to climbing, hiking and cycling. There's also a wildlife park at Daun (00 49 65 923154; www.wildpark-daun.de).
TREAT YOURSELF Try a volcano safari in a Landrover (Daun Tourist Office; 00 49 65 929 5130; www.tourismus.daun.de) or take a plane

ride to see the 'eyes of the Eifel' from above (Segelfreunde Vulkaneifel; 00 49 65 922976).
GETTING THERE From Koblenz follow signs to Trier and exit at Manderscheid on the A48/A1. From the UK you can drive to The Netherlands, through Belgium (A60) and onto Wittlich, again following signs to Koblenz and exiting at Manderscheid on the A48/A1.
PUBLIC TRANSPORT You can catch a train from Köln (Cologne), Trier or Koblenz to Wittlich, then take a bus from there to within 500 metres of the site – ask for Manderscheid-Dauner Strasse.
OPEN Early-Apr–late-Oct.
IF IT'S FULL Pulvermaarcamping (00 49 65 73311; www.pulvermaarcamping.de) is right on the edge of the Pulvermaar volcanic crater lake and has a lovely tenters' field.

**Natur-Camping Vulkaneifel**, Feriendorf Moritz, 54531 Manderscheid, Germany

| t | 00 49 65 729 2110 | w | www.vulkan-camping.de |

# müllerwiese

Alchemists and apparitions, ghosts and goblins, nefarious kings and needy water nymphs – these are just some of the characters that have tramped through the Black Forest over the centuries. Not your usual tourist demographic, granted, but then Germany's source of myths and legends is not the kind of forest you'd bring home to meet your mother. Or at least it wasn't a couple of hundred years ago.

These days, the most dangerous thing about the forest is the amount of famous gateau it serves up. And the only thing dark or mysterious about award-winning campsite Müllerwiese is the brooding bulk of its 1970s shower block at night; though the automatic lighting sort of ruins the dark part…and kills the mysteriousness a bit, too.

No, Müllerwiese is a family-run (and family-friendly) oasis; a small-but-perfectly-formed operation that's been running since 1972, headed up by the laid-back but efficient team of Friedrich Erhard and his father, Hans. In the last 30-odd years they've perfected the art of running a campsite with the vital two Ps: professionalism and passion.

The site can be found at the edge of a picturesque German village called Enzklösterle. Most of the 75 pitches are past the house and beyond the main gate, along the border of a burbling mountain brook (actually the River Enz). This section of Müllerwiese is devoted to caravans and large tents, but campers needn't go that far. You can just turn left and pitch in a grassy, car-free area that's purely for tenters.

The area resembles nothing so much as a pretty – and pretty spacious – garden. The Enz gurgles its way past here too, and fir trees provide shelter and scenery. Though the site isn't huge, it's large enough to accommodate around 30 tents (pitches range from 60 to 80 sq. metres) without it feeling like Glastonbury or The Big Chill on a Sunday morning.

The facilities are modest but adequate. A playground is built into the garden and includes table tennis, a swing and one of those small springy-bouncy thingies that young children adore springing and bouncing on. The brook makes for a nice, clean, natural distraction, and you get your own bathroom and shower (and washing-up sink), located in a brand-new block. You can also use the main shower block – it looks a lot less menacing in the daytime – which is less modern, but better equipped, with everything you could possibly need for personal and clothing ablutions.

Enzklösterle, situated between 600 and 900 metres above sea level, contains just 1,300 souls – the diametrical opposite of a sprawling metropolis. But like all small German towns it illustrates startling efficiency when it comes to services. There are local butchers selling tasty Schwarzwälder Schinken, cafés hawking eponymous gateaux, food shops, restaurants, a chemist and an extravagant three hairdressers – and a tourist office over the road from the campsite offering information as well as free Internet access.

Beyond the town lies the Black Forest 'proper': a shimmering universe of shade and light defined by proud firs, rustling woodlands, crystal-clear water, tinkling brooks, expansive lakes, flowery meadows and untouched moors. Within this wooded wonderland are over 1,800 miles (3,000 km) of hiking trails and 500 miles (800 km) of cycling tracks, all very well signposted. Black Forest towns such as Bad Wildbad (6¾ miles/11 km), Freudenstadt (17 miles/ 27 km) and others offer spas, sightseeing and relaxation opportunities, and are accessible for free by bus for those staying on the site.

Be careful, though. You might not see any ghouls or goblins en route, but there's a slice of cake around almost every corner just waiting to get you.

THE UPSIDE Charming, rural site on the doorstep of Germany's Black Forest.
THE DOWNSIDE Not many public areas and not much to do for teenagers.
THE DAMAGE A pitch costs €6.50. Over 14s pay €5; 2–14s are €3. A small tent plus car is €5.
THE FACILITIES Good clean shower block in the main camping section; brand-new facilities for campers near the main house. Onsite playground and a (shallow) stream for splashing around in.
FOOD AND DRINK There's nothing onsite, but Enzklösterle has a bakery and a butcher's as well as cafés, beer gardens and restaurants. A short drive away, Kaltenbronn's Hotel Sarbacher (00 49 7224 9339; www.hotel-sarbacher.de) offers a wide range of regional dishes, often involving local game. There are also farmers' markets in Altensteig 9¼ miles (15 km) away (Saturday mornings) and Bad Wildbad (Saturday mornings) .
FAMILY FUN 3–6-year-olds can visit the Enzklösterle kindergarten free of charge, which is just 200 metres from the campsite. Three miles (5 km) away in Poppeltal is one of the longest mountain slides in Germany, a really long thrill ride guaranteed to make the surliest child beam (00 49 7085 7812; www.riesenrutschbahn. de). Throughout August the tourist office also organises entertainment programmes for children in nearby villages and woods.
TREAT YOURSELF If you really feel like pampering yourself, check out the incredibly indulgent spa experience at the lavish Palais Thermal (www.palais-thermal.de) in Bad Wildbad.
GETTING THERE From the north, take the A8, coming off at exit Pforzheim-West and then follow the B294 to Calmbach. There you turn right and drive through Bad Wildbad. If you take the A5 from Basel or Frankfurt the campsite is reached most easily from the exit Rastatt, along the romantic Black Forest Valley Road through Freudenstadt – or take the mountain pass Gernsbach–Reichental– Kaltenbronn. From Munich take the A99 towards Stuttgart/Augsburg/Dachau follow the A8, then follow the directions as from the north.
PUBLIC TRANSPORT You can catch a train from any main German station to Bad Wildbad, 6¾ miles (11 km) from Enzklösterle. Ten buses a day run from Bad Wildbad to a stop just 300 metres from the campsite.
OPEN Early-Jan–early-Nov; 20th Dec–31st Dec.
IF IT'S FULL Try Schwarzwald Camping (00 49 7453 8415; www.schwarzwaldcamping.de), a nice, natural site near the river, 9 miles (15 km) away from Müllerwiese in Altensteig.

**Müllerwiese**, Hirschtalstrasse 3D-75337 Enzklösterle, Germany

| | t | 00 49 7085 7485 | w | www.muellerwiese.de |

# schnitzmühle

If the Black Forest is Germany's dark secret, a place of goblins and ghosts and the occasional slice of devilish gateau, its easterly cousin, the Bavarian Forest, is all easy-going charm and woody innocence. A lumberjack's violent fantasy, the forest comprises a seamless landscape of undulating hills, winsome spa towns and dense woodlands, criss-crossed with comely copses and titillating trails for bikers, hikers and cyclists.

Located slap-bang in the centre of this leafy nirvana is Camping Schnitzmühle, arguably the first really cool campsite in the country. Unlike most German sites, this one is run by young people determined to make the tenting experience considered and comprehensive, as well as energetic. The owners in question are Sebastian and Kristian Nielsen, who adopted their parents' hotel business a few years back and have lovingly transformed it into a funky one-stop-shop for all things outdoorsy. Not only did they give the hotel's interior a modernist makeover, they also overhauled the restaurant, added the capacious camping area, constructed an expansive spa and built a beach area around the site's natural lake.

The Nielsen brothers' rejuvenating spirit haunts the whole site, and in a good way.

Its several acres, located right next to a pretty section of the Schwarzer Regen river, are green and airy, peppered with trees, bushes and flowers. Even without the funky extras it would be nice, but when you discover the delights of: the Bongo Bar (a thatch-roofed drinks bar surrounded by sand and deckchairs); Stonehenge (a cheeky replica of the great British landmark that doubles as an open fire and grill place); and the Group Camping section that has adventure facilities and experienced instructors leading rope-climbing, canoeing and mountain-biking escapades – well, it's hard not to be impressed.

Being blessed with two rivers – the Regen and the Schwarzer Regen – means water-babies are going to feel totally at home here. Stroll around for a minute or two and you'll find a lovely natural swimming spot, whilst you can easily arrange canoe trips on site (€36 per canoe for 2 adults/2 adults and a child). A shuttle bus whisks you to a starting point and you make your own way back to Schnitzmühle.

The surrounding area isn't short of charming countryside or traditional towns and villages. Some leave you a bit cold, though others have high rural appeal. Arnbruck for example, is world famous for its superior glass production and a perfect place to pick up some quality wine glasses at decent prices for all your drinking exploits at home. Nearby Viechtach has some cafés and gives insight into small-town Bavarian life.

Back at the site, if you don't feel like breaking out the barbie, take advantage of the hotel-restaurant, which combines Thai and Bavarian specialities with truly superb results (the mixed tapas is especially good, though it's neither Thai nor Bavarian, but who cares?). Behind the hotel lies the

camping reception, which also boasts a well-stocked kiosk offering everything from lovely local *Weizenbier* to the equally lovely freshly baked bread.

The nearby beach and lake, located along a path on the other side of the hotel, is the perfect place to cool off and sunbathe. And if you're feeling even more indulgent, the spa is just a short aloe-vera-face-scrub-throw away. But if you don't feel like leaving Schnitzmühle to enjoy some real R&R, there's absolutely no need to.

THE UPSIDE Authentic 'cool camping' in the heart of the Bavarian forest.
THE DOWNSIDE You need a car to get around.
THE DAMAGE Tent plus 2 adults is €12 (including tent).
THE FACILITIES These are superb, including a clean (and colourful) shower block, well-stocked kiosk, onsite bar (Bongo Bar), a place for camp fires and BBQs, a playground and Internet (restaurant) – plus a hotel, spa, restaurant and lake right next door.
FOOD AND DRINK The kiosk sells fresh bread in the mornings and general camping essentials. The hotel-restaurant serves up a funky fusion of Bavarian and Thai food, and has a generous breakfast buffet each morning for €8, as well as salads and sandwiches for lunch. Bella Italia (00 49 9942 3633) in nearby Viechtach sells good pizza and pasta.

FAMILY FUN The site can organise everything from canoeing and hiking, mountain-biking, cycling and tree-climbing tours. There's a playground onsite with table-tennis tables, and you can swim in the lake. Another great option is the bobsleigh ride at the theme park Rodel Paradies (www.sommerrodeln.de; 00 49 9965 1203), a 20-minute drive away.
TREAT YOURSELF For a truly relaxing experience, try one of the many massages at Schnitzmühle's spa. Take your pick from the Yanomami (with banana leaves – €72 for 75 minutes), the Espresso (a 15-minute quickie for €14) or the Absolute High Power Massage (55 minutes for €49).
GETTING THERE From Munich take the B2R and exit onto the A9. From there take the exit 68-Kreuz Neufahrn to merge onto A92 towards Landshut, continuing on the B11. Turn left

at the B85, right at St2139 and continue on Bahnhofstrasse/St2326. Take a right towards Blosserberg, right at Schönauer Strasse and right at Leuthenmühle. Then it's a left towards Rothenbühl, left at Rothenbühl and left at Gmeinholz. From Dresden, take the A4 towards Chemnitz/Leipzig, taking exit 68-Kreuz Chemnitz to merge onto A72 towards Hof/Zwickau/Chemnitz-Süd. Take exit 4-Dreieck Hochfranken to merge onto A93 towards Regensburg/Prag/Praha/A6/Hof-Ost. Take exit 33-Schwandorf-Mitte towards Cham/Wackersdorf. Merge onto the B85, the B20/B85, turning left at St2139. Follow directions as from Munich.
OPEN All year.
IF IT'S FULL Campingplatz am Höllenstein Pirka (Leitenweg 12, 94234 Viechtach; 00 49 9942 8501) is a small, family-run site where river fishing is much more likely than Internet surfing.

**Camping Schnitzmühle**, Schnitzmühle 1, 94234 Viechtach, Germany

t 00 49 9942 94810   w www.schnitzmuehle.de

# seeperle

There are lakes, there are large lakes and then there's Lake Constance. Known as the Bodensee in German, it's central Europe's third-largest lagoon. In fact, it's so big it can be shared by three different nations – Austria, Germany and Switzerland.

Constance is ringed by the Alps and surrounded by the Black Forest. The hillsides that slope to the water's edge are dotted with vineyards, orchards and colourful hamlets with busy tourist centres. Little wonder it's one of Germany's biggest summer hotspots.

Many campsites in this area reflect Deutschland's penchant for caravan parks and commercial tourism. But Seeperle is one of the few that likes to keep things small and simple. Even better, it still occupies a prime position on the shore of the lake. Owners Claire and Manfred Maier have been running things since 1986, though Manfred's parents were operating a farm here back in 1962. The site has around 50 spots (scaled down from 80 to create more space and greater intimacy), which run along three lanes down to the lake, overlooked by apple and pear trees along the way.

The site is shared more or less evenly between tents and caravans, although – and you'll like this – the very best lakeside spots have been reserved for tenters. These are the spots to book up if you possibly can. Shaded by bowed fruit trees, they offer unobstructed views across the lake: simply pitch, crack open a bottle of the local vino and watch the boats, yachts and kayaks glide by. You'll be the envy of every caravan-owner.

A 20-minute stroll (or 5-minute bike ride) along a nature path brings you to the tourist town of Unteruhldingen. There are a few attractions here, such as the Pfahlbauten open-air museum, which is home to Neolithic and Bronze-Age pile dwellings based on local archeological finds. There's also a picturesque marina, spacious park and a happy huddle of cafés and restaurants.

The main attraction, you guessed it, is the lake, which offers a vast range of 'wet' activities to suit those who like to skim, dip, swim or plunge headlong into the water. Choose between sailing, windsurfing, diving, rowing and swimming. But one of the best ways to see the lake is to rent a bike (at the railway station in Unteruhldingen) and get pedalling. Cycle routes are easy to follow and check out the orchards, vineyards and traditional towns whilst you coast along. Towns like Meersburg (4 miles/7 km away) and Lindau (31 miles/50 km away) are some of the most prettily preserved Germany has

to offer, though they tend to be congested during peak season. Get there nice and early.

Ferries criss-cross the water every day, so you can easily take in sights like the monastic island of Reichenau and its famous Benedictine Abbey. The island of Mainau (which takes 20 minutes by boat from Meersburg) is home to one of the finest gardens in Europe, with 500 different types of tree, a maze, palm house, spurting fountains, as well as Germany's largest butterfly house. Again, it's heaving in summer, so time your visit well.

For a more relaxed day back at the ranch, you can swim or rent a kayak/boat and use the site's handy pier. When you do feel like some entertainment, take an evening stroll to nearby Spargelhof, a welcoming sort of place that serves local delicacies such as apple wine, *Wurst* and *Käse*-platters and, of course, the eponymous *Spargel* (asparagus).

When you get back you'll find your lakeside pitch appears magical under the night sky's purplish hues. And you'll be thankful that the views of this big, big lake are all yours – no sharing required.

THE UPSIDE Quiet, intimate camping on the shore of the mighty Lake Constance (Bodensee).
THE DOWNSIDE Not many facilities onsite and you'll need your own transport.
THE DAMAGE €26.60 for a tent, 2 people and car; €3.50 for youngsters aged 0–14.
THE FACILITIES Just the essentials, really: a kiosk selling the basics, an ageing (but adequate) shower block, washing-up area, plus electricity and water available.
FOOD AND DRINK The kiosk sells snacks and beer, but the Spargelhof (a 15-minute stroll away) serves great local dishes and has a warm and welcoming atmosphere. Unteruhldingen has hordes of eateries – Mainausicht is great for fish dishes. Every Saturday in Überlingen (7 miles/ 11 km) farmers get together for a morning market.

The region has good wines – try Hagnauer or the local vineyards in/near Meersberg and Birnau.
FAMILY FUN Apart from swimming in the lake, you can rent bikes in Unteruhldingen (Hotel Knaus, Unteruhldingen, Seestrasse 1; 00 49 7556 8008) as well as boats at the marina (Bottsvermietung Weber; 00 49 751013; www. bootscharter-weber.de). There's also a reptile museum in Unteruhldingen and a sealife centre in Konstanz (00 49 180 5 66 69 01 01; www. sealifeeurope.com) 1 hour by boat.
TREAT YOURSELF Fancy a ride in a Zeppelin? The DZR airline (00 49 7541 5900; www.zeppelinflug.de) offers hourly flights for up to a dozen passengers in its new Zeppelin airships from Friedrichshafen airfield. An hour-long cruise above the lake is pricey, about €250 per person

(€280 at weekends), but what treats aren't?
GETTING THERE From Munich, take the A96 towards Lindau/A8/Stuttgart. Take exit 3-Sigmarszell for the B31/B308 towards Sigmarszell/Friedrichshafen. Turn right at the B31, coming off onto the L328a/LindauerStrasse. Follow signs for Seefelden. From Frankfurt head south along the A81 taking exit 40 towards Friedrichshafen/Lindau. Merge onto the A98 and head for Friedrichshafen on the B31n, turning right for Kloster Birnau. Then follow signs for Seefelden.
OPEN Late-Apr–early-Oct.
IF IT'S FULL Camping Wirthshof (00 49 7544 9627; www.wirthshof.de) in Markdorf is set 4 miles (7 km) inland from Lake Constance, but is well organised with good facilities, including a wellness centre, heated pool and a family tent area.

**Camping Seeperle**, 88690 Uhldingen-Mühlhofen, Ortsteil Seefelden, Germany

| t | 00 49 7556 5454 | w | www.camping-seeperle.de |

# zellersee

As its name suggests, Zellersee is all about its lake. It's not a huge lake, but what it lacks in size it makes up for in sheer convenience. You can literally slide out of your sleeping bag, forward-roll through your tent-flaps and slip straight into the lake's watery embrace: the perfect way to wake up.

Afterwards, treat yourself to a nice hot coffee and fresh bread from reception whilst you decide what to do with your day. A bike ride to the Chiemsee (9 miles/15 km) where you can swim some more? A paddle boat cruise to the Herrenchiemsee – a collection of Versailles-like palaces. Or perhaps you fancy some more watery action at Lake Taubensee – just a 1,138-metre hike up the hill.

For those preferring a flight of fancy, there's the world-famous gliding school in nearby Unterwössen, offering gliding and paragliding. This is the place to catch the most amazing thermals – the kind that keep you afloat for up to 560 miles (900 km), so make sure you know how to get down before you take off.

In the evening, unwind with a beer from reception and reflect on how everyone around seems to be so smiley. Is it that there's a community ambience that fills every camper with a warm glow? Or could it be that you forgot to get dressed after your morning dip? Whichever it is, Zellersee is an open-minded place, so just keep smiling.

---

THE UPSIDE Intimate site located on a natural lake, with superb access to Germany and Austria.
THE DOWNSIDE The site is quite small, though there are some extra spaces in an adjacent field.
THE DAMAGE A tent, car plus 2 people costs €15 (plus €2 tax). Children aged 4–6 cost €2 and those aged 7–16 €3 cost plus €0.5 tax.
THE FACILITIES These are adequate for the site, if not overly modern. There's a kiosk/reception, decent shower block (toilets, showers, washing machine, dryer) and a small kitchen for general use. There is Internet available all around the site.
FOOD AND DRINK Onsite you can buy snacks and drinks, and there's a small kitchen. Gasthof

Zellerwand is about half a mile (1 km) away and sells traditional German/Austrian food. Head to Grassau's market (4 miles/7 km away; Saturday mornings) and pick up sausage, cheese and fruit.
FAMILY FUN There's a playground, tennis courts and a lake to keep kids and adults occupied, plus a climbing wall on the site (training is available once or twice a week during summer). There is also a children's park 3 miles (5 km) away in Marquartstein (00 49 8641 8234; www.kindercamp-sonnenhof.de).
TREAT YOURSELF If you're into aerial pursuits, try a gliding trip with the world-renowned DASSU school (00 49 8641 698 787; www.dassu.de).

It costs €20 for 10 minutes and €1.50 for each additional minute.
GETTING THERE From Munich or Salzburg, take the A8. Exit at 106 Bernau, towards Reit im Winkl. In Marquartstein drive towards Schleching. Exit 109 Übersee, looking out for the Zellerseeweg sign on the road between Schleching and Raiten.
PUBLIC TRANSPORT You can catch a train to Übersee and a bus from there to Schleching, getting off at Zellerwand/Mettenham. From there it's a 5-minute walk to the site.
OPEN All year.
IF IT'S FULL *Cool Camping*'s Park Grubhof (see p197) is just over the border in Austria.

**Camping Zellersee**, Reiner Möüller, Zellerseeweg 3, 83259 Schleching-Mettenham, Germany

| t | 00 49 8699 86719 | w | www.camping-zellersee.de |

# park grubhof

They say size isn't everything, but as any actress would surely say to any bishop: it can certainly help. Park Grubhof is a particularly well-endowed campsite, located in the Salzburgerland region of Austria.

Set in the former gardens of an ancient castle, it boasts over 30 acres, and is centred around a huge meadow full of alpine flowers during summer, creating a natural feel that's echoed through the chestnut trees lining the Saalach.

When you enter the site and see the broad boulevards lined with caravans and mobile homes, you may wonder why on earth you've come to Park Grubhof at all. The reason is the capacious field that's set apart from the motorhome area; it runs right down to the river and is dedicated solely to tenters. The field offers spectacular views to the Loferer Steinberge range. You can listen to the gentle splashing of the river or watch the sun going down between the Breithorn and the Loferer Alm. For wet-weather days there's even a large hut, where you can relax until the weather improves.

But that's not the only reason. Despite being one of the 'big boys' of Austrian camping, Park Grubhof does not rest on its laurels. It's excellently managed by Robert Stainer

and his staff, working tirelessly to create a communal atmosphere and look after the needs of their guests.

The facilities are quite superb, especially the shower blocks. The latest block, built relatively recently, is nothing short of spectacular: a light-filled, loo-lover's dream featuring brushed aluminium and pine-wood interiors, glass-walled showers, a baby-changing room, hairdryers and even a dry room for wet canoeists.

Whilst most campers head for the aforementioned meadow, you can also pitch in most of the site's other sections. Apart from the main boulevards there are pitches all along the riverside, subtly divided into family- and dog-friendly/-free areas. From these riverside spots you can really get a back-to-nature vibe – especially when you lie back and admire the fantastic mountain scenery surrounding the site.

The Loferer and Leoganger Steinberge mountains are one of the smaller groups in this Alp range, but what they lack in size they make up for in clout. The walks here can be steep, hard-going, and not for the faint-hearted, but they pay back multifold in terms of view – Birnhorn, at 2,634 metres, is the highest and has a 1,500-metre vertical south face, which threatens to flummox all but the most dedicated peak-baggers.

Slightly easier to explore are the region's villages and towns. St Martin (about ½ mile/ 1 km) and Lofer (just over 1 mile/2 km), both quintessentially quiet Salzburgerland towns, are quaint enough, but further afield things get more interesting. You can cycle along the 202-mile (325-km) Tauernradweg, which runs from Krimml, site of the famous waterfalls, to Passau. Salzburg itself is only 25 miles (40 km) away, whilst the fabulous

Grossglockner road can be reached in 1 hour (37 miles/60 km). Or you can just jump into the Saalach with your kayak.

Just over the German border is Bad Reichenhall, a friendly Bavarian spa town that serves as an entry point to the Berchtesgadener Land – one of the most beautiful areas in Germany and home to Hitler's notorious Eagle's Nest retreat. Yes, it's true, Grubhof might be one of Austria's camping 'big boys', but it's the kind of site that will still respect you in the morning.

THE UPSIDE Large site with separate camping area on the banks of the Saalach in Austria's Salzburgerland.
THE DOWNSIDE Park Grubhof's size and seeming penchant for caravans and mobile homes may be a turn-off, though the tent field is much more intimate.
THE DAMAGE €21.60 per night for 2 adults, car and tent and €19.20 in low season (tax included); €29.30 per night for 2 adults, 2 children, car and tent and €26.40 in the low season (tax included). There are also camping huts, costing €33/38.
THE FACILITIES These are generally excellent, with ultra-modern shower blocks, a small but info-packed reception, onsite restaurant and mini-market, playground/teenager lounge (with table tennis and TV), baby room and wi-fi access.
FOOD AND DRINK You can get tasty and reasonably priced Austrian food onsite at the restaurant, but there are also many other cafés and

inns in the vicinity, where you can gorge yourself on regional specialities like *Apfelstrüdel* and *Schnitzel*. If you want some great views and food, drive to Loferer Alm and visit Schönblick (00 43 6588 8278/ 00 43 6647 362 1214) run by Vanya, a friendly Yorkshire lass and her Austrian husband.
FAMILY FUN Take your family for some canyoning or rafting. The Motion Team (00 43 6588 7524; www.motion.co.at) organises both activities (and many more besides), and their base is just half a mile (1 km) downstream from the campsite.
TREAT YOURSELF Dine out in style at neighbouring Castle Grubhof (00 43 6588 725 90). The restaurant, Ristorante da Marcello, serves authentic Italian food in a sophisticated ambience. You can also have a relaxing spa in Bad Reichenhall's Rupertus Therme (00 49 1805 606 706; www.rupertustherme.de), 16 miles (26 km) from the site.

GETTING THERE From Munich take the A8 towards Salzburg, exit Traunstein/Siegsdorf (Germany), follow signs to Lofer. In Lofer take direction Zell am See from the roundabout and follow the signs to Grubhof. From Innsbruck take the A12, direction Salzburg, exit Wörgl West, then follow signs to Lofer; at the roundabout take the direction Zell am See and follow the signs to Park Grubhof.
PUBLIC TRANSPORT Trains do not travel to Lofer – only buses do. There are direct buses from St Johann in Tirol, Saalfelden, Zell am See, Kitzbühel and Salzburg to Lofer and the campsite. Trains travel from Salzburg to Zell am See and Saalfelden.
OPEN Late-Apr–early-Oct 2009. Then from Dec 2009 onwards open year round.
IF IT'S FULL Camping Zellersee (see p195) is another *Cool Camping* site 25 miles/40 km away, across the border in Germany.

**Park Grubhof**, 5092 St Martin near Lofer, Land Salzburg, Austria

| t | 00 43 6588 8237 | w | www.grubhof.com |

# fernsteinsee

Austria isn't exactly short of castles. From Vorarlberg to Vienna the region is swamped with Baroque citadels and Renaissance fortresses. Whilst Schloss Fernsteinsee might not be in the same league as Festung Hohensalzburg, Liechtenstein Castle or other such flamboyant Austrian venues, there's no denying it's a handsome slice of history.

It certainly says much about the place that the Bavarian King Ludwig II – no slouch himself in the castle-building business – was very fond of staying here. He came not only for the winsomeness of the castle but – as with most visitors both then and now – for its enchanting, crystal-clear lakes and the high sculpted peaks of the nearby Tyrolean mountains. Were Ludwig alive and visiting the place now, he would doubtless be highly amused to find that the castle grounds had grown a campsite. In the 19th century, combining castles with campsites wasn't the catchiest of concepts, even though nowadays the two things can go together like schnitzel and schnapps.

Set over 500 metres or so from the castle (transformed into a luxury 4-star hotel), Fernsteinsee's site is relatively new. It has 125 generously sized pitches arranged around a circular, tree-lined road. The remote end of the road has grassy pitches and a contemplative ambience; the nearer side has a sunbathing lawn and a more sociable vibe.

The site, as you might expect it being connected to a hotel, has above-average facilities. There's a heated loo block, washing machines and a well-stocked shop, as well as a bar, an outdoor terrace, a sauna and a solarium (though these cost extra). To get to the hotel and the lakes, just follow the silvery stream through the adjacent woods for 10 minutes.

Use of the hotel is pretty much restricted to the restaurant, though campers qualify for a small discount at breakfast and get a free dessert at dinner – a four-course, 4-star gourmet experience that's highly recommended when you find the outdoor life has perked up your appetite. Use of the lakes, which are unbelievably clear, with a visibility range of over 50 metres, is also somewhat restricted. The fragile nature of their ecosystem means that only diving pros with a minimum of 50 logged dives can explore the depths, though everyone is free to swim, take a boat ride, or lounge in the sun on the grassy banks. The surrounding area is certainly worth a peek – or perhaps a peak – or two. The site is ringed by the Tyrolean Alps, which can be explored from small, charming villages such as Nassereith (3 miles/5 km) and Obsteig (8½ miles/14 km), or from the town of Imst (9 miles/15 km), an attractive, mountain-surrounded spot brimming with activity opportunities such as climbing and canyoning.

Since Fernsteinsee lies close to the German border, it's also a cinch to explore pretty market towns like Garmisch-Patenkirchen (18½ miles/30 km), from where you can traverse Germany's largest mountain, the mighty Zugspitze. The hike from Garmisch-Patenkirchen takes between one and two days (lodges and food are available on some routes), though you can find shorter routes from the closer Austrian town of Ehrwald (10½ miles/17 km). The views from the summit are nothing short of spectacular.

Head east 30 miles (50 km) along the A12 and you'll arrive at Innsbruck, Tyrol's capital and a haven for skiers and mountain-hikers. Here you have museums and cafés, markets and boutiques – a colourful and vibrant dash of modern Europe in the midst of Austria's eternal landscape. With the lakes and your castle-campsite complex eagerly awaiting you upon your return, it's difficult not to feel you're living like a king.

THE UPSIDE A castle, Tyrolean Alpine scenery and some of Europe's clearest lakes.
THE DOWNSIDE Lake dives are for pros and hotel guests only.
THE DAMAGE During high season 2 people plus a tent is €18–24 (depending on the size of the pitch). In low season it's €14.40–19.20 (again, depending on the size of the pitch).
THE FACILITIES These are excellent. There is a dedicated reception/shop and shower block, a playground for the kids, lakes to swim in and a sauna/solarium, too (€6).
FOOD AND DRINK The shop sells eggs, bread, soups and sweets, as well as pizza in the evenings and fresh bread in the mornings. The adjacent castle has 2 restaurants, where campers get small discounts and special offers. There are daily markets in Obsteig and Imst (closed Sundays), both 9 miles (15 km) away.

FAMILY FUN An outdoor playground supplies free entertainment, and there are pedalos and rowing boats on the lakes. Reception can advise you on hiking, climbing and cycling routes and bicycles for rent. For bigger thrills head to Imst and book a spot on the world's longest Alpine Roller Coaster (00 43 5412 66 322; www.alpine-coaster.at).
TREAT YOURSELF Splash out on one of the Schloss's grand hotel rooms (00 43 5265 5210; www.fernsteinsee.at). Inveterate romantics won't be disappointed with the massive King Ludwig suite or the equally luxurious Kaiser Josef room. For a unique experience try a soak in the world's only Starkenberger Beer Pool at Starkenberg Castle (00 43 5412 66 201; www.starkenberg.at), 8½ miles (14 km) from the site.
GETTING THERE From Zurich, drive towards St Gallen, then Feldkirch. Pass over the border into Lichenstein and Austria. Head towards Innsbruck through the Arlberg tunnel to Imst. Turn onto the B171 towards Imst and follow signs for Fernpass. After a bridge you'll see the huge Hotel Schloss Fernsteinsee sign. From Munich take the A95, then the B2. Exit on the B23 towards Grainau/Garmisch, entering Austria. Continue onto B187/Ehrwalder-Bundesstrasse, take the ramp to B179/Fernpass-Bundesstrasse until you see the Hotel Schloss Fernsteinsee sign.
PUBLIC TRANSPORT Catch a train to Imst, and from there an hourly bus comes to Schloss Fernsteinsee (sometimes changing at Nassereith).
OPEN End-Apr–end-Oct.
IF IT'S FULL Camping Imst West (00 43 5412 66 293) in nearby Imst, is a pleasant family-run campsite. It's close to the town yet set back in a field, so it has a much more natural and remote atmosphere than you might expect.

**Fernsteinsee**, Fernstein 426, 6465 Nassereith, Austria

| t | 00 43 5265 5210 | w | www.fernsteinsee.at |

# sonnenberg

Ah, there's nothing like getting the horn amidst the thrusting peaks and sensual curves of the Austrian mountains. The horn, of course, is the alphorn – the long, wooden wind instrument used to summon cattle and serenade tourists.

Every Sunday at Camp Sonnenberg the site's owners (and friends) graciously bedeck themselves in traditional mountain livery and put on a performance. As the sombre drones echo around the site and the last rays of sun daub the summits of the surrounding Vorarlberg region, it's impossible not to get that 'I'm in Austria' feeling.

At 600 metres above sea level, Sonnenberg – appropriately translating as 'sunny mountains' – is run by the Dünser family (Matthias and Beate), and has an air of tradition and meticulousness often lacking in other campsites. Tents and small caravans mingle on the site's kempt terraces; a well-equipped reception eagerly takes care of all enquiries and a nearby bakery sells tasty, fresh German breads each morning; and the spotless facilities block sports baby-changing facilities, spacious washing and drying rooms plus Internet and library. But the best things about Sonnenberg are the views. The site is ringed by glorious peaks and no matter where you

pitch you'll be greeted each morning by the Silvretta in the south-east, the Rätikon to the south, the Lechtaler Alpen in the north... even the Swiss Alps can be spotted in the distance on a clear day.

The surrounding Vorarlberg region is easy to explore. Each valley has its own character, and every town its points of interest. Nüziders offers happy campers handy shops and eateries, though more interesting are Feldkirch (12 miles/20 km away), a medieval town full of young, hip types, and Bludenz (almost 2 miles/3 km away), the key activity town of the region where the five valleys meet. It provides the starting point for hiking, biking, skiing and snow-boarding. If you're a bit of a chocoholic, you may be happy to hear that Suchard are based here, though strictly as an after-activity reward, of course – yeah, right.

The numerous local valleys include the Klostertal, Montafon, Walgau, Brandnertal and the nearby Grosses Walsertal, which UNESCO has designated a Biosphere Reserve. Options for outdoor pursuits are nigh-on infinite, and the great news for all hikers is that you can climb almost every peak without fancy equipment. Highlights include a hike up the 'Matterhorn of Vorarlberg', the Zimba Massif – a one- or two-day hike, depending how fast and how fit you are – and the must-see Lünersee, a crater lake 1,970 metres above sea level. If you're not fond of walking, however, a cable car from Brand will get you most of the way without you feeling puffed out. And if you don't wish to walk alone, the site also organises regular group hikes.

You can also drive down to the region's picturesque capital, Bregenz (30 miles/50 km), which lies at the foot of the enormous Lake Constance (Bodensee). On the lake you can hire boats and bikes or hike up to the Pfänder (1,064 metres) for peerless views of the lake and surroundings. From here you can explore the Bregenzerwald, a gorgeous, relaxed region that's all alpine dairies (including a dedicated 'cheese route', or *Käsestrasse*), chocolate-box villages and thoroughly modern eco-buildings.

Meanwhile, back at the site, you'll find it easy to unwind on the grassy terraces, check your emails in your tent and enjoy the quietude as the sun dips and night descends on the mountains like a velvet duvet. If it's Sunday, you already know what to do – sit back with a beer and enjoy the Alphorn dirge resounding through the evening air.

THE UPSIDE Meticulous and atmospheric campsite ringed by the peaks of Vorarlberg's mountain ranges.
THE DOWNSIDE No sauna or pool, but free entry to a big outdoor pool within 2 miles (3 km).
THE DAMAGE In low season it costs €18 for 2 adults and €24 for 2 adults plus 2 children or a family of 4; in high season it's €24 for 2 adults and €31 for a family of 4.
THE FACILITIES These consist of a 2-storey building containing everything from WCs, hot showers and a baby room, to drying room, laundry room, Internet and dish-washing facilities. The reception building has a cinema room on the upper floor and a sleeping loft for 4 campers if the weather gets bad. There's also a shop selling basics, a playground, indoor games room, table tennis and wi-fi.
FOOD AND DRINK There are only basics available on site, but restaurant/café Daneu (328 yards/300 metres away) serves Austrian and international food; Angelo – a tiny Italian restaurant just over a mile (2 km away) serves tailor-made meals (closed Sundays) and in Braz (5 miles/8 km) there's a lovely place called Rössle (00 43 5552 281 050; www.roesslebraz.at). Bludenz also has plenty of cafés and shops.
FAMILY FUN Onsite you'll find a playground and table tennis, darts, table football and a weekly programme of activies for children (such as guided walks and a cinema room) 3 or 4 times a week during high season. You can hire bikes onsite. Down on Lake Constance you can also hire bikes as well as boats (ask at reception for details).
TREAT YOURSELF Why not have a night in the Frassen Hut (00 43 699 1705 1089; www.frassenhuette.at), a cosy Alpine hut (with restaurant) that lies on the hike to the Hoher Frassen? You can hike all the way or take the cable car – double rooms are available. High-flyers should head to the paragliding school in Schnifis (00 43 5556 767 17; www.tandemgliding.at) and take a tandem flight over the Montafon valley.
GETTING THERE From Munich, take the A96 towards Lindau/18/Stuttgart, following it across the border into Austria. Continue onto the A14, taking exit 58-Brandnertal. Follow signs Nüziders, then Camping Sonnenberg. From Innsbruck, take the A12/E533/E60 road, following signs to Bregenz/Garmisch/E60. Continue onto the S16 and A14, taking exit 59-Bludenz-Bürs. Follow signs Nüziders, then Camping Sonnenberg.
PUBLIC TRANSPORT There are railway stations in Bludenz and Nüziders, from where you can take a bus to just near the site. Pick-ups are possible.
OPEN Late-Apr–early-Oct.
IF IT'S FULL Camping Walch (00 43 5552 28102; www.landhauswalch.at) is a spanking new campsite with great facilities in a natural location, 8 miles (13 km) away in Braz.

**Sonnenberg**, Hinteroferst 12 A-6714, Nüziders bei Bludenz Vorarlberg, Austria

| t | 00 43 5552 64035 | w | www.camping-sonnenberg.com |

# eigernordwand

Say the phrase 'Hinterstoisser Traverse' to most people and it'll mean nothing – it could be a German action hero or a section of Belgian motorway. But say it to a few cognoscenti climbing wonks and they'll immediately know it's a section of the awesome north face of the Eiger, named in honour of the first climber to cross it successfully, in 1936.

Eiger means 'ogre' and it's easy to see where the name came from. The rock rises 1,800 metres from the valley and is so high that it creates its own mini-climate, conjuring storms on even the most placid days. It's one of the reasons why it's such a brute to climb and why you're far better off sitting in a campsite, watching others take the strain. And this is just the place for it. Camping Eigernordwand is at the foot of the Eiger. The site's run by a charming old gent, Rudi, who's been here since canvas bags and cable-knit woollies were all the climbing rage. He comes round every evening to say hello, but finds all chairs turned towards the Nordwand as campers search out tiny specks of human dust trying to clamber up the rock. Of course, there's more to Grindelwald than a huge slab of rock and the views from the site are just as inspiring if you turn your camp chair around and look down the valley. It's just that now everyone's looking at you.

THE UPSIDE Close-up views of the awesome north face of the Eiger.

THE DOWNSIDE The lower part of the site is weighed down with caravans.

THE DAMAGE Adults are CHF8 (plus CHF2.90 tax) and children aged 3–12 years are CHF4. Tents are CHF7–14, depending on size and a car costs CHF3.

THE FACILITIES Housed in a Swiss-chalet building, there are über-powerful hot showers and everything else you need after a hard day in the lounger watching the climbers.

FOOD AND DRINK There's a small hotel next to the site with a terraced bar looking up to the Eiger. Up in the village, Hotel Grand Regina (www.grandregina.ch) has a posher wood-panelled bar and terrace for evening drinks, while across the road by the railway station Hotel Kreuz und Post serves generous, good-value meals.

FAMILY FUN Try the cable car that runs from Grindelwald up to Männlichen (00 41 33 854 80 80). It's supposedly the longest one in the world and starts a 10-minute walk from the campsite.

TREAT YOURSELF Take the 35-minute ride on the cog train up through the Eiger to Kleine Scheidegg. It's the best place for views of the face, but it's not cheap at CHF83 return per person.

GETTING THERE By car, come off the A8 at Interlaken, heading for Lauterbrunnen. After about 3 miles (4.8 km), turn left towards Grindelwald. On entering the town you'll see the site down to your right. Take the right fork at the roundabout, down the hill past the railway station and follow the road over the river. There are also trains roughly every 30 minutes during the day from Interlaken.

PUBLIC TRANSPORT There are regular trains and buses to Grindelwald from Interlaken. Check for times at www.sbb.ch/en. The campsite is a 10-minute walk from the station.

OPEN Early-May–mid-Oct.

IF IT'S FULL Apparently. if you arrive before 3pm there's always room, even in high season. However, if you're unlucky there's Camping Gletscherdorf (00 41 33 853 14 29; www.gletscherdorf.ch) just outside Grindelwald, or you can head to Lauterbrunnen to the dramatic Camping Jungfrau (00 41 33 856 20 10; www.camping-jungfrau.ch).

| **Camping Eigernordwand**, 3818 Grindelwald, Switzerland | | | |
|---|---|---|---|
| t | 00 41 33 853 12 42 | w | www.eigernordwand.ch |

# petit praz

Switzerland is, of course, a little odd. It's no coincidence that Einstein developed his theory of curved space-time whilst working as a patent clerk in Bern, nor that the giant CERN particle accelerator buried in the Swiss soil has men with wild hair and perspex goggles busy with pesky little particles that may or may not exist.

There's just something a little bit weird about the place that seems to lend itself to whacky time warps and altered states of being – as if life's out of kilter and nothing's quite what it seems.

Take Camping Petit Praz, for instance. Depending on who you ask and where you are when you ask them, it turns out that this site may be called Camping Petit Praz or, alternatively, it may be called Camping Arolla. Or both. Either way, it's not actually in Arolla, but in La Monta. And Praz is somewhere else altogether.

About the only thing you can be sure of when you come here is that, as you wind up the valley road, there's a small sign with a tent on it. You follow the dirt track over a river and, hey presto, there you are. Or are you? How can you be sure? Well, who cares? Just take a look at the views and forget all about theoretical physics.

It's hardly surprising that Petit Praz has spectacular views, as it's just short of 2,000 metres up in the Swiss Alps and claims to be Europe's highest campsite.

Most of its grassy terraced pitches face back down the valley, but if you pitch your tent on the shoulder of the hill you can enjoy the views up towards the 4,000-metre summit of the north face of Mont Collon and the Pigne d'Arolla. And you'll see that hovering above the site is a very nasty spike of rock, like a vast hypodermic needle, which would certainly bring tears to your eyes if your doctor came anywhere near you with it in his hands.

Apart from the challenging climbing, there's fine walking to be had in these parts and one trip that is virtually compulsory (unless you happen to have a sick note from matron) is up to Lac Bleu, easily accessible from La Gouille. It's a relatively short walk that meanders gently through forest and meadow before climbing, admittedly pretty steeply, up to the lake.

And when you reach the top, you'll certainly need to give yourself a reward. This comes in the form of an absolutely crystal-clear lake with water tumbling over rocks into it and a series of pools running out of it down the

hill. Even more good news is that there's a pleasant little café down at the start of the walk, with the chilled beer you'll probably be in dire need of after all your exertions.

But if even that sounds like too much effort – this is supposed to be a holiday after all – there's always the luxuriant green grass of the site, which is a very comfy place to plonk yourself down on to while away the odd afternoon. Blame the altitude and all that wonderful pure air for making you feel so giddy that you feel in urgent need of a quiet, relaxing lie-down. Either that or blame the weird goings-on at CERN, where no lesser a brain than Stephen Hawking has warned that the place could create an enormous black hole that might even swallow us all up. All the more reason to get up to Arolla whilst it's still there. Or here. Or wherever it is.

**THE UPSIDE** The highest campsite in Europe, with head-clearing air and great views.
**THE DOWNSIDE** Telephone cables and electricity wires spoil some of the views.
**THE DAMAGE** CHF7 per adult and CHF4 per child. Tents are between CHF6 and CHF12, depending on size, and a car is CHF3.
**THE FACILITIES** There's a nice new facilities block with all the trimmings. The only niggle is that you'll need to equip yourself with 2 CHF1 coins to operate the showers.
**FOOD AND DRINK** There's a small *épicerie* at the site for basic provisions (you can order bread for the morning). Up the hill in the village of Arolla there's the Café du Pigne (00 41 27 283 71 00), with a sunny terrace looking up the glacier. It sells Belgian fruit beer but, that apart, it's a great little place and there's a small supermarket just next door.
**FAMILY FUN** Call Pascale Follonier (00 41 79 560 98 94). He runs organised trips for kids aged 4–12, with games, animal-spotting and walks in the hills.
**TREAT YOURSELF** If you've ever seen *The Shining* you'll enjoy a visit to the Hotel Kurhaus (00 41 27 283 70 00). It's been there since 1896, plenty of time for strange goings-on in its wood-panelled rooms. There's a bar/restaurant there if you can't face staying the night. Otherwise doubles start at CHF50 for B&B and a room with a balcony and mountain views is CHF88.
**GETTING THERE** From the main east–west E62 road take the road signed Route d'Hérens towards Vex. Carry on all the way through Evolène and Les Haudères until just before Arolla. There's a sign to the campsite on the left, just by a small hotel. Follow the dirt track over the river and back up the hill and shout 'bingo'!
**PUBLIC TRANSPORT** Hitch a ride with Postman Pierre – there's a *car postal* run by the Post Office from Sion to Arolla. Call 00 41 79 50124 82 for times and prices. Get off at La Monta and it's a 5-minute walk to the campsite.
**OPEN** June–late-Sept.
**IF IT'S FULL** There are 2 campsites back down the valley in Les Haudères (Camping Molignon 00 41 27 283 12 40; www.camping-molignon.ch) and Evolène (Camping d'Evolène; 00 41 27 283 11 44; www.camping-evolene.ch), but for another cracking Alpine site go the the *Cool Camping* site at La Fouly – Camping des Glaciers (see p215).

**Camping Petit Praz**, 1986 Arolla, Switzerland

| t | 00 41 27 283 22 95 | w | www.camping-arolla.com |

# camping des glaciers

The Swiss don't do clichés – but if they did they'd probably be the best clichés in the world. Sure, there are a few images that pop immediately into your head when you think of Switzerland – Heidi in flaxen pigtails or yodellers in tight leather shorts (delete according to taste), triangular chocolate bars and cuckoo clocks. That sort of thing.

And here at Camping des Glaciers you certainly get all the standard features – Alpine meadow, forest glade, mountain glacier, gushing river, crystal air, wild flowers underfoot, puffy white clouds overhead. But, somehow, it all resists cliché because it's just so refreshingly…refreshing.

The site is spread out like a giant green picnic blanket on the side of the hill at the end of the glacier moraine, and you can take your pick from three types of pitch – in amongst the grassy rocks thrown down the mountain by the action of ice and gravity, with views up to the mountain tops; on the open meadow looking back down the valley; or in amongst the pine trees and wild flowers, where you can't see the wood for the trees (and the bees).

The owners of the site, Agathe and Michel Darbellay, have run it for nearly 40 years and seem to have intimate knowledge of every blade of grass and flower in the place. Agathe will show you some of the seven different types of wild orchid that grow on the site and can even occasionally point you in the direction of a rarer mountain flower, such as *Campagnola thyrsoïdes*, growing wild somewhere about the place. It helps enormously that she speaks excellent English along with a number of other languages. She's always bustling about the place, popping in for a quick drink with some guests who are back for at least the 30th year in a row, showing people around, pointing out the flowers. It's a small wonder she doesn't get dizzy.

In contrast, Michel is a quieter type (you couldn't have two of them like Agathe – it wouldn't work), though his reticence results from as much modesty as from the fact that he doesn't speak English. He's also as far removed from the dizzy type as you can imagine. He was, after all, the first man to scale the north face of the Eiger solo – a feat he achieved in 1963. Luckily this was before Agathe came along, because she claims that if they'd been married then, she'd never have let him anywhere near it.

The site's a 10-minute stroll from the hamlet of La Fouly, a modest ski resort in the winter months, with a black run and a couple of

reds and blues. But it's probably even more popular in the summer, when the meadows are laced with a profusion of wild flowers and the melon-green river comes crashing down from the glacier.

There's an intricate maze of walks and climbs from the village, or from Ferret a couple of miles up the valley, and although the mountains around La Fouly are not quite in the Eiger league they can still hold their heads up high. The twin peaks above

the site and the *col* (mountain pass) that leads over to France are sufficient for most serious walkers and you'd need to do more than strap a pair of crampons to your Gucci loafers if you wanted to lunch in Chamonix. It's only 10 miles (16 km) away as the crow flies, but it will take you an hour and a half by road over the Col des Montets.

Not that you need to go all that way when everything you need is here – all those boringly bog-standard Alpine things.

THE UPSIDE Mountains, meadows, glaciers, wild flowers – everything you associate with summer in the Swiss Alps.
THE DOWNSIDE Suggestions on a postcard please.
THE DAMAGE CHF6.50 per adult and CHF3.50 per child. A pitch costs CHF10–16.
THE FACILITIES A new facilities block was constructed in 2008, so you're spoilt for choice. The newer 2 are great, the older 2 (beneath the reception area) are a little tired these days, but are perfectly serviceable. There's also a handy day-hut with a TV.
FOOD AND DRINK There's a *supermarché* in the village, about 10 minutes' walk from the campsite. Just above it is the Restaurant des Glaciers, which

has recently been taken over by a new chef who's introduced a bit of flair to the menus, which start at CHF22 for a set 3-course lunch.
FAMILY FUN Take a trip to the breathtaking Gorges du Durnand (www.gorgesdudurnand.ch), a collection of 14 waterfalls with wooden walkways connecting them. The walkways are built into the rocks and you might find some of them are pretty hair-raising, but it's worth it for the spectacular views.
TREAT YOURSELF In June and July there's an open-air cinema at Martigny (www.open-air-kino.ch). Check with them what films are on and which are dubbed into French and which in English with subtitles. Otherwise you'll end up watching *Indiana Jones et le Royaume du Crâne Cristal*

and not knowing what's what.
GETTING THERE From Martigny head for Champex-Lax and the Grand-Saint-Bernard Tunnel. Turn right at the town of Orsières (where there's also a railway station) and follow the road up to La Fouly. Drive through the village and, opposite the chair lift, veer down to the right, cross the river and you're there.
PUBLIC TRANSPORT Buses and trains run from Martigny to Orsières and there's a bus from there to La Fouly. It takes about 20 minutes and runs about 7 times a day, from 06:45 to 18:05.
OPEN Mid-May–end-Sept.
IF IT'S FULL According to Agathe it's very busy from mid-July to mid-August, but there's always room somewhere.

**Camping des Glaciers**, 1944 La Fouly, Val Ferret, Switzerland

| t | 00 41 27 783 17 35 | w | www.camping-glaciers.ch |

# silvaplana

You'd have to be pretty rich, very famous or have virtually no scruples to speak of to arrive at a campsite by private chopper. But, then again, not that many campsites have helipads. However, at Silvaplana, in the Swiss Alps, you do wonder, since these massive winged creatures are constantly materialising on the horizon like great black insects, before growing to sci-fi B-movie-size as they come closer.

But they're actually heading for St Moritz, that ultra-exclusive ski resort where royals and celebs annually snow-plough down the slopes to please the paparazzi, and which is still sufficiently scenically appealing in summer to have the big-wigs fly in just for the weekend. And who can blame them? The view's quite incredible.

When the snow has disappeared from all but the top-most peaks stretching along Switzerland's Upper Engadine Valley, the scenery revealed is as leprechaun-green as the winter is white. From the mountain tops, the melting snow cascades in long white strips down rock crevices into the majestic turquoise Silvaplana lake below.

The campsite reaps the benefit of this outstanding scenery, clinging to the shore at the bottom of the Mount Julier pass and looking across the water at waterfalls, a pine forest, grasslands so smooth that you could play pool on them and the mighty mountains, some of which tickle the clouds at 4,000 metres.

The lake, the campsite and the surrounding greenery gang up to offer perfect conditions for sport, sport and more sport. So if you are this way inclined, you've definitely come to the right place. You can have lessons in windsurfing, kite-boarding and sailing. World Cup events held here in the summer ensure your instructor has reached a fairly high standard.

Either side of peak season the campsite is quieter, and fishing and rowing attract a more retiring crowd, who sink a line from the jetty or sit quietly adrift in rowing boats offshore. The campsite is generously spread out along the lake, so that you can find some privacy and your own little piece of the view, if that's the way you like things.

Away from the lake, various Alpine walks and hikes start from the campsite itself and wend into the surrounding terrain. If you're very adventurous you can have a stab at rock-climbing, paragliding and horse-riding with local experts. Or you can try hiring a bike to explore 100 miles (160 km) of official bike and mountain-biking routes. A cable car goes up to some of the best trails, and this is a trip in itself.

The campsite is a five-minute walk from the village of Silvaplana, but St Moritz has the pick of the restaurants and bars. It might feel a little bit as though everyone has shut shop for the summer months, but the dash of glam along the streets – think Gucci and Prada – tells you loud and clear how ritzy the place is when the mercury sinks.

Distinctive architecture, including 16th-century patrician houses, gives the little villages hiding in the hillside their characteristic Swiss feel. So if you feel a little yodel tickling the back of your throat, don't feel you have to hold back.

Not to be outdone, an imposing druid stone in St Moritz, dating back to times when druids populated the Engadine Valley in the 1st century BC, hints at the historical feast you can gorge on when you visit the area's medieval walls, Roman ruins and Gothic churches and castles, including the romantic Crap da Sass in Silvaplana. These, along with more galleries and museums than you can possibly shake a stick at, should satisfy the most cultured camper, whether you own a chopper or not.

THE UPSIDE Stunning scenery with more outdoor activity than you could ever imagine.
THE DOWNSIDE Statics take up most of the waterside spots and, take heed, this is Activity Central come July and August.
THE DAMAGE It costs CHF9.90 per adult, CHF4.60–7.45 per child, depending on age, plus CHF8.15 per car and CHF5.10–7.15 per tent, depending on its size.
THE FACILITIES The question should be: what haven't they got?
FOOD AND DRINK It's hard to go past the campsite's own Mulets restaurant, with its beer garden, super lake views, schnitzels and beer. Silvaplana bars and restaurants are within walking distance, or drive into St Moritz. For brunch try the Alpine cheese dairy in nearby Morteratsch (00 41 81 842 62 73).
FAMILY FUN Take the kids to see the hut that featured in the Heidi movie; get the details from the tourist office (www.stmoritz.ch).
TREAT YOURSELF Sightseeing and glacier-landing flights depart from Samedan Airport (00 41 81 851 08 51) or indulge yourself at one of St Moritz's natural mineral spas.
GETTING THERE The campsite is easily spotted on the lakeside near Silvaplana on the S3 (which becomes the S27) through the Engadine Valley.
PUBLIC TRANSPORT Local buses run between villages in the Engadine Valley.
OPEN Mid-May–mid-Oct.
IF IT'S FULL 20 minutes' drive away, Camping Plauns Morteratsch (Ch-7504, Pontresina; 00 41 81 842 62 85; www.campingplauns.ch) offers a quieter and smaller alternative, with an emphasis on hiking.

**Camping Silvaplana**, Via Boscha 15, 7513 Silvaplana, Switzerland

| t | 00 41 81 828 84 92 | w | www.campingsilvaplana.ch |

# seiser alm

If you're not the world's greatest linguist, you can be forgiven for getting tongue-tied here. It's not the altitude, which can surely make you dizzy, but the language. You're in Italy, but with more than a hint of a Swiss–Austrian–German twist.

The cute little peak-roofed doll's houses are enough to make you start yodelling here and now, and the clanging cow bells make you wonder if Julie Andrews is about to come skipping over the nearest grassy hillock.

Seiser Alm (German moniker), or Alpe di Siusi (Italian version), is in the very heart of the Dolomites. This Italian region of the Alps is a sprawl of massive Triassic rock formations, rising like doomsday monoliths from a soft bed of pine trees and Alpine fauna.

The area has three main towns: Castelrotto, Siusi and Fie. Between them, in the foothills, sit smaller villages, and here the long shadow of the 2,500-metre Sciliar Massif falls across Camping Seiser Alm. Not too far from the base of this carbonate marvel, tiny tents are pitched randomly on a couple of grassy knolls. Despite the minor irritation of somewhat unsightly serried ranks of caravans and statics, the unhindered front-row Dolomite view almost makes you feel as if you're camping in the rough.

And so it should. This area's a real looker – gorgeous enough to take your breath away. In winter the valley's covered in thick unyielding snow, and the mountain peaks – the highest over 3,000 metres – are like fins of chocolate mud cake dusted in icing sugar. In summer cagouled-and-booted walkers arrive en masse to hike the sublime landscape. Flower-covered pastures erupt from colossal mountains of carbonate rock, the peaks, columns and crags set off against the big blue sky.

Hiking has been a happening thing here since the 19th century and it plods along today on over 210 miles (350 km) of marked tracks – take your pick from the different grades on offer. The Seiser Alm cable car – the world's longest – and connecting chair lifts are ready and waiting if you'd really rather do the whole thing sitting down. You'll have to get up off your backside, though, if you want to have a little sit-down in the Rifugio Bolzano. This is one of the oldest mountain huts in the Alps and it nestles just below the 2,300-metre Monte Pez on the backbone of the Sciliar Massif. Another clever idea is to take the easy stroll to the Punto Panoramico at the top of Chairlift Three. This has a high wow-factor, with its views to the Marmolada or Punta Di Penia, the highest peak in the Dolomites.

If serious hiking isn't really your thing, but you're a bit of a history buff, you'll enjoy rubbernecking around the fortresses, ruins, castles and pint-sized villages that dot the area. The beautiful Larghetto di Fie, a natural lake known for its intact ecosystem and excellent water quality is a must for a refreshing little dip when the weather warms up. If you're a mountain-biker or a road-cyclist, don't feel obliged to take a back seat either – the region's rocky slopes and undulating roads provide heart-pumping scenic adventures, no matter what your ability level is. Meanwhile, back at the campsite, when your throat needs a yodelling break, breakfast is served on a long terrace with truly spectacular views of the Dolomites on one side and the valley on the other. But don't be expecting cappuccino and pastries. Breakfast here is typically German – a boiled egg served up with cheese and ham. A delicious and appropriate way to build up your strength for the energetic day that lies ahead.

THE UPSIDE The front-row Dolomite view and hiking terrain.
THE DOWNSIDE Staff members aren't particularly welcoming.
THE DAMAGE €6.50–9 per adult and €3.40–7 per child per night, depending on season and age.
THE FACILITIES Restaurant, excellent bathroom and toilet facilities, plus a mini-market, wi-fi and morning newspapers.
FOOD AND DRINK The campsite's own Zur Quelle restaurant has a large outdoor patio with a view to the Dolomites. The little town of Siusi has a couple of bars and a pizza restaurant. Ristorante Bullaccia at the top of Chairlift 3 is the perfect top-of-the-world spot for a beer. There's a farmers' market every Friday at Castelrotto and every Saturday at Fie.
FAMILY FUN Take a cable car ride to the Seiser Alm plateau (Cabinovia Siusi-Alpe di Siusi, Via Sciliar 39; wwwseiseralmbahn.it). Grab a chairlift to head further afield once at the top.
TREAT YOURSELF To a 15-minute tandem paraglide down the valley (Tandem Fly; 00 39 338 604 19 79; www.tandemfly.it; or Fly2; 00 39 335 571 65 00; www.fly2.info). Alternatively, if you'd prefer something more sedate, enjoy a famed Tyrolean hay bath, an age-old peasant practice whereby relaxing in the herbs and oils of fresh-cut hay has strangely rejuvenating effects (Hotel Heubad, Fie' allo Sciliar; 00 39 0471 725 020; www.hotelheubad.com).
GETTING THERE The campsite is signposted along the SS24 between Fie and Siusi at Saint Konstantin (or San Costantino).
OPEN Dec–Nov.
IF IT'S FULL Camping Vidor (Pozza di Fassa, Trentino, Dolomites; 00 39 0462 763 247; www.campingvidor.it) over an hour's drive away, has similarly scenic Dolomite vistas.

**Camping Seiser Alm**, Saint Konstantin 16, 39050 Völs am Schlem, Italy

| t | 00 39 0471 706 459 | w | www.camping-seiseralm.com |

# bellavista

Come and make a splash at Camping Bellavista. The site sits pretty on a bay at the northern end of Lake Garda, Italy's most magnificent lake, and is in prime position for all campers who love to get wet – really wet.

It is a simple and welcoming campsite, with generous grassy plots neatly spaced under rows of shady olive trees. All have hook-ups and, given the boutique size of the site, you're never too far from anything. From the front of the property you can step onto a picturesque waterfront with blue water so clear (and cold) that you can see your tootsies sinking into the white sand.

On each side of the lake imposing limestone mountains retreat into the distant horizon, framing the 180° view. The landscape is a

perfect playground if you are keen on hiking, canyoning, rock-climbing or mountain-biking. But given the site's location, your first priority should really be all about getting wet. Windsurfing and sailing are the most popular ways of doing this and you can hire everything you need.

When you've had enough and have towelled off, you'll find a green valley of orchards and vineyards flourishing in the Mediterranean climate, surrounding the nearby town of Arco. Its old centre has a busy square and streets flanked by quaint little terraced houses sporting cute shuttered windows. End your stay on a high note with a visit to the romantic Arco castle, which teeters above the town on a sheer rock face. Just don't try high-diving off the top.

THE UPSIDE A boutique campsite just a hop, skip and a jump from the waterfront
THE DOWNSIDE An oversized hedge-cum-fence, no doubt meant for privacy, blocks the waterfront view.
THE DAMAGE €8.50 per adult, €6.50 per child aged 8–12, plus €11 per pitch.
THE FACILITIES Newly renovated shower block, laundry facilities, private bathrooms (€8 extra), recycling facilities, mini-market and play area.
FOOD AND DRINK The campsite bar and café

has al fresco seating and excellent coffee. For dinner, tempt your tastebuds at Ristorante Alla Lega (Via Vergolano, 8, Arco; 00 39 0464 516 205; www.ristoranteallalega), where Italian fare is served on a vine-covered patio.
FAMILY FUN Take a guided tour of nearby Arco Castle (00 39 0464 532 255) or head into Riva del Garda for an ice cream on the promenade.
TREAT YOURSELF Why not try out a canyoning adventure in the beautiful mountain crevices of the Upper Garda (Canyoning Adventure, Via

Matteotti 5, Sul Garda; 00 39 0464 505 406; www.canyonadv.com)?
GETTING THERE The campsite is on the waterfront at Nargo-Torbole on the SS-240 between Arco and Riva del Garda.
OPEN Apr/May–Sept/Oct.
IF IT'S FULL There is a handful of bigger campsites spread along this waterfront stretch. One of them is Camping Maroudi (Via Gardesana 13, 38069 Torbole, Lago di Garda; 00 39 046 450 51 75; www.campingmaroadi.it).

**Camping Bellavista**, Via Gardesana 31, 38062 Arco, Italy

| t | 00 39 0464 505 644 | w | www.camping-bellavista.it |

# san biagio

DH Lawrence may be best known for writing about naughty ladies and randy gamekeepers, but he was a dab hand when it came to Italy, too. The original beard-and-sandals Brit abroad, Lawrence came to Lake Garda (Lago di Garda) just before the First World War and marvelled, with arty-farty lyricism, at 'cypress trees poised like flames of forgotten darkness' and 'the green-silver smoke of olive trees' – enough to make your mouth water.

Lake Garda, Italy's largest and grandest lake, might have lost some of the romanticism of Lawrence's time since tourists started turning up in droves, but the cypress and olive trees still grow amidst the terracotta-roofed houses and now they have citrus orchards and vineyards to add extra charm.

The campsite at San Biagio is on the western side of the lake, in the lushly green region of Brescia, near Salò. It occupies its very own private, sandy peninsula, Belvedere Point, which juts northeasterly into the water, a bit like an accusing finger.

Its 165 pitches, all power-connected, extend along the narrow stretch of land, cleverly creating the intimate ambience of a much smaller campsite. Most pitches are either shimmied up against the water's edge (for

a small extra fee) or not too far from it. Others are slightly elevated so that you peer through the boughs of enormous blossoming magnolia trees to the blue water beyond, a vista enhanced by the soft, floral waft of magnolias in the fresh air.

But, wherever you end up pitching, you're never far from a bit of water-based activity. In most cases sink-your-toes-in sandy beaches allow easy access, but where sharp boulders nudge the edge of the lake, there are handy steps into the water – just the job for launching your inflatable mattress when you go for a relaxing drift around the lake.

If you can drag yourself away from the crystal-blue lake water lapping languidly on three sides of you, there's plenty in the surrounding countryside to keep you amused. Towards the east there's Rocca di Manerba, a 222-acre natural archeological park, where a re-discovered fortress dominates the skyline. How anyone lost it in the first place is a bit of a mystery, but there you go – these things happen.

At the northeastern tip of the peninsula, where six of the best pitches hide amongst the reedy waterfront, you can see Isola San Biagio, known locally as Isola dei Conigli, or Rabbit Island. It sits on the horizon,

closely resembling something straight from the tropics. When the water is low you can reach the island by picking your way along a narrow strip of white sand. When it is high, wading knee-deep with a towel around your neck and a bucket and spade in your hand makes for a perfect little adventure. Take a picnic, or use the BBQ, and have a nice snack on a well-chosen grassy lunch spot. Better still, pull up a bench seat at the island kiosk and relax whilst the hours tick by.

If you're feeling a bit more energetic, there is a smattering of small towns – complete with typically Italian piazzas, churches

and pizzerias – all a short drive away. And further afield still is Salò, the capital of Mussolini's Nazi-backed puppet state. Luckily the old man is long-gone and this beautiful town has a waterfront that will make you feel as though you've just stepped, *Alice Through the Looking Glass*-style, right into a Venetian painting. Its little lanes are full of the kinds of tempting shops, cafés and bars that exude the very essence of the Italy DH Lawrence would still recognise.

All in all, a terrific reason to strap on your sandals, with or without Brit-man-abroad socks, and go and take a look.

THE UPSIDE Prime location on a relatively small campsite.
THE DOWNSIDE A popular spot in high season (Jul–Aug).
THE DAMAGE €9–25 for tent and car, depending on tent size, site and season, plus €6–9 per adult and €3–7 per child, depending on season.
THE FACILITIES A large, clean, central block has male and female toilets, hot showers with separate changing areas, washing machines and basins. There's also a playground, supermarket and free wi-fi.

FOOD AND DRINK Mauro, the campsite's own waterside bar, with gaudy orange table cloths, is a great spot for a cold beer, espresso or pizza.
FAMILY FUN Water and swimming options are endless. In July and August the nearby village of Manerba plays host to an evening market each Tuesday night.
TREAT YOURSELF Head into nearby Salò for a typically Italian evening at Cantina Santa Giustina (Salita Santa Giustina 6, 25487 Salò; 00 39 0365 520 320). This rustic and cavernous eatery promises cheese, charcuterie, wine and, if Vasco,

the owner, has anything to do with it, a hangover.
GETTING THERE From the north, turn off SS45bis near Salò on to the SS572 towards Desenzano. Exit at Manerba and follow the camping signs to Via Cavalle. From the south, turn off the A4 towards Desenzano onto SS572 north towards Salò. Exit at Manerba and continue as above.
OPEN Mid-Mar–end-Oct.
IF IT'S FULL The SS45bis and this area of Lake Garda are riddled with signposted campsites, or head north to Bellavista, another Lake Garda *Cool Camping* site (see p229).

**Camping San Biagio**, Via Carvalle 19, 25080 Manerba del Garda, Brescia, Italy

| t | 00 39 0365 551 549 | w | www.campingsanbiagio.net |

# lo stambecco

Big Paradise Park is quite a name to have to live up to. Luckily the Parco Nazionale del Gran Paradiso in the Italian Alps is up to the challenge. On the Italian side of the Mont Blanc Massif, the park ticks so many Alpine boxes that even a meticulous Brussels bureaucrat would have trouble finding fault with its paperwork.

There are views up the valley towards the summit of Testa della Tribolazione, whose south-east wall is a favourite with climbers, despite its rather daunting name (something about tribulation). Across from the site is a steep shoulder of mountain, behind which the sun settles for the evening, and rumbling through the valley below the site is one of those high mountain rivers that is three-parts glacier melt and one-part crushed rock, giving it the distinctive grey-green mineral colour of a river of Margueritas. Dips (and sips) are not recommended, though – your various extremities would not thank you for the exposure, plus you'd end up being washed down the valley and out into the Med.

Lo Stambecco is in the tiny village of Valnontey, a stopover on one of the great summer Alpine walks – the Alta Via from Champorcher to Courmayeur. With an average altitude of over 2,000 metres and the pass of the Col Loson measuring up at 3,300 metres, the Alta Via (a literal highway) is a fairly serious multi-day walk. But thankfully you can sample the atmosphere of it by doing nothing more strenuous than waving at passing walkers from the comfort of the grassy slopes of Lo Stambecco. They're perfect for a prolonged lounge; one of those lazy ones that can last an afternoon. The thick grass is so soft and comfy that carpet slippers seem more appropriate footwear than clumpy walking boots.

There's a variety of pitches, some on the grassy slopes, some venturing into the pine cover that sneaks down the hill, threatening to engulf the whole place. The further up the hill you go, the thicker the trees. Like Hansel and Gretel you might want to leave a trail of breadcrumbs from your tent to the facilities block at night, just in case you get lost. Unfortunately things both small and furry are likely to snaffle them in the night and if the trees have surrounded you during the hours of darkness, you might have to machete your way out of the thicket by the time morning arrives.

If you are itching for a hike, there are walking maps on sale from the campsite's reception, so you can tackle anything from a half-hour stroll to a day's hard slog up the valley in search of the elusive ibex ('*stambecchi*' in Italian) – those hairy things with horns that look like upturned stacks of ice cream cones. There's actually an old hunting lodge called the Rifugio Vittorio Sella, originally owned by King Victor Emmanuel II who became the first king of a united Italy in 1861 thanks in part to the support of Garibaldi (the revolutionary, not the biscuit), and who used to come up here to hunt *stambecchi*. It's about two-and-a-

half hours' steady climb from Valnontey and there's a restaurant for fortification before the descent. Much easier is the downhill, 2-mile (3-km) walk to the bright lights of Cogne, a typically gorgeous Alpine village, which, with nearly 1,500 inhabitants, feels like downtown Manhattan after a few days up at Lo Stambecco. Fair enough, the return walk is back up the hill, but with the prospect of your carpet slippers waiting for you back at the campsite, it's a breeze.

THE UPSIDE Box-ticking Alpine camping – views, air, walks and creeping trees.
THE DOWNSIDE There's a large car park across the road from the site that is busy with day-trippers at the height of summer.
THE DAMAGE €6 per adult and €4 per child (extra between 20 July and 26 August). A tent is €3–4 (€5–6, high season) depending on size.
THE FACILITIES They're OK, but a little dark and dingy. The showers are fine, but the squat loos will test those with dodgy knees (though there are a few you can sit and read on, too).
FOOD AND DRINK There's a miniature bar/

restaurant onsite with a few tables outside for admiring the mountain view. Within Valnontey, there are several restaurants, the best-situated being the Hotel Paradisia (00 39 0165 741 58), which offers a range of standard mains such as pasta and steaks for €7–17.
FAMILY FUN Take the kids to La Ferme du Grande Paradis (00 39 3482 589 500; www. lafermedugrandparadis.it.) just across the river from the campsite.
TREAT YOURSELF To some of La Ferme du Grande Paradis's excellent collection of cheeses; it is a working farm, after all. It's all

locally produced and some of it is pretty strong.
GETTING THERE From Aosta, take the SR47 towards Cogne. Turn right in the town up the cobbled street signposted for Valnontey. After 2 miles (3 km), there's a sign for Lo Stambecco to the right, just before the village.
PUBLIC TRANSPORT Buses run from Aosta.
OPEN End-May–end-Sept.
IF IT'S FULL Camping Gran Paradiso (00 39 0165 905 801; www.campinggranparadiso.it) is another few hundred metres up the road. Further afield there's Camping Arvier (00 39 0165 990 88) on the road up towards the Mont Blanc tunnel.

**Camping Lo Stambecco**, Valnontey, Cogne, Aosta, Italy

| t | 00 39 0165 741 52 | w | www.campeggiolostambecco.it |

# internazionale firenze

In imperial times it was said that all roads led to Rome and, thanks to Italy's idiosyncratic road signs, it can often still seem to be that way. Many a T-junction will tell you that Rome is to the left. And to the right. So if you're on your way to the forum and you see a sign that says 'Firenze', be sure to take it.

No visit to Italy is complete without a couple of days in the company of Dante, Michelangelo and co, because if one city sums up Italy in all its Renaissance glory – the painting, the sculpture, the poetry, the architecture – this little city by the Arno is it.

Camping Internazionale Firenze is as 'internazionale' as the name suggests. There are more national flags aloft over reception than in an Olympic athletes' village. This is Florence (Firenze to the locals), after all, and in summer it's clogged with gaily-clad camera-clicking culture-vultures from all possible corners of the globe. But the site is a 20-minute, €1.20, bus ride from the city centre, so in the height of a Tuscan summer you'll be able to relax a little way away from all the hubbub happening in town.

The site is reasonably large and quite steep, but the good news is that the chalets are out of sight near reception and the camping area is on long, broad grassy terraces up the hill. Though you can't see downtown Florence from the site, pitch over here and you'll have views of the illuminated convent of San Paulo on one hill, or pitch over there and there's the church of Certosa. As night falls, you'll see bats on the wing, flitting between the trees with their built-in sat-navs picking out bugs and moths in the air, and you'll be winked at by the fireflies lurking in the grass. You'd be hard-pushed to find that sort of thing in a 2-star *pensione* in town.

Down the hill on one side of the site is a fairly lively bar, frequented by a youngish crowd whose attire is usually as loud as their voices. Luckily for all campers in need of a peaceful time, it's all well out of earshot of the camping area.

There's also a modest restaurant (no awards, as yet, and don't hold your breath) and a reasonably well-stocked little shop, where the basics of breakfast can be found in the morning and a cold beer in the evening, if you want to take one back, sit on the grass and Bluetooth the bats.

And when it's time to hit the tourist trail you just won't know where to start. Michelangelo at the Academia or Donatello at the Bargello? A café macchiato or a glass of Chianti?

*Prosciutto* or *formaggio*? Ponte Vecchio or Ponti's ice cream? You need to take a deep breath, lace up your most sensible walking shoes and prepare yourself for culture, Italian-style.

Florence is one of those convenient cities in which the main attractions are all handily within walking distance of each other. But unfortunately there are so many to choose from that you can easily cover the Olympic marathon distance getting from one to the next, and on to the next.

At least it's all walker-friendly; the centre's streets are largely pedestrianised or only have room for those scooters that sound like hairdryers and tiny Fiats that look like upturned bathtubs. Neither seems capable of more than 15 mph, even with a tailwind, so you're in more danger of tripping on the ancient cobble stones than anything else.

Just pick up a map and don't pay too much attention to the road signs. They'll just point you to Rome.

THE UPSIDE On the doorstep of the finest collection of Renaissance art and architecture in the world.

THE DOWNSIDE There's a large electricity pylon slap-bang in the middle of the site and, being Florence, the site does cater for bus-loads of visitors. There is a bit of noise from the motorway.

THE DAMAGE €9.50–10 for adults and €6.50–6.80 for children aged 3–12 years. A pitch is €16–16.80, depending on the season (the higher price is charged early-June–late-Sept).

THE FACILITIES Not bad. Decent showers and WCs and plenty of washing facilities (clothes and dishes) in a central block.

FOOD AND DRINK Eat on the hoof when in town. Just by the Duomo there's a great little *enoteca* (wine bar) called Alessi (Via delle Oche), which serves delicious bruschetta and quality wines by the glass. For something near the Uffizi, try Giulliano Centro, a small café with local grub – spiced and herbed chicken, local sausage, rosti and a dollop of spinach and broccoli mashed up with garlic and olive oil. Just opposite is a great stand-up place serving Tuscan nibbles like artichoke and truffle on bread and help-yourself chianti at €2 a go. A few streets along is a great little café-bar called Naimi, where net nuts can enjoy free wi-fi.

FAMILY FUN Climb the dome of Brunelleschi's Duomo, explaining as you go how the twin-skinned structure was built without scaffolding, and then regain your breath by enjoying the views from the top.

TREAT YOURSELF To seeing Donatello's über-camp statue of David – a far cry from Michelangelo's massive muscular marble version at the Academia. Donatello's androgynous little imp has undergone an 18-month restoration programme and is back on display at the Bargello.

GETTING THERE Come off the A1 Roma road at the Certosa exit. As you pass through Bottai, the campsite is signposted to your left. Follow the road back under the motorway and the campsite is on your right.

PUBLIC TRANSPORT A number 37 or 68 bus (depending on the day) runs from the train station in Florence to Bottai. It's a 10-minute walk to the site from the bus stop.

OPEN All year.

IF IT'S FULL Camping Michelangelo (00 39 0556 811 977) is just under the Piazzale Michelangelo, 20–30 minutes' walk in sensible shoes from the Ponte Vecchio. It's large and a bit noisy, but the pitches are mainly under olive trees.

**Camping Internazionale Firenze**, Via San Cristofano 2, 50029 Bottai-Impruneta, Italy

| t | 00 39 0552 374 704 | w | www.florencecamping.com |

# stella mare

Not a man to twiddle his thumbs, Napoleon Bonaparte spent his year-long exile on the island of Elba compiling crossword clues and planning a range of branded luxury goods. Of the former the only memorable example is the rather neat palindrome 'Able I was ere I saw Elba' and of the latter all that survives is the modish logo that adorns the gates of his villa.

Sadly, the range of quality high heels and handbags for the WAGs of his favourite generals never made it to the production line because, after a year on the island, the little general decided to escape and go double-or-quits with one last fling at Waterloo.

Italy's third-largest island, Elba is a craggy volcanic outcrop off the Tuscan coast, covered in lush, almost tropical, vegetation. It's a little like the Caribbean, but without the bananas, and is a perfect getaway from the hustle of the mainland.

The Emperor's villa on Elba is now a museum (€6 to enter and closed on Mondays) and the fancy wrought-iron gates are still topped off with the rather stylish Napoleonic logo of an 'N' in a crown of laurel leaves. He obviously liked to remind himself who was boss. But you can't help wondering, as you walk up the impressive cobbled drive, past bamboo stands, sprigs of wild flowers and the odd eucalyptus, quite why he wasn't happy just to put his feet up and settle down here. A more modest man would almost certainly have stayed put.

Napoleon wasn't the first wanderer to land on Elba. Legend has it that Jason and the Argonauts stopped off for a bit of shore leave back in the mists of time. And you'll be quite happy to have made landfall here, too.

From the picturesque town of Portoferraio you can head up west into the volcanic highlands, east towards the hilltop town of Capoliveri or south, over the shoulder of the hills towards Lacona, where you'll come across the quiet little bay that Camping Stella Mare overlooks.

The bay's water is only knee-deep (waist-deep if you happen to be as short as Napoleon) and perfect for kids to splash about in whilst you keep a weather-eye on them from the narrow strip of beach. There's a host of bars and restaurants to choose from right by the water. Round the back of the site there's also what is effectively a private beach (and one where it seems occasionally people 'forget' their swimming cozzies). This can be reached by some steep steps from the campsite.

And when you're done sunning yourself for the day, it's only a short stroll up to the campsite, where the pitches are alphabetised, and the further you go beyond ABC, the higher you climb up the cliff. The 'A's are down near the beach, if you don't want to have to walk too far, and can't be bothered with the climb. By the time you get to the far reaches of the alphabet – particularly the 'S's and the 'U's – you're into pitches that are raked into steep terraces overlooking the water and dotted with dinner-plate-sized cactus plants and all manner of different trees. Most of these pitches are inaccessible to caravans and camper vans; you have to park your car up top and carry your gear down the steps to your pitch. But it's worth it.

And so if you were Napoleon, surely you'd be quite happy to retire from all that gallivanting about in stiff breeches and a bicorn hat. You'd lie back, let Josephine feed you sculpted melon balls for breakfast on the sun terrace of your lavish villa, and think to yourself, yep, Elba will suit me just fine.

THE UPSIDE Crumbly cliff-top camping overlooking a quiet bay on a wonderful little island.
THE DOWNSIDE It can be a long, steep and rocky trip to the shower block in the middle of the night.
THE DAMAGE Depending on the season it's €8.50–14.50 per adult, €5–10 per child (2–8 years) and €9.50–14 for a tent.
THE FACILITIES Three shower blocks: they're fine and the showers are hot. There's not much dish-washing capacity, though – but then, you are on holiday.
FOOD AND DRINK Apart from a restaurant and snack bar on the site (and the restaurants by the beach), the best option is to head to Capoliveri. Le Piccole Ore (via P. Gori 22) is an atmospheric

bar with decent brunch items before 2.30pm. Most of the locals seem to eat at Ristorante Pizzeria da Michele (via Calamita 6). Though it's a standard pasta/pizza joint, it's where you'll catch all the local gossip.
FAMILY FUN There's a funky glass-bottomed boat run by Aquavision (00 39 3287 095 470) with an underwater viewing gallery, which sails from either Portoferraio or Marciana Marina on 2-hour marine-life spotting trips. Great for learning how to identify *scorfano rosso* from its dorsal fins alone and other salty trivia. It's €15 for adults and €8 for kids under 12.
TREAT YOURSELF To an upgrade from canvas at the 4-star Park Hotel Napoleone (00 39 0565 911 111; www.parkhotelnapoleone.com) at the

bottom of the drive up to the Emperor's villa. Standard rooms start at €65 per night and there are suites for about €100. There's a good restaurant and a pool, but better still there's a shuttle bus to the hotel's private beach at La Biodola.
GETTING THERE The ferry runs from Piombino up to 16 times each day and takes an hour. From the port, follow the dual carriageway out of town heading for Porto Azzurro. Turn right at the traffic lights, where the road heads for the hills and Lacona. Once over the hills, turn right at Lacona and just past Camping Lacona is the turn-off on the left for Stella Mare.
OPEN End-Apr–end-Oct.
IF IT'S FULL Camping Lacona (00 39 0565 964 161) is just next door, with a really nice pool.

| **Camping Stella Mare**, Lacona, Isola d'Elba, Italy | | | |
|---|---|---|---|
| | t | 00 39 0565 964 007 | w | www.stellamare.it |

# costiolu

It's such a long and winding road that leads to the door of this organic working farm, situated high in the central Sardinian hills, that even Macca and the other lovable Liverpool moptops might feel somewhat dizzy. The trek up the narrow, snaking bends will have you more than ready for a glass or two of home-made wine when you arrive, courtesy of Giovanni di Costa, the Azienda's hospitable owner.

A colourful character, Giovanni is a friendly kind of guy, and doesn't let the small matter of speaking completely different languages pose a barrier when he chats away to his foreign guests.

The delight he takes in showing you around is infectious, and it's easy to see why the farm, which has been in his family for generations, is his pride and joy. Its roots go way back, with a small enclosure of rocks in front of the house once forming part of a *villaggio* dating back to 1,000 BC, when the first Nuragic settlers found their way up to this fertile terrain.

Apart from the odd piece of new-fangled farming equipment about the place, Costiolu's unspoilt nature gives the impression that things haven't been updated all that much in 3,000 years.

A proper retreat from the hectic trappings of everyday life, the Azienda offers a calm, country experience alongside its simple, old-fashioned farming ways, and has won Giovanni several awards, including the much-coveted Agrituristica Plein Air di Qualita, a kind of Michelin star for farm-based holidays.

Although the local town Nuoro, Sardinia's cultural capital, remains visible from the Azienda's lofty perch, the views are mostly taken up with its sprawling olive groves, cereal fields and grazing land peppered with languid cows, sheep and goats.

The camping area consists of nine adjacent pitches on a flat plain above the small herd of bell-tinkling goats, and there's room enough for a good spattering of tents behind the farmhouse, too. The clean bathrooms are to be tracked down in a simple stone building nearby, and picnic tables are set on the Azienda's terrace for dining al fresco, *a la* Giovanni.

Breakfast, lunch and dinner are all available for your delectation and feature mouth-watering home-grown delicacies, such as traditional Sardinian sheep's cheese, goat's yogurt, hung meats and bottles of fruity wine. Every so often Giovanni puts on a huge hog roast, whilst he teaches local kids the Barbagian way to make ricotta cheese and look after the animals.

If you fancy a trip back down the bendy hills into civilisation, Nuoro (which means 'home' in the town's ancient dialect) is well worth a visit. Known as the 'Sardinian Athens' for its rich cultural history, many artists have lived and worked here over the years, including Giovanni's brother. You can inspect his twisty sculptures as they are dotted around the farm, as well as decorating a piazza in town. Grazia Deledda, winner of the 1926 Nobel Prize for Literature, was born in Nuoro, and her old house has been converted to a museum to celebrate her life and work.

You will find further doses of culture in the town's museums of and ethnography (which explore the life and traditions of Sardinians, dating back to the 1800s) and contemporary art. But for those more in favour of sipping a coffee and watching the sleepy Sardinian world go by, there are delicious little cafés scattered about the town where you can enjoy a caffeine fix.

This region's rugged beauty may be a far cry from Sardinia's publicised coastal splendour, which sees footballers and WAGs flocking to the island's beaches. But for a true taste of Sardinian culture and farming life, it's Azienda Costiolu and its affable owner that'll make you want to 'twist and shout'.

---

THE UPSIDE The warmest of welcomes, stunning views and complete tranquillity
THE DOWNSIDE Difficult to get to without a car.
THE DAMAGE Tents, camper vans, caravans with 1 person, €7–10. Discounts of 20–30 per cent for kids under 8. No pets allowed. Lunch and/or dinner can be provided from €30–45.
THE FACILITIES A small but clean shower block (1 women's, 1 men's), and nearer the house there's a disabled toilet.
FOOD AND DRINK Giovanni cooks up feasts in the restaurant, and there are lots of home-grown goodies to be had. Or nearby Oliena's Su

Gologone restaurant, which features a 500-year-old fireplace, has a delicious seasonal menu and local speciality: Cannonau wine.
FAMILY FUN Become Clint Eastwood for the day by hopping onto one of Giovanni's horses for an excursion.
TREAT YOURSELF Just for a change, treat yourself to a day on the Costa Smeralda, Sardinia's most beautiful coastline. Frolic on the beach for the day, then head for drinks or a slap-up dinner at the exclusive Cala di Volpe Hotel (Costa Smeralda, Porto Cervo 07020; 00 39 0789 976 111), and be prepared to spot one or two celebs there, too).

GETTING THERE It's approximately 5½ miles (9 km) along the SS389 from Nuoro to Bitti and thankfully there are a couple of Costiolu signposts along the way.
PUBLIC TRANSPORT ARST A1 buses run from Bitti to Nuoro (route Q.511). And the R2 runs from Nuoro to Bitti. They run very irregularly and on Sundays there isn't always a service, so it's advisable to check ahead.
OPEN All year, but you must book ahead.
IF IT'S FULL Another *agriturismo* site nearby is Roccas, which has 5 pitches available (00 39 3495 781 623; www.roccas.it).

**Azienda Agrituristica Costiolu**, 08100 Nuoro, SS389 (Nuoro to Bitti), Sardinia

| t | 00 39 0784 260 088 | e | roccasagriturismo@tiscali.it |

# il falcone

Some people may think that Umbria hasn't got the same good looks or popularity as its flashier Tuscan cousin, but its rolling hills and scattered lakes do have one clear advantage over what's rightly known as Chianti-shire – you won't find hordes of braying toffs unloading hampers of champers from the boots of their Chelsea tractors out here. You're more likely to find some crumple-faced old farmer humping crates of olive oil out of the back of a battered Fiat, whilst the silence is broken only by the chirrup of unidentified birds, the gentle stir of olive leaves and poppies nodding their heads in the breeze.

At Camping Il Falcone you get the olives and poppies, but it would simply be uncharitable to describe owner Carlo Valeri as a crumple-faced old farmer. He's far too young and chipper. Mind you, he does harvest the olives from the trees that are planted along the terraced rows of the campsite, though he claims there's only enough of the resulting oil for 'family'.

The site at Il Falcone is a lasso-shaped slice of hill, terraced between youngish olive trees and dotted with crimson poppies. Caravans and camper vans are mainly confined to the outer reaches of the site, leaving the steep terraces for the canvas crew.

You have to ditch your wheels at the top and clamber down the hill with your gear to pick a pitch on grass as thick as sprigs of spring onion. If you choose the left-hand side of the site, there are sumptuous views down to the lake and across to the village of Civitella del Lago; one of those ancient shadowy villages populated by nothing but old folk and kittens.

If you wander over to the village and look west over Corbara lake (Lago di Corbara) you can just make out, through the heat haze, the outline of another hilltop community – Orvieto. It's a larger version of Civitella del Lago, but houses one of the most visually stunning of Italy's many cathedrals. In candy-stripes of grey and white stone, the massive *duomo* and its ornate mosaic front look good enough to eat. Inside is that marvellous church smell of old pew and cold stone mingling with centuries of burnt incense and evaporated candle wax.

Back at Il Falcone, you might – as you sip your olive-garnished martini – wonder about the name. The image of the falcon adorns the walls of the village and there's a weather-washed old stone falcon at one of the village's viewing points over the surrounding countryside. What does it all mean? Well, this mountainous region was once a medieval hunting ground. While our Norman ancestors were busy breeding racing pigeons and stick-thin whippets, the Italians were pulling on long leather gloves and feeding bits of minced-up field mouse to beaky birds of prey. You're unlikely to see any now, though, as the locals have taken to the more sedate pursuits of growing olives and raising kittens. As evening falls and the suns sets directly behind the village, sinking through the smoke from BBQ fires, you'll spot little geckos darting around your feet, looking for a warm rock for the night, and thanking their lucky stars that all the hungry falcons have gone.

THE UPSIDE Pitches in poppies and olives, with views of the lake and a medieval hilltop village.

THE DOWNSIDE Olive trees don't provide much in the way of shade.

THE DAMAGE Adults are €5.10–6.20 and children 3–10 years are €4.10–5.20. A tent is €5.10–7 and a car is €2.20. The higher prices apply in July and August.

THE FACILITIES One well-maintained block with good showers (though only 3 each in the men's and women's). There are separate clothes- and dish-washing areas. The site now has a new swimming pool.

FOOD AND DRINK A tiny bar (but with really cold beer) is onsite and there are several stone BBQ pits, but you really need to head to Orvieto to indulge. Maurizio's (00 39 0763 341 114), just by the *duomo*, serves a great 'taster' menu for €30 – Umbrian cured meats and entrecôte steak cooked with Sagrantino wine. For coffee and snacks try Café Barrique at 111 Corso Cavour (00 39 0763 340 455). Both are incongruously modern for such an old place – but nice all the same.

FAMILY FUN Thirty miles down Autostrada 1 at Bomarzo is the Parco dei Mostri (Monster Park; www.parcodeimostri.com). Dating back to the 16th century, it's a weird collection of stone monsters and woody groves set in a 'sacred wood', aka the grounds of an old estate.

TREAT YOURSELF Brush off your plummiest wine-tasting phrases by sampling some bottles of Orvieto Classico, the local tipple, which dates back to the time of the Etruscans. It's available in most places, especially Orvieto itself. Quaff a glass, or 2 or more, and practise saying 'Mmmm, it's as lively as a wet spaniel'.

GETTING THERE Come off the A1/E35 main road between Florence and Rome and just past Orvieto take the SS448 towards Todi. After approximately 3 miles (5 km) turn right up the SP90 towards Civitella del Lago. As you approach the village, veer right and follow the road round the hill (towards Melezolle). The site is signposted to your right.

OPEN Early-Apr–late-Sept.

IF IT'S FULL Down by the lake on the road to Orvieto – about half a mile (1 km) past the turn-off for Civitella del Lago – is Scacco Matto (00 39 0744 950 163), which is pleasant enough. Slightly further afield is the *Cool Camping* site of Il Collaccio (see p257).

**Camping Il Falcone**, Vallonganino 2/A, Civitella del Lago 05020 Baschi, Italy

| t | 00 39 07449 502 49/00 39 0758 436 90 (off-season) | w | www.campingilfalcone.com |

# il collaccio

Il Collaccio is what estate agents would call 'marvellously appointed'. Hidden deep in the valleys of the Umbrian hills, where the villages are so out of the way and ancient that you half expect a Roman legionnaire to come marching up the road and hail you in the name of Caesar, this *agriturismo* site lies across the hills from the pointy little village of Preci and keeps a wary eye up the valley for the distant approach of Caesar's renegade legions.

Like a number of Italian *agriturismo* sites, this is a complex, which combines a small family-owned truffle farm with a modest hotel and restaurant, a stunning pool, some basic chalets and cabins, and plenty of terraces for campers, caravans and tents. To be honest, tents are in the minority. However, the site is so steep that once you're settled into your little terraced bolt-hole, you can quite easily forget all about the two-wheelers behind you and just enjoy the peace and quiet.

The site's right on the doorstep of the Parco Nazionale Monti Sibillini, which is slap-bang in the middle of Umbria's heavily wooded gorges and fairly serious Appenine mountains. At just under 2,500 metres, the highest of them, Monte Vettore, commands a bit of respect and certainly isn't something

you should undertake wearing a pair of trainers and a mac that folds up into its own little pocket.

You can get a sense of the scale of things by taking the road up from Visso beyond the tree line and onto a broad, shallow plateau of rocky meadow, at the end of which the town of Castelluccio pricks the skyline. Carry on over the ridge and there's a 1,500-metre-high mountain pass on Vettore's southern flank that can eventually bring you back in a loop to Preci, via the comely town of Norcia. It's a great little taster menu of the à la carte delights that Umbria has to offer.

If it's Italian heritage you're after, then you can always call in at the medieval town of Spoleto, which claims yet another of Italy's 'finest' cathedrals – though this time the boast holds water. Holy water at that. The campanile was built from Roman remains, the bulk of Spoleto's *duomo* was built around AD1200 and the portico was added during the Renaissance.

Whereas so many Italian cathedrals have been tinkered with over the years – with their Romanesque façades tarted up with Gothic bling – this mishmash of styles is a surprisingly pleasant success. Inside it's cool and white, with some wonderfully ornate little chapels at the back if you feel like a quiet word with 'him upstairs'. Spoleto itself is a more 'lived-in' town than the rather pickled and preserved touristy spots like Orvieto. The shops are aimed less at passing travellers eager for a souvenir and more at the locals' ironmongery and haberdashery requirements. So other than the narrow, twisty cobbled streets leading up to the *duomo*, it's not the prettiest place, but at least it's authentic 21st-century Italy. Elsewhere you'll find the throwbacks to Italy's darker and rockier past. This is the land of fortified towns built into the sides of hills, their defences telling you something about how precarious existence was for much of Italy's history.

From the time of Caesar, right through to the Allied campaign up the spine of Italy in 1944, these places have seen some action. Thankfully, the locals are far from defensive and you'll get a cheery wave from the Baldoni family at Il Collaccio when you arrive. And, if you're lucky, they might even treat you to a truffle.

THE UPSIDE Real off-the-beaten-track Umbrian camping with the Baldoni family.
THE DOWNSIDE Coach-loads of people stay in the hotel, leaving campers in the minority.
THE DAMAGE Depending on the season, €5.50–8.50 per adult and €2.50–5 for children aged 3–12 years. A tent is €5.5–8.50.
THE FACILITIES A little outdoorsy, but fairly good and well tended. The showers are fine and hot and there are washing machines at €4 a pop.
FOOD AND DRINK There's an OK restaurant, Al Porcello Felice (The Happy Pig), onsite (which serves good river-caught trout as well as pasta and wood-oven pizza) and a small shop with very basic provisions, but the village of Preci's not much good for eateries. So, if you want to eat out, head up the road to Visso for a wider range of cafés and bars.
FAMILY FUN Try mule-riding with La Mulattiera (00 39 339 451 3189; www.lamulattiera.it). They're based in Norcia and run various trips in the Sibillini National Park, following ancient tracks and pathways.
TREAT YOURSELF If you feel you need a little education whilst on your hols, try one of the courses run at Il Collaccio. If you time your stay right, you can put your hand to anything from cookery to extreme sports and photography with award-winning photographer David Noton.
GETTING THERE From the SS3 road running south of Perugia, take the SS685 just before Spoleto and then veer back north on the SS209 heading for Visso. Just before Pontechiusita, turn right towards Preci. Just before the village, turn left up the hill and follow the signs for a mile or so (2 km) over undulating roads.
OPEN All year.
IF IT'S FULL Further up in the hills is the dramatic Monte Prata campsite (00 39 073 797 00 62; www.camping.it/marche/monteprata) on the road up to Castelluccio. Just past Gualdo, it's signposted on the right.

**Camping Il Collaccio**, 06047 Preci, Perugia, Italy

| t | 00 39 0743 939 005 | w | www.ilcollaccio.com |

# riva di ugento

Riva di Ugento is less of a campsite, more of a *gigantissimo* camping village. Nestled away from the peacock-blue Ionian sea in 79 acres of pine woods and Mediterranean scrub, it's so big you may feel the urge to pick up a map at reception and even perhaps make use of that boy scout's compass. But don't let that put you off; the site's so roomy there's plenty of space for all, with many a cone-studded lane to jog down or dunes and woods that are perfect for family treasure hunts. Visit the playground after a scrumptious breakfast in the yurt-style cafeteria, or hire bikes and go cruising. Another idea is to hire a catamaran or kayak; the shallow water suits all ages and the powder-fine beach goes on forever.

The mini-mart here spills over with fresh local farm produce, so no need to worry about finding good, healthy nosh. And should boring old work come a-calling there's handy Internet access and wi-fi. In the evening the restaurant is a cheerful chaos of *bambinos* and swiftly devoured pizzas. Outside they show films for the kids every night, which is great for them and a boon if you want a little me-time at the end of a hard day's family holiday. In short, this wooded haven is the kind of place you can really kick back and breathe in the rugged air without worrying too much about anything – the site might be big enough for your kids to get a bit lost sometimes, but it's small enough for them to find their way back again.

THE UPSIDE With its twisting Aleppus pine woods, beautiful rugged beach and dunes, there's endless scope for R&R.
THE DOWNSIDE If you're here in search of tranquillity make sure it's outside the school holidays. And don't get lost!
THE DAMAGE Two people, a tent and child (optional) will cost €19–40, season-dependent.
THE FACILITIES In a word: lots. There is a newsagent, first aid, supermarket, swimming pool, launderette, kids' playground, tennis courts, BBQ pits, Internet and wi-fi, bikes for hire, long sandy beach, restaurant, games room, outdoor cinema, water sports and boutiques.
FOOD AND DRINK There's a nice restaurant onsite, with a great selection of pizzas and pasta dishes, not to mention the supermarket, which encourages self-catering under the stars. But for more foodie options try the beautiful town of Lecce or the neighbouring village of Ugento.
FAMILY FUN The old town of Gallipoli is 15½ miles (25 km) away – it's well worth a visit.
TREAT YOURSELF If you're driving south you can't miss a visit to Lecce. The picturesque town, crammed with baroque-wedding-cake-style buildings and moody, deserted piazzas, seems to have leapt from the lens of a Merchant–Ivory film. Wander down the narrow alleyways, passing mouth-watering *gelateries*, shadowy *brasseries* and fine-art shops, with children scampering here, there and everywhere in the shadows of shuttered town houses.
GETTING THERE By car, if you're heading south, take the E55 to Lecce, then follow signs to Gallipoli and Ugento. In Ugento you'll see and should follow the signposts.
OPEN Early-May–end-Sept.
IF IT'S FULL Impossible – given that there are as many pitches (1,000) as Berlusconi scandals.

**Camping Riva di Ugento**, Ugento, Italy

t    00 39 0833 933 600   |   w    www.rivadiugento.it

# koren

You can't go far in northwestern Slovenia without running into the Soča: this enchanting, 84-mile (136-km) aquamarine artery snakes from its source in the soaring Julian Alps, through Triglavski Narodni Park (Triglav National Park) and northern Italy before finally splashing into the Adriatic.

Situated along the Soča's banks, not far from the quaint historical town of Kobarid, rests Kamp Koren. Vast yet chilled, the site is overseen by the passionate Lidija Koren, whose penchant for exploring the needs of camping folk seems peerless.

Lidija's 'baby' was born two decades ago. It was originally started in partnership with her family, though she has been running (and expanding) it solo for the last 10 years. Having developed step by step, bit by bit, the site is subtly divided into sections and is deceptively sprawling. Past the wooden reception, the main camping area caters chiefly for caravans and larger family tents, but skirt left up the bank and you'll find a charming wooded area made up of trees, fields, terraces and private camping pitches, all interconnected by natural walkways and wooden bridges.

In similarly subtle fashion, the site has incorporated an impressive array of features and facilities: an 8-metre climbing wall (plus a smaller one for little kids); volleyball court; *boules* pitch and viewing benches (cheekily ensconced in the wooded river bank); and, last but not least, separate loo blocks for the camping area.

Once you've snuggled into one of Koren's cosy camping alcoves, you can start getting to know the local area. The Soča valley, an important trading route for many centuries and the site of some significant World War I frontline action, is today an outdoor enthusiast's dream. To get an early taste, hike to the Kozjak waterfall (half an hour one way), tackle nearby peaks like Krasji Vrh or Krn (both solid three- to four-hour hikes) or hire a mountain bike and burn some rubber through the forest.

Nearby Kobarid is famous for the decisive battle between the Central Powers and the fascists in 1917, a scene immortalised by Hemingway in *A Farewell To Arms*. Today it's a small but pleasant historic town with a smattering of decent eateries, cafés, grocers, a world-class museum on Slovenia's role in the First World War and several places to arrange adventure sports. History buffs will enjoy the local history trail: a five-hour walk that takes in Roman archeological sites, waterfalls and World War I trenches.

It's easier to arrange trips via Kamp Koren, however, since the site offers tailored tours for small groups exploring off-the-beaten-track spots such as cave complexes and traditional villages, as well as historic towns like Tolmin. The site can also arrange activities including mountaineering, Alpine climbing and paragliding, plus, of course, river-based shenanigans such as kayaking, rafting and swimming.

You definitely won't get bored here, though you might get a little tipsy. An hour's drive from the site will bring you to one of Slovenia's best-known wine regions, Goriška Brda, which produces some very notable reds. Aim for the main town, Dobrovo, to check out the 17th-century Renaissance castle and its annexed stone-walled *enoteca*, which sells not only most of the local wine varieties but also the extremely tasty regional cheeses and meats.

Proactive as you might be, however, be warned that you may not get far past reception. This unassuming wooden hut is a marvel of hospitality, where charming Slovenian women cheerfully hand out everything from great coffee and on-tap beer to local information and Internet passwords. They can even order you a kebab from the local takeaway if you can't be bothered to cook – now that's *Cool Camping*.

THE UPSIDE A relaxed and comprehensive site slap-bang in the Soča valley that arranges everything from sports activities to kebab delivery.
THE DOWNSIDE Very busy in the summer.
THE DAMAGE In low season, it's €8.50 per adult and children aged 7–13 are €4.25. In high season, it's €10 per adult and 7–13-year-olds are €4.25. Kids 0–7 are always free.
THE FACILITIES Hot, free, modern showers, spotless toilets, bio food in the kiosk and wi-fi at reception are just some of the top facilities here at Kamp Koren. The site also has play facilities for kids and arranges specially devised tours and trips.
FOOD AND DRINK The onsite shop has a good range of organic products. Apart from the (much-publicised) kebab delivery service, you'll also find several places to eat in the centre of Kobarid (a 15-minute walk). Above-average Italian 'slow food' can be found in Hiša Franko (00 386 5389 41 20; www.hisafranko.com), located in the village of Staro selo 1, less than 3 miles (5 km) from the campsite on the road to Italy.
FAMILY FUN There are a couple of climbing walls onsite (plus an instructor daily through summer), as well as volleyball, table tennis and *boules*. You can also hire bicycles for adults and children onsite and arrange a horse-riding guide. For family kayaking and rafting try Positive Sport in Kobarid (00 386 4065 44 75; www.positive-sport.com). You can also visit the elaborate and world-renowned Postojna Caves 43 miles (70 km) away, which organise treks and tours (00 386 5700 01 00; www.postojnska-jama.si).
TREAT YOURSELF To some high-octane fun. The Adrenaline Club in Drežnica (00 386 5384 86 10; www.drustvo-adrenalin.si) can arrange tandem-paragliding for you. Or if you like keeping your feet on the ground, stay in a cottage on the mountain Krn (2,248 metres) – see reception.
GETTING THERE From Ljubljana take the A1, turning off onto the 102 and following it through Logatec, Idrija, Tolmin and Kobarid. From Kobarid, follow the signs for Kamp Koren. From Klagenfurt (Austria), take the A2/E55 towards Villach, then the 83, turning left past Hart onto the 109 towards the Slovenian border. On the Slovenian side take the 201 to Kranjska Gora, turning right onto the 206. Follow the 206 to Bovec (unless you are in a caravan or mobile home, in which case take the 203 directly), merge onto the 203 to Kobarid, then follow signs for Kamp Koren.
OPEN Mid-Mar–early-Nov.
IF IT'S FULL Kamp Nadiža (00 386 5384 91 10; www.kamp-nadiza.com) in Podbela is close to the Italian border and has nice, natural spots directly by the river.

**Kamp Koren**, Drežniške Ravne 33, 5222 Kobarid, Slovenia

| t | 00 386 5389 13 11 | w | www.kamp-koren.si |

# liza

If you're planning on pitching at Slovenia's Kamp Liza it might pay to bring along your personal kayak. With so many others lying around, without one you might feel a bit left out. The site offers access to two rivers: the emerald-green Soča and the clear, wild Koritnica, making it a serious boon for all aqua aficionados. Surrounded by the thrusting peaks and lush pastures of the Bovec valley, this site is a large, laid-back space. Groups are usually directed to the lower terrace, next to the burbling Soča; families gather in the central area, whilst independent tenters head to the furthest field, to strum guitars, sip cold beers and break out the barbie.

Nearby Bovec is tiny, but it's 800 years old and one of the area's key centres for adventure sports. This means not just kayaking, but mountain-biking, canyoning, white-water rafting and even skiing in winter. Bovec also has an array of cafés, shops and restaurants, as well as a daily dairy market and helpful tourist office. From here you can get up to the gorgeous Julian Alps (watch out for the windy roads!) and the attractive Triglavski Narodni Park.

Yep, Kamp Liza, with its wonderful access to so much natural beauty and relaxed ambience, is a truly inspiring place to be – kayak or no kayak.

THE UPSIDE Attractive, friendly site on the banks of the Soča: perfect for water babies.
THE DOWNSIDE Facilities are a bit limited.
THE DAMAGE 2 adults plus a tent costs €20; children 6–14 years cost €8 and a family of 4 costs €36 per night.
THE FACILITIES These are a little bit lacking, – there are toilets and hot showers and disabled facilities, but they're limited. There's a children's playground and a washing machine and dryer. A restaurant is under construction for 2009.
FOOD AND DRINK The nearest eating spot is Martinov Hram (00 386 5388 62 14; www.martinov-hram.si) en route to Bovec selling many traditional dishes. Bovec itself (just over a mile/2 km away) has several cafés and restaurants;

noteworthy are Bar Kaverna (00 386 5388 63 35), Bar Skripi (kaninview@gmail.com), pizza/grill Gostilna pod and Lipco (00 386 5389 62 80).
FAMILY FUN You can rent bikes for cycling tours around Bovec, and you can organise white-water activities like canyoning, kayaking and rafting through reception. You can also hike, swim in the pool at Hotel Kanin (00 386 5389 68 80; www.hotel-kanin.com), play tennis (also near Hotel Kanin, €10) or take the kids for a round of golf (there's a course 3 miles/5 km from site, 18 holes €40, 9 holes €25 weekdays).
TREAT YOURSELF To a room at Bovec's only boutique hotel, Dobra Vila (00 386 5389 64 00; www.dobra-vila-bovec.com). There are only 12 rooms, but space for a cinema, library and cellar.

GETTING THERE From Klagenfurt (Austria), take the A2/E55 towards Villach, then the 83, turning left past Hart into the 109 towards the Slovenian border. On the Slovenian side take the 201 to Kranjska Gora, turning right onto the 206. Follow the 206 to Bovec, then follow signs for Kamp Liza. From Ljubljana, take the E61/A2 north, past Bled, merging onto the 201 to Kranjska Gora. Take a right at Kranjska Gora onto the 206, which brings you past the town of Soča and directly to Bovec. Follow signs for Kamp Liza.
OPEN Early-Apr–late-Oct.
IF IT'S FULL Kamp Lazar in Kobarid (00 386 5388 53 33; www.lazar.si) offers a peaceful location, not far from the spectacular sights and sounds of the Kozjak waterfall.

| **Kamp Liza**, Vodenca 4, 5230 Bovec, Slovenia | | |
|---|---|---|
| t | 00 386 5389 63 70 | w | www.camp-liza.com |

# menina

'Welcome', says the laminated sign pinned to the door of the wooden reception. 'If we're not present you can find us in bar...just find nice spot for you and see you later...'

The sign says a lot about Camping Menina. It tells you that the site is laid-back; it suggests that the owners – Jurij and Katja – are open-minded, trusting and probably very busy. And it reveals a beautiful truth – that this is a campsite with a bar.

Indeed, Menina buzzes in the way a campsite should. It's a wonderfully sprawling place that has developed slowly and organically within a section of natural forest in Slovenia's striking Upper Savinja Valley. Like the region, Menina has retained much of its sylvan charm. Branches flutter flirtatiously in the valley breezes, dapples of sunlight dance on the grassy floor and a silver brook tinkles merrily by. It's the kind of scene that makes you reach immediately for your acoustic guitar.

Though it's divided vaguely into sections – a tipi camp (complete with friendly ponies in an adjacent meadow) lies in one area, a row of comfortable wooden cabins lines another – visitors generally do as the sign says: find a spot wherever looks nicest...and pitch. There are plenty of options; with 180 spots in total Menina tends to have room for everyone, though the site doesn't feel as big as that figure might suggest, due to the haphazard layout.

Menina prides itself on being a thoroughly sociable place. There's a nice, natural lake to gather around instead of a formal swimming pool; an extensive outdoor playground close to the bar/restaurant so you can grab a coffee and chat whilst keeping an eye on the kids; and the staff take a fairly spontaneous approach to organising everything from discos and concerts on the lake to guided tours and excursions.

In the evenings, people hang out at the bar/restaurant, taking advantage of the very decent food (fish, meat and vegetarian dishes on offer) or just to sip a cold beer from the bar. This attitude engenders a broad demographic. Everyone from kids and teens to young families and older folk – an international mix – feel comfortable here, which all makes for a friendly ambience.

As well as tents, you'll notice an abundance of canoes, kayaks, bicycles and climbing gear lying around. The site is perfectly placed to explore not only the gorgeous Upper Savinja Valley, but also the Kamnik-Savinja Alps and the nearby Logarska Dolina

(Logarska Valley). The Upper Savinja Valley is in total over 21 miles (35 km) long and, as well as the River Savinja, it also boasts the Dreta – double-bubble on the water-sports front. Unsurprisingly, then, swimming and kayaking are popular here, and since it tends to rain at least once a week in the valley, rafting is, too.

If you are an enthusiastic hiker you'll love the surrounding mountains, which offer a multitude of paths and mountain-biking treks, some including overnight stays in huts. The site can arrange tours and supply maps, and it also caters for more extreme interests such as canyoning and paragliding.

Slovenia's diminutive but cosmopolitan capital, Ljubljana, is just an hour's drive away (50 miles/80 km). Whilst you may be hell-bent on getting away from city life, if you haven't seen this charming city before, you really should. With its stunning architecture, alluring history plus a multitude of cool boutiques and hip coffee shops, it's still a world away from Menina's feel-good idyll but is a complementary delight all the same.

THE UPSIDE Buzzing site set in a beautiful natural valley.
THE DOWNSIDE You need your own vehicle and the facilities are a bit rickety.
THE DAMAGE In low season it's €15 for 2 adults plus a tent. Kids aged 5–15 cost €3.50. A family of 4 costs €22. In peak season it's €18 for 2 adults plus a tent and kids are €5. Kids under 4 are free.
THE FACILITIES The toilets and showers are a bit of a let-down (adequate but ancient) but everything else is tip-top. The children's playground is comprehensive (swings, slide, covered sand-pit, trampoline), the reception and bar serve cold beer and hot food, and washing machines and bike hire are available at reception.
FOOD AND DRINK The onsite restaurant is open every night and sells meat, fish and vegetarian dishes, usually with a local spin. You can order fresh breads from reception, and also buy salami, cheese, butter and jam. The nearest shop and bakery is just 300 metres from the campsite; just over a mile (2 km) away are 2 self-service shops. For a culinary treat try Raduha (00 386 3838 40 00; www.raduha.com). It's 9 miles (15 km) away in the village of Luče, and serves delightful local dishes under the 'slow food' banner.
FAMILY FUN Topolšica (9 miles/15 km) is a thermal resort with 5 pools (indoors and outdoors), toboggans and waterslides. The site can organise rafting and canyoning for families, and also has regular children's entertainers and playground attendants onsite. An hour away, in Mežica, there's a mountain-bike park (00 386 2870 30 60; www.mtbpark.com) with a plethora of trails and routes, including rides through mineral caves.
TREAT YOURSELF Get hot and sweaty in the sauna at Sunny House in Luče (9 miles/15 km away). Romantics can try the 3-hour special, which includes a bottle of champagne and roses.
GETTING THERE From Ljubljana take the direction Maribor. Around 34 miles (55 km) from Ljubljana, turn left onto the Mozirje–Nazarje road. After about 2 miles (3 km) take the direction Ljubno and follow the signs for Camping Menina.
OPEN Mid-Apr–mid-Nov.
IF IT'S FULL ŠMICA (00 386 3 584 43 30; www.camp-smica.com) is a relaxed and natural recreation camp in Luče, 30 minutes from Menina.

**Camping Menina**, Varpolje 105, 3332 Rečica ob Savinji, Slovenia

| t | 00 3863 583 50 27 | w | www.campingmenina.com |

# glavotok

When the campsite lights are switched off at 11pm, it'll feel like you're in Dalmatian heaven. All you'll hear are the waves softly crashing against the grey stone sea walls of Krk island. All you'll see are the twinkling lights on the island of Cres and the denser illuminations of Rijeka city on the mainland.

It hasn't always been so peaceful in Croatia. Various wars have affected the country's economy, and throughout history numerous countries have jostled for a piece of this Adriatic jewel. Victims of the 1991–2001 Yugoslav Wars (including the civil war that overthrew communism) and the 1999 NATO bombing of Serbia, are countrymen who have had to fight long and hard to reclaim their ancestor's land.

Camp Glavotok's owner Sanjin Barbalić is one such man. It took him seven years, with the help of lawyers, to win back his campsite. Now back in the family, the restaurant is watched over by a portrait of great uncle Dr Anton Milohnić, accused of being a spy and shot on this spot in 1945.

Sanjin's 12-year operation is a model Croatian campsite, and don't people know it. The best views, seen from pitches 263–280 and 327–334, are usually booked a year in advance. To bag one of these spots, aim for a June or late-August visit, otherwise make do with one of the woodland pitches. Jump off the jetty, enroll in diving classes and swim your heart out. At night, it's just you, your book and the softly crashing waves.

THE UPSIDE Croatian hospitality is generally welcoming and here it is as polite and as friendly as you could wish for.
THE DOWNSIDE They have their own sewage operation, which can get a bit whiffy, so ask for a plot away from the sanitation blocks.
THE DAMAGE From 108kn to 206kn per night for 2 adults with a car, depending on the time of year and the pitch. Pets on leads 15–20kn daily.
THE FACILITIES Of the 336 pitches 120 are used by permanent 'leaseholders'. Smart washing facilities. Hot showers (2kn), laundry/drying (20kn), Internet (250kn), basketball and beach volleyball. There are also 4 new mobile homes (sleeping 4–6).
FOOD AND DRINK Pre-order the 3-hour slow-cooked octopus speciality. The onsite restaurant also offers 25 different pizza flavours and has a TV screen showing football or films if it rains.
FAMILY FUN Do a diving course with the onsite dive school (00 385 51 869 289; www.correct-diving.com).
TREAT YOURSELF Combine shopping in Krk town with a little Roman and 4th-century history.
GETTING THERE From Trieste by car, cross the bridge that links to Krk island, heading towards Glavotok. Daily ferries from Lopar on Rab to Krk Town cost 225kn one way with a car, or 72kn per foot passenger (www.splittours.hr).
PUBLIC TRANSPORT Regular buses travel from Trieste to Rijeka, from Rijeka to Krk, then to Brzac, which is just over a mile's (2 km) walk to the campsite. Expect to pay around 300kn for a taxi from Rijeka airport to Glavotok.
OPEN Apr–Sept.
IF IT'S FULL Glavotok is all about the trees, but for a lighter, less-rustic vibe try Camp Bor (Crikvenička 10, 51500 KRK; 00 385 51 221 581; www.camp-bor.hr).

**Auto Camp Glavotok**, Glavotok 4, 51511 Malinska, Krk, Croatia

t  00 385 51 862 117  w  www.kamp-glavotok.hr

# straško

Most of the year, the sheep on Pag island outnumber the residents three-to-one. Until the summer, that is, when thousands of Croatians hit Novalja. Not called the Croatian Ibiza for nothing, Novalja's Zrće beach is home to three open-air dance venues, where the music never stops. Buses run regularly to and from the campsite, so dancing 24 hours a day, every day of the week, is a lure for many young campers.

This site isn't only great for party-people; the family facilities are just as appealing. A kids' club will take yours off your hands whenever you need a siesta, and there are numerous playgrounds and games rooms to run amok in throughout the site. But if screaming children are the antithesis of your dream holiday, just decamp to the mile-long naturist section to skinny-dip in the silky seas in peace. New arrivals are driven around the site in a buggy so they can choose a spot. Front pitches under the pines offer great ocean views, but just be aware that they'll also amplify the early-morning clamour of beachside excitement. Anyone after greater privacy parks near the entrance at the top left, under the ancient Dalmatian oaks.

The narrow sunbathing strip won't win this campsite any best-beach accolades, but you'll find you're not short of alternatives, since Pag boasts the longest coastline in the Adriatic. By servicing a variety of demographics, you're guaranteed to find a truly varied clientele here – from frazzled ravers to frazzled parents, and all the frazzled bits in between.

THE UPSIDE There's something for everyone – 24-hour party-people, families and naturists.
THE DOWNSIDE The campsite looks like a big sandy car park; you may have to hunt hard for a pretty spot.
THE DAMAGE For 2 adults and a tent it costs 76.22–152.44kn per night. You can hire mobile homes (sleeping 4–5) for 281.20–777kn per night.
THE FACILITIES Across the 140-acre site there are 400 pitches, each with electricity points and TV connections. Plus, there's a bakery, supermarket, restaurants, bars, bike and scooter hire, souvenirs, gas petrol, sports courts, Internet, mini-golf, 12 shower blocks and even a pet shower.
FOOD AND DRINK Salty sheep's cheese is the local delicacy. For fish, spend an evening in a restaurant built like a boat at Straško's Starac i more ('The Old Man and the Sea'; Braće Radić; 00 385 53 662 423).
FAMILY FUN Hire a banana boat or, for older kids, a jet-ski.
TREAT YOURSELF To an 'exotic' massage in the onsite beauty parlour (open 9am–9pm).
GETTING THERE From Zadar drive over the Pag bridge 16 miles (26 km) away from the magistrala motorway and keep going straight. Or, from the mainland, board a ferry at Prižna (110kn one-way) to connect to Žigljen on the island.
PUBLIC TRANSPORT From Zadar 3 buses run every day (it's a 90-minute journey).
OPEN Apr–Oct.
IF IT'S FULL Croatians call Lopar on the neighbouring island Rab 'paradise'; it's home to one of Croatia's few sandy beaches (pictured), which explains why it's so busy. Campsite San Marino (00 385 51 66 77 88; www.imperial.hr).

**Kamp Straško**, Novalja, Otok Pag, Croatia

| t | 00 385 53 663 381 | w | www.turno.hr |

# mala milna

Croatia might be a top summer destination amongst younger Brits, but for the wealthy Croatians, the ones who can afford holidays, the island of Hvar is the place to be. Of the country's five million population, around 10 per cent of them travel across the waters to top up their tans in the swankiest French-Riviera-style resorts every year.

Top-end restaurants and bars and bijou designer hotels fill the coastal towns. Not surprisingly, the cost of living on this island is high: a coffee can cost twice as much as on the mainland. But you can hang out with the jet set without the price tag if you camp at Mala Milna. It's so much better than paying over the odds for a tacky apartment or chancing your luck with one of the hawkers who meet people off the ferries.

Past guests have raved about Mala Milna. Efficiency here happens behind the scenes; no one ever seems to answer the phone, but bookings are promptly confirmed by email. Simple to find from the Stari Grad ferry port, on the road to Hvar Town and on the edge of a well-signposted bay, it's attractively tucked in amongst a thicket of trees. A track separates the raised camping levels from the sea, whilst a few lucky camper vans get to park right alongside the water's edge. Cars are parked within easy reach of pitches

without spoiling the view and the enveloping woods help to keep temperatures bearable for anyone sleeping under canvas.

It's worth coming to Mala Milna for the exclusive beaches alone. Many campers are willing to put up with the not-so-clean facilities here in return for this fabulous, affordable location a pebble's throw away from the inviting water. Although perhaps it's not the ideal site for young families; on the other hand, the fact that sewage isn't pumped into the sea meets the approval of most ecologically minded wayfarers.

Many campers pitch up at Mala Milna on their island-hopping journey to the breathtaking Peljesac Peninsular or before retreating to the beachside campsites on the mainland between Omiš and Brela.

Happily for those who don't fancy hiring a car, staying close to camp is easy. There's the choice of two small pebble beaches – Mala Milna and Vela Milna – on either side of the campsite. The restaurants open as soon as the first guest arrives, so you've not got to travel far from your towel for any food or drink, either. And spending lazy days on the beach will help preserve energy for the impressive four-hour walk to Hvar Town to experience its moneyed glamour. There is a bus stop next to the site, but the service can be sparse (sometimes you just can't squeeze on, because the seats are full), so be willing to explore the coastal paths on foot. Yes, you can smell the money in Hvar but you'll find the scenery equally priceless.

After driving out the 13th-century pirates who landed along Dalmatian shorelines and looted whatever they could, the islanders were encouraged to move closer to the sea. Malo Grablje is one of their former abandoned villages and since it opened to

the public in 2005 it has fast become one of the island's major attractions. Give yourself the night off cooking and set off in the early evening (armed with a torch for the short walk back home later) to enjoy some simple, atmospheric home-cooking at the popular restaurant of Stori komin.

*Condé Nast Traveller* magazine once named Hvar as one of the 10 most beautiful islands in the world. This campsite is your budget-friendly option. To Hvar good facilities or to Hvar not – that is the question.

THE UPSIDE A taste of Hvar, without paying through the (concrete) roof.
THE DOWNSIDE A church bell tolls loudly on the hour every hour from 6am.
THE DAMAGE From 18.10kn for 2 adults with a tent and car; electricity 20–25kn.
THE FACILITIES Virtually non-existent, just 4 showers and 6 toilets; in August only, the owners sell coffee and snacks.
FOOD AND DRINK A week's worth of restaurants line the bay, 2 serving breakfast from 8am. Moli

Onte run by fishermen guarantees the freshest catch (00 385 21 745 025). Stori komin at Malo Grablje is open 4–11pm, May–Oct (00 385 91 527 6408).
FAMILY FUN Swimming and ice creams – what more does a family need?
TREAT YOURSELF Make like the jet set and hire a private speedboat. The cost is 2,200–3,600kn for 4 hours, depending on where you choose to go, with room for up to 10 people (Avantura; 00 385 92 113 5383; avantura@hi.t-com.hr).

GETTING THERE From Split, catch a ferry (00 385 51 660 111; www.jadrolinija.hr) to Stari Grad (328kn return with a car, or just 42kn per person without), then catch a bus to Hvar Town, disembarking at the turn-off to Mala Milna. The campsite is on the right side of the bay.
OPEN All year, but campers start arriving in May.
IF IT'S FULL Camping Vira (00 385 21 741 803; www.suncanihvar.com/auto-camp-vira-hvar), just under 4 miles (6 km) north, is a larger, more expensive campsite, with clean washing facilities.

**Auto Camp Mala Milna**, Mala Milna bb, 21450 Hvar, Croatia

| t | 00 385 21 643 531 | w | www.hvar.hr/mala-milna |

# pod maslinom

The Croatian word for 'sea' is *more*. Which seems apt when it's permanently glistening beside you on the 4,000-mile-long Dalmatian coast. The Adriatic Sea provides Croatia with its biggest income (from tourism, not fishing; the local fisherman with their tiny boats are no competition for the huge Italian vessels on the other side of the water). But before you imagine these shores to be a mecca of sandy beaches, a quick word in your ear: Croatia is a rather rocky, pebbly paradise.

Simply do as the natives do and throw down your beach towel on any spare bit of sea wall, concrete jetty or pebbly cove you can find. Such a free-for-all mentality means that everyone can get a spot, at any time of day. If this sounds too far removed from your personal comfort zone, wait until you see the incredibly azure-crystal bays where sea horses dance on the waves like sparkling diamonds. You'll be sure to change your attitude. This country defines the word 'picturesque' and sunning yourself under its craggy cliffs in the mid-30°C heat is a heavenly pastime that is hard to beat.

To reach this patch of Croatia you can fly into Dubrovnik and catch three buses to reach the coastal road (it's a lot easier than it sounds). Better still, arrive on a no-frills morning flight to Split, then take the scenic five-hour bus ride southwards along the coast. Grab a seat on the right-hand-side of the coach and, from your elevated view, be prepared for the visual assault of beautiful bays on every bend.

Right beside the bus stop at Orašac is Autocamp Pod Maslinom. Gently starting its descent to sea level, this hilltop campsite has been a labour of love for the owner, Božo, who grew up in this village and could, by all accounts, have been a successful gardener. His conversion of an olive-tree jungle into an appealing landscaped, limestone-walled holiday ground is an enchanting find.

Whatever size wheels you arrive on (bike, motorbike, car or bus) you can set up camp in the spacious privacy of the top, flat sections at Pod Maslinom. Down past the pristine washing blocks is a woody area that offers shade and sound-proofing from the traffic above. There's room for 250 guests here, but they usually only allow 30–35 tents or motor homes in at any one time, so it never feels too busy.

The limits on numbers means that the vibe feels inclusively laid-back. Inside a reception cabin, which is manned by the duty manager along with any number of village friends who happen to drop by, there are ice creams and drinks for sale. Follow the road until it ends at a viewing platform; it's a great spot to sit and idly watch the boats ferry people along their life paths in between the three small Elafiti islands opposite.

Most Croatian campsites are within a stone's throw of a beach. Here, that stone is falling down down down, since there is a steep hill to a cove accessed only along a stony ridge. Tiny tots will deem this hill to be nothing short of a mountain, and pushing a pram up is not an option, unless you're super-fit. However, any efforts will be rewarded with a private beach, offering you a bay to call your own. You can swim easy here knowing that

without any buildings nearby, there is no sewage – the sea is as clean as clean can be.

Offsite, you'll want to check out the UNESCO World Heritage City of Dubrovnik. It'll become glaringly obvious why it was once a vital port of call amongst European glitterati and nobility. Modern campers on a budget will be equally fascinated by the city's Renaissance, Gothic and Baroque architectural mix, all framed by the shimmering ocean.

And, should you wish to see even more *more*, then wend your way back to Split by ferry, for a smashing view of Croatia's coastline.

# dionysus

In mythical days gone by, the final leg of Odysseus' journey shipwrecked him on the peaceful island of the Phaeacians, where the kindly princess Nausicaa took him to her palace to tell his tale, before letting him set sail on to the island of Ithaca. Nowadays, that same island is commonly known as Corfu, but you can still find the same gentle hospitality there.

This Ionian island became a major player in Greek affairs because of its handy location in the Mediterranean and when you are ambling through the old town's sandy neo-classical buildings you'll be sure to feel the breath of history touching your cheek. Well, Corfu's seen a fair few tourists since the late sixties, but you can still catch a glimpse of the Greece of that era by taking random turns off the main drag. All sorts of time-stands-still scenes greet you – from the crumbling, washing-strung piazza to an octogenarian bedecked in black, measuring out her years with a string of beads. The real Greece is never very far away.

Corfu actually means 'peaks' and Corfu's Old Town is sandwiched between two natural promontories on which stand two mighty fortresses, strong enough to repel the aggression of five Ottoman sieges. If you get tired of drinking frappés in the stylish cafés or haggling over evil eyes and alabaster gods, there's a rich mix of options to take your interest. Be it water sports, walking, museum-hopping, monastery-peeping or just basking on the beach, Corfu is a large island and you can easily lose yourself in the flower-filled meadows, crags and secret, hidden coves, leaving the hustle and bustle (if the Greeks have such a thing) of the resorts far behind you.

Five and a half miles (9 km) out of Corfu Old Town and a mere five minutes from chock-full, glistening-bodied Dassia beach, is Dionysus Camping. If this is a name to conjure up images of near-naked nymphs popping grapes into one another's mouths to the accompaniment of a lyre, you may, perhaps, be a little disappointed. But in every other aspect this serene spot, set in a tiered 400-year-old olive grove, more than justifies its evocative name.

The facilities offered at the campsite are excellent. There are two pristine shower blocks with hot water round the clock, a handsome bar overlooking a good-sized swimming pool, plus you have the choice of pitching your tent in the terraced meadows or – and these are terrific value for couples – taking one of Dionysus's 50 well-appointed Polynesian-style *cabanas* or *tikis*.

The site is in a former olive grove run by Nikos, a warm and welcoming manager. A true Corfiot, he knows the island like the back of his hand. As well as having a wealth of printed info for your perusal, he can point you in the direction of the best beaches and charter a boat to take you up to the north of the island – or pretty much anything else that your heart desires.

During the busy months of July and August the site's bar and restaurant host traditional Greek dancers and are buzzing with a Babel of languages. The atmosphere's wonderfully convivial and lends itself to friendly and lengthy conversations and the formation of fond bonds. So, in that respect, Corfu's hospitality is just like days of old.

But, unlike solo traveller Odysseus, be careful you don't find yourself on the back of a Honda Goldwing headed for a new life in Munich with a big bloke called Hans.

THE UPSIDE Warm hosts, peaceful settings and near lovely Corfu Old Town.
THE DOWNSIDE The beach nearby is a little on the rocky side (but sandy Dassia beach is just a moped-ride away).
THE DAMAGE Two sharing a tent can expect to pay between €13 and €16 per night, season-dependent. The quirky *tiki* huts are great value at €18–23 per night.
THE FACILITIES These are good and include a communal cooking area, fridge, BBQ pits, Internet and laundry facilities plus mini-mart, bar/ restaurant and Olympic-sized swimming pool.
FOOD AND DRINK Earthy Restaurant Rouvas (00 30 266 103 1182) just around the corner from M&S in the Old Town, is a well-kept secret (the meatballs are life-affirming). The magical Starenio Bakery near the Town Hall Square on Guilford Street is fab for afternoon coffee and croissants.
FAMILY FUN Take your own odyssey on the Kalypso Star (00 30 266 104 6525), a glass-bottomed-boat experience that takes in the underwater delights of the island's marine life.
TREAT YOURSELF For classic, romantic, al fresco dining head to San Giacomo (00 30 266 103 0146) in Town Hall Square.
GETTING THERE The No. 7 bus from San Rocco Square in Corfu town stops outside Dionysus every half hour. From Corfu port follow the main coastal road (to the right) north until, after 5 miles (8 km), at Tsavros junction, turn right. Just over half a mile (1 km) on you'll find Dionysus.
OPEN Early-Apr–late-Oct.
IF IT'S FULL Karda Beach Camping (00 30 266 109 3595; www.kardacamp.gr) just up the road is clean, shaded and near Dassia beach.

**Dionysus Camping**, Dassia, Corfu, Greece

| | t | 00 30 266 109 1417 | w | www.dionysuscamping.gr |

# enjoy-lichnos

Parga's whitewashed, Venetian-style buildings huddle on the higgledy-piggledy hillside, forming an amphitheatre of fragrant bougainvillea, magical alleyways and enticing trinket shops tumbling in profusion down to the bay. Like nearby Corfu, the town is well known for its cosmopolitan atmosphere and ultra-friendly locals. Because it's so close to Igoumenitsa Port for ferries to Italy, the little town echoes with a cacophony of Mediterranean languages and has long been a favourite of the Brit pack.

With its freaky pillars of rock jutting from the emerald sea, the little church-crowned island of Panagia in the bay and the sentinel ruins of a Byzantine fort on the hill, the place is beyond romantic. And it's not just a pretty face either; you can laze away the days on a sandy beach, indulge in some water-skiing or exercise those calves in a little bargain-hunting or museum-hopping. But here's another question for the oracle – why so many hat shops in Parga? Maybe there's a multi-headed, multiplying Hydra, or two, concealed about the place, with an insatiable headwear habit.

A short distance south of Parga you'll find Enjoy-Lichnos Camping. If there was a

*Cool Camping* award for the friendliest campsite welcome, Lichnos's manager, Georgia, would surely win hands-down. This peaceful haven, set within an olive grove, has a sugar-fine pebbled beach just a stone's throw away and is hemmed in on one side by rose-coloured cliffs and on the other by a tangle of cypress and olive trees. The water is unbelievably clear – you can see the sandy bottom when you're floating on the surface. What's more, the beach's gentle incline makes it a safe place for children to splash and paddle.

Enjoy-Lichnos is well catered for, having a friendly al fresco bar and a sizeable mini-mart and restaurant in the main building. It's *so* seventies in style you're convinced Leonard Rossiter and Joan Collins must have filmed a Cinzano ad here. Pitches are equally close to the gently lapping sea in an RV-free field festooned with tiny amber lights; by night they look like fireflies as you cross the little wooden bridge through the pergola into the magical meadow. The 500-year-old olive trees provide much-needed shade from the blistering sun of the summer and the very occasional rain.

Greek legends are at every turn and, if you're that way inclined, you can hire a catamaran, pedalo or kayak and explore the famous cave of Aphrodite just around the bay – apparently she used to bathe here. Or take the ferry that putters to Lichnos beach.

Georgia speaks great English and will happily organise trips of your choice. If you fancy a bit of self-propelled time travel, whizz back a few thousand years to the days of legend by visiting the creepy ruins of the Necromantion – a 2,500-year-old oracle of the dead. Half an hour's drive south of Parga, this hilltop haunt is reminiscent of that Tuscan graveyard in *The Omen* in which the pack of Rottweilers tuck into Gregory Peck's forearm.

A short ride across the fertile, chestnut-bordered plain is the turquoise River Acheron. What may now look like a beautiful, eucalyptus-fringed river was once a much-feared tributary of the River Styx, the subterranean route the dead took to Hades. The dead now travel a different route, or so it's said, leaving you in safety to snack on fabulous grilled fish at one of the riverside tavernas before dipping your toes in the glacial blue water.

THE UPSIDE Parga could get arrested for being so beautiful. The campsite is perfectly situated and its staff are genuinely incredibly helpful.
THE DOWNSIDE If you're travelling by bus you'll get dropped at the main road and it's murder on your knees walking down to the site.
THE DAMAGE Two people with a tent will pay €14.40–15.50, season-dependent, paying a further €2.80–3.30 for a car. Electricity costs €4.
THE FACILITIES Two restaurants, mini-mart (freshly baked bread), beach-bar, disabled and baby-changing facilities, first-aid post, tourist advice, immaculate shower and toilet block;

24-hour electricity, kayak and pedalo, water-ski.
FOOD AND DRINK Stroll down Lichnos beach to Coral Restaurant (00 30 268 403 2068). In Parga your choice is more varied.
FAMILY FUN A visit to the Necromantion is the classical equivalent of a Scooby Doo adventure! Finish off with lunch by the icy River Acheron, then head up the trail and ride its rapid currents down the mountain in a natural wet 'n' wild environment.
TREAT YOURSELF To a trip on schooner Captain Hook (00 30 694 488 4597). The cruise begins at Parga, taking in the blue caves and beautiful islands of Antipaxos and Paxos. Adults

are €25, kids €12.50.
GETTING THERE Situated a mile or so (2 km) before Parga, between Igoumentisa and Preveza off the E55. Driving north on the coastal road Enjoy-Lichnos is after Aghia Kyriaki on the left-hand-side. If you find yourself in Parga you've overshot.
PUBLIC TRANSPORT Catch a bus from Preveza bus station (last one is 8pm). Ask the driver to let you out at the top of the winding lane to the site.
OPEN Early-May–end-Sept.
IF IT'S FULL Valtos Camping (00 30 268 403 1287; www.campingvaltos.gr) beside Valtos Beach in Parga is also near a lovely taverna.

**Enjoy-Lichnos Camping**, Parga, Greece

| t | 00 30 26840 31171 | w | www.enjoy-lichnos.net |

# poros beach

Lefkada, neighbouring island to the more famous Ithaki and Kefalonia, is a quiet and authentic little place to plant your trident; at times so bucolic, with its endless meadows, crumbling shepherds' huts and twisting groves, you half expect Pan to be perched in the nearest tree.

Vassiliki, your arrival point on the island, is a pretty waterside village festooned with lights, tavernas and a vibrant spirit. It's a lovely spot to ponder the sage-green smudge of nearby Ithaki before hiring a car and exploring the island. Nine miles (15 km) away from Vassiliki is Poros. A snake-like road slithers past shady groves, dozing horses and somnolent villages on its way down to

Poros' fine-pebbled beach, the air thick with honeysuckle and thyme and the foreground resplendent with fluorescent butterflies. A spit from the water, Poros Beach Camping draws an eclectic mix of visitors (mostly Italian, with the occasional Brit thrown in for good measure).

By day, relax in the shaded comfort of the site's stylish restaurant or just flop on the beach, watching the blue horizon and turquoise sea fight for supremacy. There's no real need to move at all, since you can start your day with fresh bread and honey in the restaurant and finish it off with souvlaki and salad at the nearby Café del Mare come night fall.

THE UPSIDE  This hidden-away gem has a perfect beach, great restaurant and lovely pool.
THE DOWNSIDE  There are no buses to the site, so it's necessary to rent a moped or a car in Vassiliki.
THE DAMAGE  Two adults sharing a tent can expect to pay €17 in low season and €28 July–Aug, with an additional €3 for a car.
THE FACILITIES  There are plenty: a bar, restaurant, shower block/WC (hole in the floor), disabled facilities, post office, first aid, Internet, laundry services and kayak rental.
FOOD AND DRINK  Café del Mare, the nearby

taverna on the beach, is unpretentious and friendly, with a great menu leaning heavily towards seafood, plus a healthy wine selection.
FAMILY FUN  Why not take a trip with Seven Island Cruises (www.sevenislandscruises.gr; €15 per person)? True to their moniker, they will take you around the surrounding 7 islands, including Ithaki, Kefalonia's beautiful port of Fizcardo and Scorpio, exclusively owned by the Onassis dynasty.
TREAT YOURSELF  Ever fancied being a bit of an Ahab, but never got your land-lubber self around to it? Join a 2-day basic course in sailing

with Lantisworld (www.lantisworld.com) in Nidri.
GETTING THERE  There is no direct bus to the campsite (when you descend the mountain lane you'll see why) so your best bet is to hire a moped or car in Vassiliki or catch a cab. From Vassiliki turn right out of town heading for Lefkada, passing Kastri Camping (see IF IT'S FULL) en route. Poros is 9 miles (15 km) away, signposted to the right. Or catch a cab from Nydri 7 miles (11 km) away
OPEN  May–end-Sept.
IF IT'S FULL  Kastri Camping (00 30 264 503 1900; www.camping-kastri.gr) offers plenty of privacy, near a Robinson Crusoe beach.

**Poros Beach Camping**, Poros, Lefkada, Greece

| t | 00 30 264 509 5452 | w | www.porosbeach.com.gr |

# tartaruga

Zakynthos, or Zante, as it's known locally, is one of the more emerald isles in the Ionian Sea. In times gone by it was called 'the Venice of the East' because of its buildings, which resemble something out of a Canaletto painting – you almost feel like casting about for a gondola to take a ride in.

Like many Greek islands its tenure has been mixed and colourful, running through Roman, Ottoman, Byzantine, Turkish and British rulers. The old town of Zante was reduced to rubble in the earthquake of 1953, but luckily the locals loved it enough to do a great restoration job, one that St Dionysios, the island's patron saint, would be justifiably proud of.

Every August the islanders hold a festival to celebrate their patron saint St Dionysios (aka St Dennis). This night-time festival sees the atmosphere charged with Greek Orthodox fervour as the long-deceased, strangely preserved, saint is led through the candle-flickering streets safe and snug in a glass cabinet – rather like an old-fashioned Pope-mobile.

But, before you get stuck into Zakynthos' cultural highlights, you'll be needing to set up camp. If, on hearing Tartaruga Camping's pack of ferocious guard dogs heralding your arrival you think Cerberus is at your heels, be reassured, you couldn't be further from Hades; in fact, you may have just happened upon the Elysian Fields.

Run by Veit and Anna Santner, Tartaruga boasts one of the best views of any campsite in Greece; you can gaze down at the epiphany-inducing sea from the giddy heights of their al fresco restaurant, unblemished but for the odd deserted island and occasional puttering fishing boat.

As if to qualify its pedigree, loggerhead turtles have chosen the turquoise waters beside the campsite as a safe enclave in which to play their mating games. There's a floating platform to swim out to and wait on for the turtles to come, or use Veit's goggles and fins, which he leaves by the rocks for anyone to borrow. There are old diving shots from the seventies pasted on the walls of the basic eaterie, which also doubles as a TV room when there's a sporting event on.

In summer, when the witchy olive trees are crawling with children, there are weekly table-tennis tournaments, with ice cream for the lucky winners. Anna is a brilliant cook – if food is made with love, then Aphrodite has certainly taken up residence in her kitchen. The menu contains whatever Anna brings

back from her daily visit to nearby butchers and fishermen, and you can be sure there'll be plenty to get your taste buds going.

The mainland feels a long way away, even though you can see it just over the water. So, too, do the trampled, over-harvested tourist traps like nearby Laganas. But here on the campsite, amongst the chattering of cicadas, the hypnotic scent of thyme and calm whispering of pine trees, you could easily have travelled back 30 years. And since you're on the island's southern tip you benefit from a much-needed breeze.

When it comes to putting up your tent, you have a considerable choice of pitches. You can try a spot in the shadow of pines, the light around you dappled like a Monet painting; or set up near the beach where a fallen olive tree, bleached whalebone-white by the sun, lies surrounded by sentinel rock sculptures that look as if they've been filched from the Tate Modern.

Zakynthos or Zante, St Dionysios or St Dennis – whichever you prefer, Tartaruga Camping is a tenters' paradise. Come on in, the water's lovely.

THE UPSIDE  Great cuisine and arguably the best view of any campsite in Greece.
THE DOWNSIDE  Not great if you're travelling by public transport. The only option is a taxi and it's mighty expensive.
THE DAMAGE  Two adults sharing a tent can expect to pay €13.80–16.50, depending on season; children under 4 are free. Cars are charged €2.50–2.90.
THE FACILITIES  Clean communal shower block, bakery, limited mini-mart, disabled toilet, al fresco restaurant, TV room, Internet, laundry services, playground and, of course, the beach.

FOOD AND DRINK  You may not want to leave the confines of Tartaruga after tasting Anna's cuisine, but the Village Inn, on the waterfront in Zakynthos Old Town, is good for traditional food.
FAMILY FUN  You can play table tennis, go snorkelling, visit the peacocks or noodle about on the trippy beach before you explore this idyllic island. You can see turtles in the spring/summer.
TREAT YOURSELF  Let Golden Dolphin Tours (00 30 269 508 3248) take you to the Blue Caves and Shipwreck Beach, a heavenly strip of fine sand bordered by high cliffs and finished off with the postcard-esque wreck of an old boat.

GETTING THERE  Zakynthos is the southernmost island in the Ionian Sea; head for Killini port to reach it by ferry. From Zakynthos town it's 8 miles (13 km) to Camping Tartaruga. Head for Keri – there's a sign for Tartaruga followed by a windy lane.
PUBLIC TRANSPORT  There is a bus twice a day. A taxi costs €15–18.
OPEN  April–end-Oct; it is possible to camp between November and March by arrangement.
IF IT'S FULL  Zante Camping (00 30 269 506 1710; www.zanteweb.gr) in Tragiki, 3 miles (5 km) north of Zante Old Town, is a safe bet.

**Tartaruga Camping**, Keri, Zakynthos, Greece

| t | 00 30 269 505 1967 | w | www.tartaruga-camping.com |

# areti

The charming little town of Neos Marmaras is kissed with blue waters and bobbing schooners. On Thursday mornings a fruit-and-veg market bubbles to life by the palm-studded wharf, and it's easy to feel like one of the locals as you marvel doe-eyed at calamari and haggle over your pot of indigenous honey.

Interesting to think, as you gaze out at the distant wooded hills, that 2,500 years ago this was Alexander the Great country. Macedonian people are fiercely proud of this fact, too, so don't be surprised if their grasp of history is greater than the average classics student. If your local hero once ruled half the world before he was 30, you'd probably be the same.

Camping Areti, just 7 miles (11 km) down the road, is sleepier than a *raki*-laced bouzouki player; the pace here is joyfully slow. Its spotless taverna is both welcoming and atmospheric, with locally caught fish sizzling away on the grill to the acoustic accompaniment of crickets and the Aegean lapping right near your table. On a clear morning the distant peak of Mount Olympus beckons you to breakfast with the gods. And if they could relocate, well they'd probably want to plant their trident in these pine-scented waters.

Areti sits amongst acres of mature eucalyptus trees and hibiscus-bordered pathways. You can throw up your tent in various locations, depending what takes your fancy. If you'd like to be near enough to the water to smell the salty air, then pitch up near the sea beside a sugar-sand beach, dramatically screened by gnarled olive trees. For the less watery inclined, head for the back of the meadows for a little more privacy.

If the heat becomes too much, try a night off in one of the Crusoe-style log cabins. There's about a dozen of them scattered across the site, choking in orchids and flora. Inside they're cosy and functional, with a kitchenette, separate double bedroom and WC, with an extra berth that could come in handy for a smaller person.

You'll find that Areti's mini-mart is well-provisioned, plus there's a wealth of amenities including a kids' playground and tennis courts, as well as hidden recesses for cheeky romance and inviting lookout points with benches pointing seaward just begging to be sat on at sundown. It's just the kind of quiet, forgotten patch in which you can regain some sense of yourself without fear of being disturbed by anyone.

If you've had enough introspection and philosophising and are gagging for something more physical, then challenge yourself to the swim to one of the three deserted islands across the cobalt-turquoise-chequered bay. It's a fair old distance, but then it wouldn't be a challenge if it wasn't, would it?

Two and a half thousand years ago, a stubborn little collection of states known as Hellas were about to be disciplined by the Persian Empire. The attacking armada was stayed, albeit briefly, by the alleged sea monsters in the foaming reefs. These days it's a little safer to venture out into the sea. And if you want to see more of the island life beloved of the locals then talk to Giorgos, the softly spoken manager, about chartering an old schooner for the day to take you round the triple peninsulas. Before you know it you'll be hailing everyone with *Yassas* and drinking *ouzo* like a local.

THE UPSIDE With its view, private beaches, distinct cuisine and charming, old-school management, you can't fault it.
THE DOWNSIDE We couldn't find one.
THE DAMAGE €12 per tent per night, €9 per adult, €4.50 per child. A family cabin (sleeping 4) will cost you €60. Prices are lower off-season.
THE FACILITIES There's a mini-mart, kids' playground, launderette, BBQ area, volleyball and tennis courts, twin beaches, restaurant and immaculate toilet block.
FOOD AND DRINK Neos Marmaras has plenty of good places to eat. For freshly caught fish, head

for the Bays Restaurant (00 30 237 507 1291; www.sithonian.gr) on the waterfront.
FAMILY FUN Jet-ski and windsurfing are available on demand. Nearby Nireas Diving School (www.nireas.gr) can be contacted for local dives.
TREAT YOURSELF Charter an old boat (it takes up to 30 people) plus a captain to take you on a trip around the triple peninsulas. It costs about €25 per person and food is included.
GETTING THERE From Thessaloniki head for the Sithonian Peninsula via Neo Modenia. Kassandra is the first peninsula; avoid this and push on to Sithonia, the second. Seven miles

(11 km) beyond the turn-off for Neo Marmaras you'll find the sign for Camping Areti. It's nestled at the bottom of a pine-clad road.
PUBLIC TRANSPORT On arrival at Thessaloniki head for Chalkidiki bus station to catch a bus to the Sithonian Peninsula. Make sure you're headed for Sykia or Neo Marmaras and let the driver know where you're going so he can drop you off. If you end up in Neo Marmaras then you'll have to get a 10-minute cab to the campsite.
OPEN Early-May–early-Oct.
IF IT'S FULL Camping Stavros (00 30 237 507 1975) is around the corner, with its own beach.

| | **Camping Areti**, Neos Marmaras, Chalkidiki, Greece | | |
|---|---|---|---|
| | t | 00 30 237 507 1573 | w | www.camping-areti.gr |

# chrissa

Climbing the scarily steep, twisty road towards the famous oracle at Delphi is an enchanting experience, and you're in excellent company, too. People from the times of Heracles to Alexander the Great have made the same trip during the last 3,000 years. By night, the mountain eyrie of Delphi village glitters like jewels heaped at the feet of the mythic Pythia (clairvoyant crones) in the hope of soliciting a favourable reading. This might be somewhat different from checking out your horoscopes in the evening paper.

Myth has it that a serpent or dragon called Python once lived at Delphi before being slain by Apollo, the sun god. Thereafter, for nine months of the year he uttered prophecies by whispering through a laurel bush. A rich Athenian family built a magnificent columned temple in his honour and people came from far and wide to seek answers to their problems. Perching over the hallucinogenic fumes billowing from a fissure within the mountain, the Pythia (withered clairvoyant crones) were thrown into ecstatic raptures – think Russell Grant in drag – whereby they were able to divine the future.

The amazing ruins are more than worth the arduous climb; you almost feel as if you're in a Ray Harryhausen movie with plasticated Minotaurs and Cyclops heading your way. And if you make it as far as the stadium at the top, you'll rightly deserve a refreshing sorbet at the *gelaterie* by the ruin's entrance. Crouch down in the narrow chamber of Apollo's temple and mouth your questions into the ghostly darkness. Like, why do our Japanese friends wear Darth Vader macs and gloves in 30°C heat? And why is the euro so supernaturally strong against the pound? Answers came there none.

Four miles down the road in Chrisso village, Chrissa Camping boasts an unfeasibly beautiful view of the silvery-green olive plain below, broken only occasionally by spears of cypress trees. The site's quirky central building could be a Bond villain's hide-out. In fact, there's an almost palpable seventies vibe here – it's quite easy to imagine Roger Moore in a safari suit popping up amongst its geometric lines, armed with a quip and a Beretta.

The balconied restaurant, reeling in bright-orange orchids, is the perfect place to rest your history-embattled calves, nurse a Mythos beer and watch one of the most divine sunsets in Greece: the light turning pastel pink and salmon as the sun goes down over waterside Ieta village. The food complements the view, with a simple traditional Greek menu plus some Italian dishes thrown in for good measure. You can stay in one of four Serengeti-style *cabanas* (they can sleep four), whilst for all you tent-purists there are more terraced pitches than the proverbial hanging gardens. Just be warned, though, that with the gravel earth harder than a Minotaur's hoof, you'll need a pretty sturdy mallet in order to hammer those tent pegs in.

Facilities are good, with a decent mini-mart and good-sized shower block, plus laundry and Internet. If you need any information about anything at all, the best source is Chrissa's manager, Katerina. Her English

is terrific and she's full of ideas about how to make your stay a memorable one. Give yourself some time to cool off in Chrissa's sparkling swimming pool before taking a trip to explore the diminutive two-tiered village of Delphi, which clings precariously to the mountainside. The village itself holds plenty of other less-arduous diversions in the form of boutiques and restaurants, their windows dominated by handsome-browed verdigris gods.

High up in the clouds here, you may even start some of your own whisperings – here's one suggestion: Chrissa Camping is, like the oracle, one of a kind.

THE UPSIDE One of the most stunning views in Greece. Classic.
THE DOWNSIDE The campsite could be a little closer to the ruins, to save your legs.
THE DAMAGE Two adults sharing a tent cost €18–20 per night, depending on season. Family-size cabins cost €60–65 per night (€80 in Aug).
THE FACILITIES Decent mini-mart, launderette, good-sized shower block, plenty of pitches on different levels, each with a terrific view. Swimming pool, baby pool, kids' play area, nearby tennis courts and basketball court. Internet.

FOOD AND DRINK The campsite's restaurant is great, but you've come here for the ruins, let's face it. And Delphi village does not disappoint gastronomically either. Stop at one of a clutch of tasteful tavernas (see TREAT YOURSELF).
FAMILY FUN Visit the ruins and museum of Delphi, with its artefacts from the golden days of Greece. Or head to the beach in neighbouring Itea, 10 miles (16 km) across the olive grove.
TREAT YOURSELF Head for Epikouros (00 30 226 508 3250), the most stylish restaurant in town. This well-situated watering hole serves up

wild boar and onions as its house speciality.
GETTING THERE By car: take the E962 towards Livadeia, then head to Itea. Chrisso village is below Delphi.
PUBLIC TRANSPORT Buses from Athens travel directly to Delphi and can drop you outside the site if you ask the driver.
OPEN All year.
IF IT'S FULL Apollon Camping (00 30 226 508 2750; www.apolloncamping.gr) on the outskirts of Delphi has good facilities, great views and its own swimming pool.

**Chrissa Camping**, Delphi, Greece

| | t | 00 30 226 508 2050 | w | www.chrissacamping.gr |

# nicholas

Welcome to the Peloponnese, land of orange groves, myths and Heracles. If you need your fix of ruins and classic tales, this place has a higher concentration than anywhere else in Greece. It's spooky going past the ruins of ancient Tiryns – the dreaded palace where Heracles had to return on completing each labour, only to be given another.

You'll see the sign for Tiryns as you head towards sleepy Epidavros. For most of the year this water-lapped town is a somnolent tableau of old-timers flicking their worry beads at the end of the jetty. Then comes July and the population explodes with the fireworks of the annual festival of theatre; culture vultures from across the globe come to witness the spectacle of Aeschylus, Euripides and Sophocles performed Greek-style in the two ancient theatres. Of the two theatres, the largest is amongst the best-preserved in Greece and has hosted some famous names and performances during the 20th century. Built in the 4th century BC in amphitheatre style, the acoustics are astonishing; actors can play to 15,000 people at a time and everyone can hear a pin drop, even from the very back.

A 10-minute wander from the town, through a shady grove, past the small theatre, and along the beach, and you'll find Nicholas Camping. Formerly an orange grove, its mulberry and orange trees provide plump natural arbours in a series of enchanting, sleepy hollows. And whilst the site might lack tennis courts, swimming pools and the sophistication of some campsites, Nicholas more than makes up for it with its luscious setting. How many campsites have you been to in which you can pluck a ripe orange from the leafy canopy then plop into a silk-calm bay a stone's-throw away?

Nicholas is run by husband-and-wife team, Christina and Yiannis Gikas. Christina left the hubbub of Toronto to re-discover her Peloponnesian roots, and looking out through the palm-studded gardens, taking in the orange-scented air as you gaze at the nearby sea, it's easy to see why. She can organise visits to the theatre and diving trips for you.

If you fancy yourself as a bit of a Jacques Cousteau, then go exploring scuba-style. Just down the beach there are the remains of a sunken city, the victim of an earthquake and subsequent tsunami in AD 175. Follow the curve of the beach away from town, don your mask and weave past sea urchins with Sid Vicious hairstyles lurking on the squat underwater ruins. You never know, you might just find something exciting; there are over 1,000 shipwrecks in Aegean and Ionian waters, and potentially so much hidden treasure that most wrecks are off-limits to commercial divers.

If you need more than underwater entertainment, take yourself off to nearby Nafplio – a beautiful old town choking on Venetian architecture, bougainvillea and tamarind trees. The shops are tasteful and sometimes intriguingly quirky, with narrow little walkways for you to escape from the sun in glorious midday shadows. Take your pick from half a dozen great restaurants, then after lunch work off the calories with a brisk walk up to the Palamidi (the fortress ruins) and a refreshing dip in the sea on the other side of the hill. Nafplio has become something of a favourite with Athenian urbanites. If you spend an afternoon here you'll soon see why they like to keep it a secret from the package crowd.

THE UPSIDE The proximity to the beach (any closer and you'd be underwater).
THE DOWNSIDE Because the site is a bit more intimate than most (100 pitches), in high season you'll have to try that bit harder to find a spot away from the RV gang.
THE DAMAGE Two people sharing a tent will pay €16 –20 per night, depending on season.
THE FACILITIES There's a clean shower block, BBQ, mini-mart, Internet, 24-hour hot water and it's near to a bus stop.

FOOD AND DRINK The Mouria Restaurant, next door, is a favourite haunt for visiting actors, who sit beneath the mulberry tree practising lines between mouthfuls of moussaka. The menu leans heavily towards seafood. The food is fresh and delivered with a smile.
FAMILY FUN Head for the theatre, lunch by the pretty harbour in town or drive to Nafplio for a taste of Aegean chic.
TREAT YOURSELF Epidive Center (00 30 275 304 1236; www.epidive.com) offers dives at all

levels, plus introductory courses for beginners.
GETTING THERE If you're driving from Athens take the E94 motorway and drive via Argos and Nafplio. Then follow signs for Nea Epidavros.
PUBLIC TRANSPORT If you're taking public transport you'll have to change at Nafplio and catch a local bus.
OPEN Apr–Oct.
IF IT'S FULL Camping Bekas (00 30 275 309 9930; www.bekas.gr) at the bottom of the beach has 130 pitches in an old olive grove.

**Nicholas Camping**, Epidavros, Peloponnese, Greece

| t | 00 30 275 304 1218 | w | www.nicolasgikas.gr |

# antiparos

Clambering off the boat in the whitewashed harbour of this diminutive Aegean jewel you can hardly believe your eyes. Everything you see is Greeker than Greek: old fishermen with crinkly faces and Charles Bronson eyes, cats stretching in the shadows, fruit spilling from colourful crates, plus an azure sky pure enough to melt the heart of a Mississippi lifer. Welcome to Antiparos, possibly Greece's best-kept secret.

It would be breaking a promise to Theo Kalygros, son of the owner of Camping Antiparos, to disclose who's been quietly buying up land here to hide away from the paps. But let's just say that Antiparos has attracted its own pantheon of A-list deities.

The central, pedestrian-only street is a curious mix of tavernas, stylish cafés, home-made ice-cream parlours and boutiques offering anything from jewellery made just for you to – curiously – fairies. There's no explaining it, but these now-you-see-them-now-you-don't little winged people pop up on every bougainvillea-clad corner.

Wandering around the ruins of the old castle, which intimately hug the town's backstreets, you get a chance to soak up the history of this proud idyll. Back in the 15th century the island fell prey to pirates, who used it as a base, so the locals built a near-impregnable squat castle to keep them out – yes, even Cap'n Jack Sparrow is banned. Defending themselves against a more contemporary nemesis during World War II, Antiparians were amongst the first Greeks to pledge themselves to the cause of the Resistance, and there's still a sense of proud independence today.

No less enchanting is Camping Antiparos. Pitch up under a tangled canopy of cedars or find a secret spot in the site's bamboo field. OK, so the facilities are a touch basic but, to be honest, that's all part of the place's charm.

Theo can show you grainy footage of music festivals and football matches at the site back in the seventies; an endless summer of music and flares, afros and super-8 glare. Maybe the stoned ghosts of those hippies are still lurking somewhere in the ether or gazing up at the enormous 400-year-old giant cedar twisting its stairway to heaven, but music and free-spiritedness is still a feature, with Theo organising festivals and impromptu jam sessions for visiting troubadours.

There are three main beaches on Antiparos: the nearest is to be found through a weave-world of paths running through the dunes and vanilla-scented scrub. And if you like to don your nothing in particular for beachwear, then you're in luck – this first beach is of the naturist variety. But if people decked out in their birthday suits give you the willies, then head for the beach beyond the windmill, just past the edge of town.

Camping Antiparos' restaurant is a honey-pot of home-made indulgence (try the wonderful squid stuffed with rice and raisins), so a stay without a night or two sampling their fare would be remiss. Kindly Mrs Kalygros, when she's not alchemising delicacies to melt your taste buds, is usually found benignly knitting. However, she's well known for secretly pressing home-made biscuits into your hot, sticky palm, too; it would be rude to refuse, wouldn't it? It's also a tranquil place to sit and chat with the eclectic mix of visitors, or simply to sit and listen, like the Greeks do, to the melancholic chords of the bouzouki.

THE UPSIDE The campsite oozes 'escape' and the management couldn't be more friendly.
THE DOWNSIDE It's a long ferry ride to get to Paros (about 4 hours from Piraeus (Athens).
THE DAMAGE Depending on the season, expect to pay €10–15 each for 2 people with a tent.
THE FACILITIES Myriad options for pitches: under the trees, in the reed fields…Launderette, 24-hour hot water, mini-mart, bar, self-catering facilities, plus what must be some of the best home-cooking in Greece.
FOOD AND DRINK For traditional seafood, which probably swam past you earlier in the day, head to Taverna Yorgis (00 30 228 406 1362) on the main street.
FAMILY FUN Check out the nightly open-air Cinema Oliaros (00 30 228 406 1717) up on Mr Pantelakis's rooftop; it's a wonderful way to watch your favourite films. Sea-kayaking is available through the aptly named Argonauts Blue Sea Kayaking (00 30 228 406 1364; www.argonautsblue.com).
TREAT YOURSELF Charter the old schooner, Alexandros, helmed by Captain Antonis (00 30 22840 61273). The boat takes you around the neighbouring island and hidden bays and includes a BBQ lunch. It's €50 per adult and €25 per child.
GETTING THERE Take the 4-hour ferry (€29) from Piraeus (Athens) to Paros, then catch the 5-minute shuttle boat to Antiparos at the tip of the island. The campsite is a 10-minute walk from the harbour.
OPEN May–end-Sept.
IF IT'S FULL There are 200 pitches, so it's unlikely, but book ahead since Camping Antiparos is the only option on the island.

| **Camping Antiparos**, Antiparos, Cyclades Islands, Greece | | |
|---|---|---|
| t | 00 30 228 406 1221 | w | www.camping-antiparos.gr |

# useful words

| ENGLISH | PORTUGUESE | SPANISH | FRENCH | DUTCH |
|---------|-----------|---------|--------|-------|
| campsite | parque de campismo | un camping | un camping | camping |
| pitch | alvéolo | una parcela | un emplacement | kampeerplaats |
| large/small/family tent | tenda grande/pequena/familiar | una tienda grande/pequeña/familiar | une grande/petite tente/tente de famille | kleine/grote/familie tent |
| facilities | instalações/serviços | unas instalaciones | le bloc sanitaire | badkamers |
| toilets | casas-de-banho | unos aseos | les toilettes | toiletten |
| showers | duches | unas duchas | les douches | douches |
| washing-up/laundry sink | lavandaria/tanque | un fregadero/lavadero | un bac lave vaisselle/lave linge | afwas/wasplek |
| drinking water | água potável | agua potable | l'eau potable | drinkbare water |
| beer | cerveja | una cerveza | une bière | bier |
| wine | vinho | un vino | du vin | wijn |
| sleeping bag | saco-cama | un saco de dormir | un sac de couchage | slaapzak |
| campfire | lareira | una hoguera | un feu de camp | kampvuur |
| train | comboio | un tren | un train | trein |
| car | carro | un coche | une voiture | auto |
| petrol (unleaded) | gasolina (sem chumbo) | gasolina (sin plomo) | l'essence (sans plomb) | benzine (ongelood) |
| diesel | gasóleo | diesel | diesel | diesel |
| bicycle | bicicleta | una bici | un vélo | fiets |
| left | esquerda | izquierda | à gauche | links |
| right | direita | derecha | à droite | rechts |
| straight on | em frente/a direito | todo recto | tout droit | rechtdoor |

# useful words

| GERMAN | ITALIAN | SLOVENIAN | CROAT | GREEK |
|---|---|---|---|---|
| Campingplatz | un campeggio | kamp | kamp | Κάμπινγκ (Camping) |
| Zeltplatz | una piazzola | postaviti | postaviti, razapeti | Θέση για σκηνή (Thési gia skiní) |
| ein kleines/grosses/ Familien-Zelt | una tenda grande/piccola/ familiare | velik/majhen/družinski šotor | veliki/mali/obiteljski šator | Μεγάλη/Μικρή/Οικογενειακή σκηνή (Megáli/mikrí ikogeniakí skiní) |
| Sanitärbereich | i servizi | ugodnosti, ponudba | sadržaji | Παροχές (Parochès) |
| Toiletten | i bagni/WC | WC, toaleta | WC, toaleti | Τουαλέτες (Toualètes) |
| Duschen | le doccie | tuši | tuševi | Ντούς (Doùs) |
| Abwaschwanne/ Wäschereiwanne | la lavanderia/il lavello | pomivanje/odtočni jašek pri pranju | Pranje/umivanje/Praonica rublja | Πλυντήριο/Σκάφη (Plintírio/skáfi) |
| Trinkwasser | acqua potabile | pitna vod | voda za piće | Πόσιμο Νερό (Pósimo neró) |
| Bier | la birra | pivo | pivo | Μπύρα (Bíra) |
| Wein | il vino | vino | vino | Κρασί (Krasí) |
| Schlafsack | un sacco a pelo | spalna vreča | vreća za spavanje | Σλίπινγκ μπαγκ (sleeping bag) |
| Lagerfeuer | il falò | taborni ogenj | logorska vatra | φωτιά (Fotià) |
| Zug | il treno | vlak | vlak | Τρένο (Tréno) |
| Auto | l'automobile | avto | auto | αυτοκίνητο (Aftokínito) |
| Benzin (bleifrei) | la benzina (verde) | bencin | bezolovno (gorivo) | Βενζίνη (αμόλυβδη) Venzíni (amólivdi) |
| Diesel | il gasolio | diesel | dizel | Πετρέλαιο (Petréleo) |
| Fahrrad | una bicicletta | kolo | bicikl | Ποδήλατο (Podílato) |
| links | a sinistra | leva | lijevo | Αριστερά (Aristerá) |
| rechts | a destra | desna | desno | Δεξιά (Deksiá) |
| geradeaus | avanti dritto | naravnost | ravno | Ευθεία (Efthía) |

# useful phrases

| ENGLISH | PORTUGUESE | SPANISH | FRENCH | DUTCH |
|---|---|---|---|---|
| Hello | Olá | Hola | Bonjour | Hallo |
| How are you? | Como está?/Como estás? (formal/informal) | Cómo está?Cómo estas? (formal/informal) | Comment allez-vous?/ Comment ça-va? (formal/ informal) | Hoe gaat het? |
| Do you speak English? | Fala ingles?/Falas ingles? (formal/informal) | Habla inglés?/Hablas inglés? (formal/informal) | Est-ce-que vous parlez anglais?/Est-ce-que tu parles anglais? (formal/ informal) | Spreekt u Engels?/Spreek je Engels? (formal/ informal) |
| Why not? | Porque não? | Por qué no? | Pourquoi pas? | Waarom niet? |
| Sorry, I don't speak [… whatever language]. | Desculpe, não falo português. | Lo siento, no hablo español. | Désolé, je ne parle pas français. | Sorry, ik spreek geen Nederlands. |
| Some of my best friends are […nationality] | Alguns dos meus melhores amigos são portugueses. | Algunos de mis mejores amigos son españoles. | Quelques-uns de mes meilleurs amis sont français. | Sommige van mijn beste vrienden zijn Nederlanders. |
| What's the local tipple? | Qual é a bebida típica da região? | Quál es la bebida típica por aquí? | Qu'est-ce qu'on boît ici? | Wat drinken jullie hier graag? |
| Cheers! | Tchim-tchim (pron.: tcheen-tcheen) | Salud! | Santé! | Proost! |
| Mmm, that tastes lovely. | Humm, sabe muito bem. | Mm, es muy sabroso. | Mmm, c'est délicieux. | Hmm, dat smaakt heerlijk. |
| I am lost! | Estou perdido/perdida! | Me he perdido! | Je suis perdu! | Ik ben de weg kwijt! |
| Help! | Socorro! | Socorro! | Au secours! | Help! |
| The bill, please. | A conta, por favor. | La cuenta, por favor. | L'addition, s'il vous plaît. | De rekening alstublieft. |
| It's all Greek to me. | Isso para mim é chinês. | Me suena a chino. | C'est du chinois pour moi. | Ik versta er geen moer van. |
| Aren't you a little overdressed for beach volleyball? | Não estão demasiado vestidos para jogar voleibol de praia? | No vas demasiado vestido/a para jugar a vóley playa? | Est-ce-que tu n'es pas un peu trop couverte pour le beachvolley? | Ben je niet wat warm gekleed voor beach volleybal? |

# useful phrases

| GERMAN | ITALIAN | SLOVENIAN | CROAT | GREEK |
|---|---|---|---|---|
| Hallo | Salve, ciao | Živjo | Zdravo | Γειά σου (Yá soo) |
| Wie geht es? | Come stai/state? (formal/informal) | Kako si? | Kako si? | Τι κάνεις? (Ti kánis?) |
| Sprechen Sie Englisch?/ Sprichst du Englisch? (formal/informal) | Parla inglese? | Govorite angleško? | Da li govoriš engleski? | Μιλάς Αγγλικά? (Milás aglikà?) |
| Warum nicht? | Perché no? | Zakaj ne? | Zašto ne? | Γιατί όχι? (Ghiatí óchi?) |
| Ich spreche kein Deutsch. | Mi dispiace, non parlo italiano. | Oprostite, ne govorim slovensko. | Oprosti, ne govorim hrvatski jezik. | Λυπάμαι, δεν μιλάω Ελληνικά. (Lipáme, then miláo eliniká.) |
| Einige meiner besten Freunde sind deutsch. | Alcuni dei miei migliori amici sono italiani. | Nekaj mojih najboljših prijateljev je slovencev. | Neki od mojih najboljih prijatelja su Hrvati. | Μερικοί από τους καλύτερους φίλους μου είναι Έλληνες. (Merikí apó tous kalíterous fílous mou íne élines.) |
| Was trinkt man hier? | Cosa si beve da queste parti? | Katera je vaša lokalna alkoholna pijača? | Koje je lokalno alkoholno piće? | Ποιό είναι το τοπικό ποτό? (Pió íne to topikó potó?) |
| Prost! | Grazie, molto gentile! | Na zdravje! | Živjeli! | Γειά μας (Yá mas!) |
| Hmm, das ist lecker. | Mmm, è delizioso. | Mmm, to je zelo okusno. | Mmm, to je veoma ukusno. | Μμμ, είναι πολύ νόστιμο. (Mmm, íne polí nóstimo.) |
| Ich habe mich verlaufen! | Mi sono perso! | Sem zgubljen/a! | Izgubio/la sam se! | Έχω χαθεί (Ého hathí) |
| Hilfe! | Aiuto! | Na pomoč! | Pomoć! | Βοήθεια! (Voíthia!) |
| Die Rechnung bitte. | Il conto, per favore. | Račun, prosim. | Račun, molim. | Το λογαριασμό παρακαλώ. (To logariasmó parakaló.) |
| Ich verstehe nur Bahnhof. | Non capisco un acca. | To je zame španska vas. | To je sve špansko selo za mene. | Δεν καταλαβαίνω τίποτα. (Den katalavéno tìpota.) |
| Bist du nicht zu warm angezogen für Beachvolley? | Non sei un tantino elegante per una partita di beach volley? | Ali nisi malo preveč oblečen za odbojko na mivki? | Nisli li malo previše obučen/a za odbojku na pijesku? | Δεν είσαι πολύ καλά ντυμένος για μπιτς βόλευ? (Den íse polí kalá ntiménos gia 'beach volley'?) |

# acknowledgements

Cool Camping: Europe 1st edition
Series Concept & Series Editor: Jonathan Knight
Commissioning Editor: Keith Didcock
Researched, written and photographed by:
Sophie Dawson, Keith Didcock, Sam Pow,
Paul Sullivan, Richard Waters & Penny Watson
Project Manager: Nikki Sims
Editor: Jo Godfrey Wood
Proofreader: Leanne Bryan
Publishing Assistants: Sophie Dawson &
Catherine Greenwood
Design and artwork: Kenny Grant
PR: The Farley Partnership

Punk Publishing would like to thank the following for
reviewing country sections:
Nicola Williams (France, Switzerland); Matthias
Lüfkens (Germany, Switzerland); Neal Bedford
(Austria); Dulce Dias (Portugal); Chiara Buttiglione
Reid (Italy); Miles Roddis (Spain); Jeroen van Marle
(Luxembourg/The Netherlands); Visnja Arambasic
(Croatia); Barbara Zlender (Slovenia); and Vangelis
Koronakis (Greece).

Published by:
Punk Publishing, 3 The Yard, Pegasus Place, London
SE11 5SD

Distributed by:
Portfolio Books, Suite 3/4 Great West House, Great
West Road, Brentford, Middlesex TW8 9DF

All photographs © Sophie Dawson / Keith Didcock /
Sam Pow / Paul Sullivan / Rui Teimao / Richard Waters
/ Penny Watson except the following (all reproduced
with permission): Ilha da Berlenga (p.21) © Luis
Figueiredo; Ilha de Tavira (p.29) © Câmara Municipal
de Tavira; Asseiceira (p.30) © Chris Langton; Marvão
(p.32) © Marvão Tourist Office; Termas da Azenha (p.38
and p.40) © Daniela Meester; Lugar Várzeas (p.44) ©
Hannah McDonnell (www.lushplanet.com); BelRepayre
Trailer Park (p.107 and back cover) © BelRepayre
Airstream & Retro Trailer Park; Mas de la Fargassa
(p.110) © Mas de la Fargassa; Tipis at Folbeix (p.130
and p.133) © Nigel Harding/Tipi Holidays in France;
Zellersee (p.194) © Reiner Müller; Park Grubhof (p.196
and p.199) © Kerstin Joensson, Walter Schweinoester
and Robert Stainer.

Front cover: Cala Llevadó © Keith Didcock

Many of the photographs featured in this book are
available for licensing. For more information, see
www.coolcamping.co.uk

The publishers and authors have done their best
to ensure the accuracy of all information in *Cool
Camping: Europe*, however, they can accept no
responsibility for any injury, loss, or inconvenience
sustained by anyone as a result of information
contained in this book. Please note that public
transport entries within the practicalities boxes are
included only where you can get to the site without
your own car/moped.

Punk Publishing takes its environmental
responsibilities seriously. This book has been printed
on paper made from renewable sources and we
continue to work with our printers to reduce our
overall environmental impact. Wherever possible we
recycle, eat organic food and always turn the tap off
when brushing our teeth.

No campers were hurt in the production of this book.

---

HAPPY CAMPERS?
We hope you've enjoyed reading *Cool Camping:
Europe* and that it's inspired you to get out there.

The campsites featured in this book are a personal
selection chosen by the *Cool Camping* team.
None of the campsites has paid a fee for inclusion,
nor was one requested, so you can be sure of an
objective choice of sites and honest descriptions.
We have visited hundreds of campsites across
Europe to find this selection, and we hope you like
them as much as we do. However, it hasn't been
possible to visit every single European campsite.
So, if you know of a special place that you think
should be included, we'd like to hear about it.

Send us an email telling us the name and location
of the campsite, some contact details and why it's
special. We'll credit all useful contributions in the
next edition of the book, and the best emails will
receive a complimentary copy. Thanks and see
you out there!

europe@coolcamping.co.uk